A book for your bedside

Layers

A Collection of Psalms and Scriptures

Milagros Nanita Kennett

Editor: Wanda (Tolefree) Ward
Photos: Greg Allikas

Published by Xlibris Corporation 2005

The Scripture quotations contained herein are from the New American Standard Bible 1995 and are used by permission. The transcription of these Scriptures were done with BibleLink software. Other credits and acknowledgements are included in the Bibliography of this book. All were used by permission.

Copyright © 2005 by Milagros Nanita Kennett

Library of Congress Number: 2005905729

ISBN: Hardcover: 1-4134-9872-8
Softcover: 1-4134-9871-X

All rights reserved. No part of this book may be reproduced or transmitted in any form or by any means, electronic or mechanical, including photocopying, recording, or by any information storage and retrieval system, without permission in writing from the author.

To spread the word of God, provide comfort to those in need, and bring joy to those that delight in His word are the main intentions of this book.

To my children

TABLE OF CONTENTS

Introduction   v

From the Old Testament:

   First Collection: Psalms

Petition	I-3
Praise	I-22
Thanksgiving	I-38
Recovery	I-44
Protection (against enemies)	I-46
Nations	I-61
Favorites	I-70
Keys for Psalms	I-81

   Second Collection: Bible Stories

The Creation	II-3
The Creation of Adam and Eve	II-5
The Fall of Man	II-5
Cain and Abel	II-7
Noah and the Great Flood	II-8
The Doom of Sodom and Gomorrah	II-10
The Offering of Isaac	II-12
The Birth of Moses	II-13
The Passover	II-14
Exodus and the Crossing of the Red Sea	II-16
The Ten Commandments	II-17
The Golden Calf and Moses' Anger	II-18
The Conquest of Jericho	II-21
Samson and the Philistines	II-22
David and Goliath	II-24
Bathsheba, David's Great Sin	II-26
Solomon's Wisdom	II-29
Daniel in the Lions' Den	II-31
Jonah's Disobedience	II-33
Key for Bible Stories	II-35

From the New Testament:

Third Collection: Scriptures

Love	III-3
Jesus' Deity	III-7
The Holy Spirit	III-15
Grace	III-18
Sin, Forgiveness, and Redemption	III-25
The Second Coming and Judgment	III-32
Exhortations	III-37
Petitions, Miracles, and Faith	III-43
Worries	III-49
Compassion	III-51
Prayers	III-52
Key for Scriptures	III-55

Fourth Collection: Parables

The House on the Rock and on the Sand	IV-3
The Sower	IV-4
The Tares	IV-4
The Leaven	IV-5
The Hidden Treasure	IV-5
The Pearl of Great Price	IV-5
The Drag Net	IV-5
The Old Gifts Used in a New Way	IV-6
The Unmerciful Servant	IV-6
The Laborers in the Vineyard	IV-7
The Two Sons	IV-8
The Vineyard	IV-8
The Marriage of the King's Son	IV-9
The Ten Virgins	IV-9
The Talents	IV-10
The Sheep and Goats	IV-11
The Seed Growing Secretly	IV-12
The Mustard Seed	IV-12
The Fig Tree	IV-13

Watchfulness	IV-13
The New Cloth and an Old Garment and the New Wine in Old Bottles	IV-13
The Two Debtors	IV-14
The Candle Under a Bushel	IV-14
The Good Samaritan	IV-15
The Importunate Friend at Midnight	IV-16
The Rich Fool	IV-16
The Servants Watching	IV-16
The Steward	IV-17
The Fig Tree in the Vineyard	IV-17
The Great Supper	IV-17
Building a Tower and a King Going to War	IV-18
The Lost Sheep	IV-19
The Lost Piece of Silver	IV-19
The Prodigal Son	IV-20
The Unjust Steward	IV-21
The Rich Man and Lazarus	IV-21
The Master and Servant	IV-22
The Unjust Judge and the Importunate Widow	IV-22
The Pharisee and the Tax Collector	IV-23
The King's Trust in His Servants	IV-24
The Good Shepherd	IV-25
Key for Parables	IV-26

Appendix 1: Rare words and ancient places from the Bible found in this book

Appendix 2: Brief biographies of the main characters in the Old Testament found in this book

Appendix 3: Brief biographies of Jude, James, Matthew, Mark, Luke, John, Paul, and Peter

Bibliography

Introduction

What is *Layers*? The concept of layers emerges from the way that many of us read the Bible: we mark our favorite passages and return to them when we have specific needs or longings. This action of linking together Bible passages with similar messages is what I have called layers.

Layers are very obvious in the Book of Psalms. The psalms have been rewritten during different periods of history. For example, David expanded many psalms that existed before his time, which were brought into completion in the time of Ezra. Psalms were written by different authors to cover multiple purposes. A psalm may have been written as a hymn, lament, a psalm of confidence, thanksgiving, or wisdom. Layering the different purposes and voices that may be found in one single psalm was the fundamental effort in preparing the collection of psalms.

In the Bible Stories collection, an effort was made to group significant stories of faith and highlight the voices of the prophets and the writers of the Old Testament. Likewise, for the New Testament, an attempt was made to lift up Jesus' divine teachings and messages, as well as the voices of the apostles, gospel writers and the many figures that lived and walked with Jesus.

◀ PURPOSE AND ORGANIZATION

The layers used in this book comprise inspirational quotes from scriptures to provide comfort and nourishment to those searching for the Truth and to those who already know the Good News. They allow the reader to have quick access to the "right" psalm, Bible story, scripture, and parable. The selected arrangement allows key verses and passages to be available in times of need, when we want to praise or give thanks to the Lord. These passages also apply to when we are under attack by our enemies, and when our dear ones are ill, as well as being available when we just need to listen to the voices of the great prophets or thirst for Jesus' teachings.

Layers comprises four collections: *Psalms, Bible Stories, Scriptures, and Parables.* To tailor the different collections, I selected 107 Psalms out of the 150 Psalms included in the Psalter, 19 Bible stories from the Old Testament, and 238 scriptures and 24 parables from the New Testament. To facilitate the reading of the selected material, I have included a key at the end of each collection which contains detailed information on the verses and scriptures used in the layers found in this book.

Throughout this book, each psalm, Bible story, scripture or parable is preceded by a brief introduction to guide the reading of the materials in each collection. In addition, this book includes three appendices containing useful facts, general references, and historical information to assist in the reading of each collection.

◀ PSALMS

The Collection of Psalms in this book are grouped in the following layers: *Petition, Praise, Thanksgiving, Recovery, Protection, Nations,* and *Favorites.* This organization permits the reader to select a psalm according to a particular need. For instance, the layer for *Nations* includes psalms that can be used to pray for our Nation and Israel. The layers for *Favorites,* comprises a collection of the most beautiful psalms in the Psalter. *Petition, Praise, Thanksgiving, Recovery,* and *Protection* are layers that address these particular needs.

To read the Book of Psalms is to get a glimpse of heaven. The Psalter provides comfort and joy to people who delight in the Word of God. This Book talks about God, addresses God or makes us think about God. It helps to pour out our soul to God in anticipation of His grace and thanksgiving, and to understand eternity.

Psalms are ancient songs and prayers. The word "psalms" in original Hebrew means song. They were meant to be played by musical instruments, mainly the harp, flute, pipe, horn, trumpet, timbrel, and cymbal. About two-thirds of the Psalter have been ascribed to David. Other important authors of the psalms are Asaph, the sons of Korah, Solomon, Moses, and Ethan.

The Psalter is divided into books of various lengths. They can be classified as hymns of praise; prayers of supplication, thanksgiving, confidence, and wisdom; and as processional hymns and entrances to liturgies. The psalms classified as hymns, frequently begin and end with a call to joyful worship; they consist of praise to God based upon His great deeds. They usually center upon life and joy. Laments or supplications exhibit a strong prophetic influence, especially from Jeremiah in which Israel came to realize that suffering provoked by sin, individual or national, has a positive role in returning the people to God and in appreciating His compassion. Confidence and thanksgiving are central to a smaller series of psalms. They express gratitude, a response of Israel to the love of God. Psalms of wisdom are usually concerned with virtue and retribution for sin.

The Book of Psalms is largely the work of David. A body of evidence indicates that a few psalms adjudicated to David were in existence before his time, but he was responsible for greatly enlarging this body of literature. After David, other inspirational poets worked on the psalms bringing the Psalter to completion during the time of Ezra and Nehemiah. The whole collection extends over a period of about 1,000 years.

The Psalter is composed of five Books, each one comprising 41, 31, 17, 18, and 44 psalms. Book one consists almost exclusively of the Psalms of David. The second focuses on Jerusalem's Temple liturgy in the psalms of the sons of Korah and Asaph. Book three belongs almost exclusively to Asaph and the sons of Korah, while the psalms in book four are almost completely untitled. Book five is mostly liturgical with attention to Jews in the Diaspora on pilgrimage to Jerusalem. These Books were made at times of high religious life: the first, probably, near the close of David's life; the second in the days of Solomon; the third by the singers of Jehoshaphat; the fourth by the men of Hezekiah; and the fifth in the days of Ezra.

In the New Testament, there are 116 direct quotations from the Psalter. Jesus was particularly fond of the Psalms and they were part of His nature. During His Agony on the Cross, Jesus quoted Psalms 22:1 and 31:5. Through His life, He expressed that many things in the Psalms spoke of Him.

◄BIBLE STORIES

The Collection of Bible Stories are part of the Books of Genesis, Exodus, Joshua, Judges, 1 Samuel, 2 Samuel, 1 Kings, Daniel, and Jonah. The stories explain the mysteries of heaven and earth and the relationship between God and man. They explain the covenant and the need to fear God and follow His Law. They disclose the meaning of praise, thanksgiving, grace, forgiveness, and redemption. *The Bible Stories* selected for this book highlight the teachings in which our Judeo-Christian traditions are based. For example, the Creation shows a timeless picture of God and illustrates His dimension and infiniteness. The Fall of Man unveils God's intention of a perfect world and the boundaries that separate the divine and the human world. The Conquest of Jericho conveys that God chooses to intervene in man's struggle and provides a powerful expression of faith and deliverance. Bathsheba, David's Great Sin, renders an account of man's contrition and God's grace.

The Christian Old Testament contains exactly the same books as the one followed by the Jewish faith but they are arranged differently. The Hebrew Old Testament is arranged in 5 books reflecting the Law (the Pentateuch), 8 books containing the Prophets teaching, and 11 books devoted to the "Writings" which is a miscellany of Israelite literature which uses incidents in the Bible to derive principles of the Law or to teach moral lessons. The Septuagint Translators --seventy translators responsible for translating the Hebrew Old Testament into Greek-- re-classified the Old Testament books according to subject matter. English translators, following the Septuagint Translators, provided

The Torah and the Talmud

The word Torah means teaching. In its most limited sense, Torah refers to the Five Books of Moses: Genesis, Exodus, Leviticus, Numbers and Deuteronomy. But the word torah can also be used to refer to the entire Jewish Bible. The Torah is also known as the Chumash, Pentateuch or Five Books of Moses.

The Jewish community suffered horrendous losses during the Great Revolt against Rome in 6-41 A.D. and the Bar-Kokhba rebellion in 132-135 A.D. Over a million Jews were killed along with thousands of their rabbinical scholars and students. This decline in the number of knowledgeable Jews seems to have been a decisive factor in writing the Oral Law, that is, the legal commentary on the Torah. For centuries, Judaism's leading rabbis had resisted writing down the Oral Law. But with the deaths of so many teachers in the failed revolts, it was feared that the Oral Law would die unless it was written down. In the Mishna, the name for the sixty-three tractates in which the Oral Law was set down, subjects were arranged topically.

Talmud originally signified "doctrine" or "study". It meant the justification and explanation of religious and legal norms. When in the third century the recorded Mishna became the chief object of study, the expression "Talmud" was applied chiefly to the discussions and explanations of the Mishna. Finally, it became the general designation for the Mishna and the collection of discussions concerned with it. The Talmud comprises six sections, each section is called a Seder

the final arrangement as we now know them, which is:

- Historical: Genesis, Exodus, Leviticus, Numbers, Deuteronomy, Joshua, Judges, Ruth, 1 Samuel, 2 Samuel, 1 King, 2 Kings, 1 Chronicles, 2 Chronicles, Ezra, Nehemiah, and Esther

- Poetical: Job, Psalms, Proverbs, Ecclesiastes, and Song of Solomon

- Prophetic: Isaiah, Jeremiah, Lamentations, Ezekiel, Daniel, Hosea, Joel, Amos, Obadiah, Jonah, Micah, Nahum, Habakkuk, Zephaniah, Haggai, Zechariah, and Malachi. Malachi was the last prophet before the advent of Christ. He wrote his prophetic piece 409 years before Jesus' birth.

Although many teachings can be derived from the Old Testament, it involves three fundamental concepts:

- God's promise to Abraham that in his seed all nations should be blessed. This promise converted Israel in the Messianic Nation of the world.

- God's covenant with the Hebrew Nation promising that if Israel remained faithful to Him, they would prosper as a nation.

- God's promise to David that his family should reign over God's people forever.

◄SCRIPTURES

The Collection of Scriptures comprises a series of passages from the New Testament, fundamental to the Christian faith. It includes layers related to *Love; Jesus' Deity; the Holy Spirit; Grace; Sin, Forgiveness, and Redemption; the Second Coming and Judgment; Exhortations; Petitions, Miracles, and Faith; Worries; Compassion; and Prayers.*

The New Testament consists of four Gospels: Matthew, Mark, Luke, and John. It includes the Book of Acts; the teachings of Paul (Romans, 1 Corinthians, 2 Corinthians, Galatians, Ephesians, Philippians, Colossians, 1 Thessalonians, 2 Thessalonians, 1 Timothy, 2 Timothy, Titus, Philemon, and probably Hebrews); the books of James, 1 Peter, and 2 Peter; and 1 John, 2 John, and Revelation which are attributed to John.

Matthew, Mark and Luke are usually known as the Synoptic Gospels. Synoptic comes from the Greek language and means to present or take the same common view. The Synoptic Gospels all provide a similar account and narrative of the life of Jesus. Although these Gospels have additions and omissions, when compared, they have a strong correlation with each other.

Scholars have different opinions about the authorship and age of the Synoptic Gospels. The most commonly accepted perspective is that Mark was the first of the written Gospels, and that Matthew and Luke were based on Mark. To comprehend the additions and omissions found in the text of the Synoptic Gospels, we need to understand that these gospels were written from a certain

Other Books in the New Testament

Others books in the Bible found in *Layers* include the following:

James: The author was James, Jesus' brother. The place and time of the writing was Jerusalem. The object of the writer was to enforce the practical duties of the Christian life.

1 Peter: Peter has been called "the apostle of hope," because I Peter abounds with words of comfort and encouragement to sustain a "lively hope." It was written from Babylon, on the Euphrates, at the time of Christian persecution. This Epistle was written shortly before Peter's own martyrdom, exhorting Christians not to by defeated by suffering.

2 Peter: It gives Peter's account of the Transfiguration of Christ. It was written to combat the belief and activities of certain heresies which were a threat to the emerging Church. The Epistle ends by expressing the imminent Second Coming of Jesus and the New Heaven and Earth.

1 John: This loving letter from John to the brethren, was written in Ephesus when he was in advanced age. This letter addressed concerns against incipient heresies which were produced by a corrupt and paganized form of Christianity. John emphasizes that Jesus is the actual, material, authentic manifestation of God in the flesh.

2 John: This letter includes a series of notes to persons whom John expected soon to visit. This epistle makes reference to the Elect Lady, who may have been a well known prominent woman living near Ephesus. The letter focuses on the "truth" and warns against false teachers.

Jude: The author was Judas, the brother of Jesus. The epistle is addressed to Christians in general to put them on their guard against certain threats posed by heresies that were trying to turn the grace of God into an excuse for open immorality.

Revelation: This is the last and only prophetical book of the New Testament. John wrote this book on the Isle of Patmos when he was over 100 years old. This book is apocalyptic. It shows the supreme conflict between good and evil and chronicles what will happen in the end.

point of view. For instance, Matthew was written for the Jewish people and its main purpose was to convert Jews to Christianity. Mark is the most straightforward of the gospels. It provides a narrative of Jesus' life. Mark's gospel records the preaching of Peter, who was part of the inner circle of Jesus and was always very close to His heart. Luke is the only author of the Bible who is a Gentile. Luke saw Jesus as the Savior of the World, a cornerstone, where the barriers between Jews and Gentiles were broken. His teachings are directed at converting Gentiles to Christianity.

The fourth Gospel is quite different from the other three. To grasp the difference of the Fourth Gospel we need to understand the setting and time when it was written. John wrote this Gospel in Ephesus about the year A.D. 100. By that time Christianity had gone out into the Gentile world and the Christian church was no longer Jewish but predominantly Gentile. The purpose of John's Gospel is to restate Christianity, to convert a Greek audience, and to rectify certain heresies that had emerged in the Church as Gentiles and pagans had joined the faith.

The fourth Gospel is the most precious book in the New Testament. It teaches us about the abundant love that Jesus has for us. It tells us that Jesus was present during the creation of the world and that because He loved us so much He gave us the Holy Spirit before His departure to the Father. In John, the speeches of Jesus are often a whole chapter providing us with enough insight to understand His heart. For John, the miracles performed by the Lord showed the glory of God, breaking the boundaries between heavenly and human affairs.

Another major part of the New Testament is Acts of the Apostles, the Epistles of Paul and the work of John. The Acts of the Apostles was called "The Acts," "The Gospel of the Holy Spirit," and "The Gospel of the Resurrection." The Book starts with the appearance of Jesus to His disciples after His death. It describes Pentecost, innumerable manifestations of the Holy Spirit, and the history of the foundation of churches. In terms of its authorship, it is generally agreed that Luke wrote Acts from his personal observations. The opening sentences of the Acts are just an expansion and an explanation of the closing words of Luke's Gospel. It reflects a continuation of the history of the church after Christ's ascension.

Paul was the most prolific writer of the New Testament. Fourteen Books are attributed to Paul. The conversion of Paul on the road of Damascus, Paul, formerly Saul, was the triggering point that later lead him to become the cornerstone of the Church of Christ. Before his miraculous conversion, Saul was determined to erase Christianity from the face of the earth. When the Lord Jesus suddenly appeared and asked him, , 'Saul, Saul, why are you persecuting Me?' Saul inquired from the Lord 'Who are You, Lord?' and the Lord responded 'I am Jesus the Nazarene, whom you are persecuting.' After this divine moment, Paul's life was changed. With zeal and devotion unparalleled in history, he went up and down the highways of the Roman Empire preaching Christianity to the Gentiles and winning multitudes to Christ.

◄PARABLES

The Collection of Parables introduces parables included in the New Testament. They include, the House on the Rock and on the Sand, the Sower, the Unmerciful Servant, the Seed Growing Secretly, The Mustard Seed, The Fig Tree, the Candle Under the Bushel, and the Good Samaritan. Parables are a very important part of the New Testament. Jesus used parables as a preferred method of teaching. The Old Testament includes several parables such as the Moabites and Israelites in

Numbers, Trees Making a King in Judges, the Vineyard Yielding Wild Grapes, and the Lion's Whelps, spoken by Balaam, Jotham, Samson, Jehoash, Nathan, Isaiah, and Ezekiel, among others.

Our Lord explained the reasons for using parables in Mark 4:10-12. He said to His disciples and followers "To you has been given the mystery of the kingdom of God, but those who are outside get everything in parables, so that while seeing, they may see and not perceive, and while hearing, they may hear and not understand, otherwise they might return and be forgiven."

◄ THE BIBLE

This introduction would not be complete without a brief reference to the Bible as a whole. The Bible is the sacred Book of Christianity and the greatest book in the world. For many centuries, it has enlightened and provided comfort to humanity. It is the Word of God, supernaturally given to men. It reveals the nature, character and purpose of God. The Bible deals with God's relationship with man and His concern for nature, needs, duties, and destiny of mankind.

For about thirty years after Christ ascended to the Father, information about Him was transmitted orally. Seventy years after the Crucifixion, Christianity had grown so large that it was difficult for the Apostles to continue to spread the gospel by word of mouth only. Thanks to the letters of Paul and others, and the Gospels written by Matthew, Mark, Luke, and John, the records of Christ's life and teachings became the written word.

After the ascension of Christ, several hundred years passed before the Church became officially organized. Two major councils in North Africa, in Hippo in 393 and in Carthage in 397 established the canons of the Old and New Testaments. The word canon was applied to the Scriptures because they contained the rule of faith and practice. The oldest surviving complete text of the New Testament is the Codex Sinaiticus, dating back to the middle of the fourth century. The oldest fragments, the Bodmer and Beatty Papyri and Papyrus 52, date back to the second century but only contain portions of the Gospel of John. All of these texts are in Greek. However, Jesus' native tongue was Aramaic, and it is almost certain that He spoke it to His disciples. Although the Bible accurately reflects the thinking, life and purpose of the Lord, without any surviving Aramaic text, the actual words of Christ are, unfortunately, lost forever.

There are many ancient Christian writings that do not form part of the Bible. Only certain books passed the measuring rules required for 'canonization'. The general rules to be included in the canons were:

- It had to be written or sponsored by an apostle.
- It had to have orthodox content.
- It had to be publicly used by a prominent church or a majority of churches.

The first list of New Testament books ever to be compiled is the Muratorian Canon, which dates about A.D. 170. This first canon included the four Gospels, fourteen letters of Paul, two letters of John, Jude, Revelation, the Wisdom of Solomon, and the Revelation of Peter (somewhat contested).

The decision to decide on the final biblical canon took around 200 years. Many voices were influential in the selection of the canons. At Hippo and Carthage, Augustine and Jerome were very influential. Later on, Tertullian, Origen, Clement of Alexandria, and Irenaeus had major voices in the decision of the writings. It was Irenaeus who first declared that there could only be four gospels.

The list of books in the canon continued to be debated throughout the third century until Eusebius published a list at the beginning of the fourth century. Books still in question included James, 2 Peter, 2 and 3 John, and Jude. Another canon was released by consensus in 367 A.D. which names the 27 books we know today. Additional books, the *Didache*, the *Shepherd of Hermas*, *I Clement*, and the *Letter of Barnabas* were considered suitable for study but not as scripture. This last list of books was finally accepted by the Council of Hippo in 393 A.D. and the Council of Carthage in 397 A.D.

■ A FINAL NOTE

This book was made possible by the inspiration and guidance of many men and women that had participated in the preparation of the English version of the Bible and many outstanding Christian studies that have followed. Credits and acknowledgments at the end of this book describe these merits. I humbly declare, that the preparation of Layers was also possible by the divine intervention of the Holy Spirit and the blessing of our Lord Jesus Christ. Layers was put together in a three month period.

My love to you all. Thank you Heavenly Father.

LAYERS

- Petition
- Praise
- Thanksgiving
- Recovery
- Protection
- Nations
- Favorites

First Collection

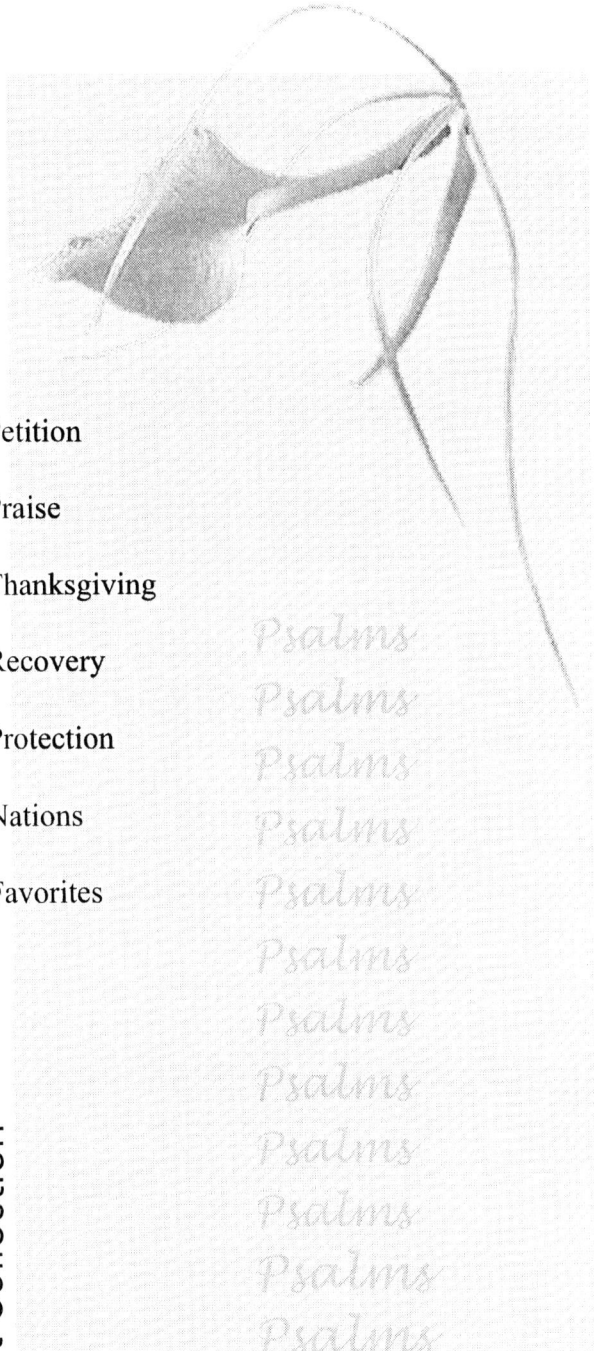

David, Asaph, Sons of Korah, Solomon, Moses, Ethan

† It shows all the verses from a particular Psalm are included

✻ It shows that only selected verses from a particular Psalm are included

First Book, Second Book, Third Book, Fourth Book, Fifth Book

Petition

Psalm 4 †

In this Psalm, a call for help is followed by reflections addressed to adversaries. It asks for protection and deliverance and expresses trust in the Lord. A good night prayer.

1 Answer me when I call, O God of my righteousness! You have relieved me in my distress; Be gracious to me and hear my prayer.
2 O sons of men, how long will my honor become a reproach? How long will you love what is worthless and aim at deception? Selah.
3 But know that the Lord has set apart the godly man for Himself; The Lord hears when I call to Him.
4 Tremble, and do not sin; Meditate in your heart upon your bed, and be still. Selah.
5 Offer the sacrifices of righteousness, and trust in the Lord.
6 Many are saying, "Who will show us any good?" Lift up the light of Your countenance upon us, O Lord!
7 You have put gladness in my heart, more than when their grain and new wine abound.
8 In peace I will both lie down and sleep, for You alone, O Lord, make me to dwell in safety.

Psalm 5

This Psalm includes words of supplication for help in times of trouble. It ends with a plea for renewal. A good morning prayer.

1 Give ear to my words, O Lord, consider my groaning.
2 Heed the sound of my cry for help, my King and my God, for to You I pray.
3 In the morning, O Lord, You will hear my voice; In the morning I will order my prayer to You and eagerly watch.
4 For You are not a God who takes pleasure in wickedness; No evil dwells with You.
5 The boastful shall not stand before Your eyes; You hate all who do iniquity.

8 O Lord, lead me in Your righteousness because of my foes; Make Your way straight before me.

Psalm 6

This Psalm includes words of emotional intensity. The petitioner is close to death and asks God for deliverance.

1 O Lord, do not rebuke me in Your anger, nor chasten me in Your wrath.
2 Be gracious to me, O Lord, for I am pining away; Heal me, O Lord, for my bones are dismayed.
3 And my soul is greatly dismayed; But You, O Lord-- how long?
4 Return, O Lord, rescue my soul; Save me because of Your lovingkindness.
5 For there is no mention of You in death; In Sheol who will give You thanks?
6 I am weary with my sighing; Every night I make my bed swim, I dissolve my couch with my tears.
7 My eye has wasted away with grief; It has become old because of all my adversaries.
8 Depart from me, all you who do iniquity, for the Lord has heard the voice of my weeping.
9 The Lord has heard my supplication, the Lord receives my prayer.

Psalm 13

This is a lament asking God for deliverance when sorrows are overwhelming. It concludes with words of grace and salvation.

1 How long, O Lord? Will You forget me forever? How long will You hide Your face from me?
2 How long shall I take counsel in my soul, having sorrow in my heart all the day? How long will my enemy be exalted over me?
3 Consider and answer me, O Lord my God; Enlighten my eyes, or I will sleep the sleep of death,

5 But I have trusted in Your lovingkindness; My heart shall rejoice in Your salvation.
6 I will sing to the Lord, because He has dealt bountifully with me.

Psalm 17

This Psalm includes words of supplication and establishes a relationship between deliverance and righteousness. It calls for God's protection. A good bedtime prayer.

1 Hear a just cause, O Lord, give heed to my cry; Give ear to my prayer, which is not from deceitful lips.
2 Let my judgment come forth from Your presence; Let Your eyes look with equity.
3 You have tried my heart; You have visited me by night; You have tested me and You find nothing; I have purposed that my mouth will not transgress.
4 As for the deeds of men, by the word of Your lips I have kept from the paths of the violent.
5 My steps have held fast to Your paths. My feet have not slipped.
6 I have called upon You, for You will answer me, O God; Incline Your ear to me, hear my speech.
7 Wondrously show Your lovingkindness, O Savior of those who take refuge at Your right hand From those who rise up against them.

Petition   *Psalms*

8 Keep me as the apple of the eye; Hide me in the shadow of Your wings,

15 As for me, I shall behold Your face in righteousness; I will be satisfied with Your likeness when I awake.

Psalm 18

This Psalm includes a request for protection during times of distress and when life might be in danger. It establishes a relationship between deliverance and righteousness. It shows that God saves the afflicted and provides protection from evil.

1 "I love You, O Lord, my strength."
2 The Lord is my rock and my fortress and my deliverer, my God, my rock, in whom I take refuge; My shield and the horn of my salvation, my stronghold.

4 The cords of death encompassed me, and the torrents of ungodliness terrified me.
5 The cords of Sheol surrounded me; The snares of death confronted me.
6 In my distress I called upon the Lord, and cried to my God for help; He heard my voice out of His temple, and my cry for help before Him came into His ears.

20 The Lord has rewarded me according to my righteousness; According to the cleanness of my hands He has recompensed me.
21 For I have kept the ways of the Lord, and have not wickedly departed from my God.
22 For all His ordinances were before me, and I did not put away His statutes from me.
23 I was also blameless with Him, and I kept myself from my iniquity.
24 Therefore the Lord has recompensed me according to my righteousness, According to the cleanness of my hands in His eyes.
25 With the kind You show Yourself kind; With the blameless You show Yourself blameless;
26 With the pure You show Yourself pure, and with the crooked You show Yourself astute.
27 For You save an afflicted people, But haughty eyes You abase.

28 For You light my lamp; The Lord my God illumines my darkness.
29 For by You I can run upon a troop; And by my God I can leap over a wall.
30 As for God, His way is blameless; The word of the Lord is tried; He is a shield to all who take refuge in Him.
31 For who is God, but the Lord? And who is a rock, except our God,
32 The God who girds me with strength and makes my way blameless?
33 He makes my feet like hinds' feet, and sets me upon my high places.
34 He trains my hands for battle, so that my arms can bend a bow of bronze.
35 You have also given me the shield of Your salvation, and Your right hand upholds me; and Your gentleness makes me great.
36 You enlarge my steps under me, and my feet have not slipped.

Psalm 20

This is a prayer of confidence and supplication. It calls for God's protection and deliverance. It asks God to "grant you your heart's desire."

1 May the Lord answer you in the day of trouble! May the name of the God of Jacob set you securely on high!
2 May He send you help from the sanctuary and support you from Zion!
3 May He remember all your meal offerings and find your burnt offering acceptable! Selah.
4 May He grant you your heart's desire and fulfill all your counsel!
5 We will sing for joy over your victory, and in the name of our God we will set up our banners. May the Lord fulfill all your petitions.
6 Now I know that the Lord saves His anointed; He will answer him from His holy heaven With the saving strength of His right hand.
7 Some boast in chariots and some in horses, but we will boast in the name of the Lord, our God.

Psalms   *Petition*

8 They have bowed down and fallen, But we have risen and stood upright.
9 Save, O Lord; May the King answer us in the day we call.

Psalm 22

This Psalm starts with words that Jesus quoted while on the cross. It is a prophetic Psalm since some of its verses describe the crucifixion. It calls for help in time of distress or when death is near. It provides assurance that God is listening in spite there is no immediate answer.

1 My God, my God, why have You forsaken me? Far from my deliverance are the words of my groaning.
2 O my God, I cry by day, but You do not answer; And by night, but I have no rest.
3 Yet You are holy, O You who are enthroned upon the praises of Israel.
4 In You our fathers trusted; They trusted and You delivered them.
5 To You they cried out and were delivered; In You they trusted and were not disappointed.
6 But I am a worm and not a man, a reproach of men and despised by the people.
7 All who see me sneer at me; They separate with the lip, they wag the head, saying,
8 "Commit yourself to the Lord; Let Him deliver him; Let Him rescue him, because He delights in him."
9 Yet You are He who brought me forth from the womb; You made me trust when upon my mother's breasts.
10 Upon You I was cast from birth; You have been my God from my mother's womb.
11 Be not far from me, for trouble is near; For there is none to help.
12 Many bulls have surrounded me; Strong bulls of Bashan have encircled me.
13 They open wide their mouth at me, As a ravening and a roaring lion.
14 I am poured out like water, and all my bones are out of joint; My heart is like wax; It is melted within me.
15 My strength is dried up like a potsherd, and my tongue cleaves to my jaws; And You lay me in the dust of death.
16 For dogs have surrounded me; A band of evildoers has encompassed me; They pierced my hands and my feet.
17 I can count all my bones. They look, they stare at me;
18 They divide my garments among them, and for my clothing they cast lots.
19 But You, O Lord, be not far off; O You my help, hasten to my assistance.
20 Deliver my soul from the sword, my only life from the power of the dog.
21 Save me from the lion's mouth; From the horns of the wild oxen You answer me.

Psalm 23 ✝

This is a Psalm of great beauty. It is a Psalm of confidence which brings comfort to the soul.

1 The Lord is my shepherd, I shall not want.
2 He makes me lie down in green pastures; He leads me beside quiet waters.
3 He restores my soul; He guides me in the paths of righteousness For His name's sake.
4 Even though I walk through the valley of the shadow of death, I fear no evil, for You are with me;
   Your rod and Your staff, they comfort me.
5 You prepare a table before me in the presence of my enemies; You have anointed my head with oil;
   My cup overflows.
6 Surely goodness and lovingkindness will follow me all the days of my life, and I will dwell in the
   house of the Lord forever.

Psalm 25

This Psalm includes words of supplication in times of distress or persecution. It asks God for forgiveness and to "remember" His compassion.

1 To You, O Lord, I lift up my soul.
2 O my God, in You I trust, do not let me be ashamed; Do not let my enemies exult over me.
3 Indeed, none of those who wait for You will be ashamed; Those who deal treacherously without
   cause will be ashamed.
4 Make me know Your ways, O Lord; Teach me Your paths.
5 Lead me in Your truth and teach me, for You are the God of my salvation; For You I wait all the day.
6 Remember, O Lord, Your compassion and Your lovingkindnesses, for they have been from of old.
7 Do not remember the sins of my youth or my transgressions; According to Your lovingkindness
   remember me, for Your goodness' sake, O Lord.
8 Good and upright is the Lord; Therefore He instructs sinners in the way.
9 He leads the humble in justice, and He teaches the humble His way.
10 All the paths of the Lord are lovingkindness and truth To those who keep His covenant and His testimonies.
11 For Your name's sake, O Lord, pardon my iniquity, for it is great.
12 Who is the man who fears the Lord? He will instruct him in the way he should choose.
13 His soul will abide in prosperity, and his descendants will inherit the land.

14 The secret of the Lord is for those who fear Him, and He will make them know His covenant.
15 My eyes are continually toward the Lord, for He will pluck my feet out of the net.
16 Turn to me and be gracious to me, for I am lonely and afflicted.
17 The troubles of my heart are enlarged; Bring me out of my distresses.
18 Look upon my affliction and my trouble, and forgive all my sins.

20 Guard my soul and deliver me; Do not let me be ashamed, for I take refuge in You.
21 Let integrity and uprightness preserve me, for I wait for You.

Psalm 27

This Psalm includes a request for protection. It has words of confidence, longing, and trust in God. It urges to "wait for the Lord."

1 The Lord is my light and my salvation; Whom shall I fear? The Lord is the defense of my life; Whom shall I dread?

4 One thing I have asked from the Lord, that I shall seek: That I may dwell in the house of the Lord all the days of my life, to behold the beauty of the Lord and to meditate in His temple.
5 For in the day of trouble He will conceal me in His tabernacle; In the secret place of His tent He will hide me; He will lift me up on a rock.

7 Hear, O Lord, when I cry with my voice, and be gracious to me and answer me.
8 When You said, "Seek My face," my heart said to You, "Your face, O Lord, I shall seek."
9 Do not hide Your face from me, do not turn Your servant away in anger; You have been my help; Do not abandon me nor forsake me, O God of my salvation!

13 I would have despaired unless I had believed that I would see the goodness of the Lord In the land of the living.
14 Wait for the Lord; Be strong and let your heart take courage; Yes, wait for the Lord.

Psalm 28

This is a Psalm of supplication and confidence. It shows that God provides protection to His people.

1 To You, O Lord, I call; My rock, do not be deaf to me, for if You are silent to me, I will become like those who go down to the pit.
2 Hear the voice of my supplications when I cry to You for help, when I lift up my hands toward Your holy sanctuary.

6 Blessed be the Lord, because He has heard the voice of my supplication.
7 The Lord is my strength and my shield; My heart trusts in Him, and I am helped; Therefore my heart exults, and with my song I shall thank Him.
8 The Lord is their strength, and He is a saving defense to His anointed.
9 Save Your people and bless Your inheritance; Be their shepherd also, and carry them forever.

Psalm 30

This is a prayer of supplication and deliverance. It offers prayers of thanksgiving for a return to health. It calls for grace and trust in the Lord.

2 O Lord my God, I cried to You for help, and You healed me.
3 O Lord, You have brought up my soul from Sheol; You have kept me alive, that I would not go down to the pit.
4 Sing praise to the Lord, you His godly ones, and give thanks to His holy name.
5 For His anger is but for a moment, His favor is for a lifetime; Weeping may last for the night, But a shout of joy comes in the morning.

6 Now as for me, I said in my prosperity, "I will never be moved."
7 O Lord, by Your favor You have made my mountain to stand strong; You hid Your face, I was dismayed.
8 To You, O Lord, I called, and to the Lord I made supplication:
9 "What profit is there in my blood, if I go down to the pit? Will the dust praise You? Will it declare Your faithfulness?
10 "Hear, O Lord, and be gracious to me; O Lord, be my helper."
11 You have turned for me my mourning into dancing; You have loosed my sackcloth and girded me with gladness,
12 That my soul may sing praise to You and not be silent. O Lord my God, I will give thanks to You forever.

Psalm 31

Our Lord Jesus quoted this Psalm during the crucifixion. It calls on God to provide protection and recites the petitioner's sorrows and afflictions. It shows God's disregard for inequity and His caring for His people.

1 In You, O Lord, I have taken refuge; Let me never be ashamed; In Your righteousness deliver me.
2 Incline Your ear to me, rescue me quickly; Be to me a rock of strength, a stronghold to save me.
3 For You are my rock and my fortress; For Your name's sake You will lead me and guide me.
4 You will pull me out of the net which they have secretly laid for me, for You are my strength.
5 Into Your hand I commit my spirit; You have ransomed me, O Lord, God of truth.
6 I hate those who regard vain idols, But I trust in the Lord.
7 I will rejoice and be glad in Your lovingkindness, because You have seen my affliction; You have known the troubles of my soul,
8 And You have not given me over into the hand of the enemy; You have set my feet in a large place.

9 Be gracious to me, O Lord, for I am in distress; My eye is wasted away from grief, my soul and my body also.
10 For my life is spent with sorrow and my years with sighing; My strength has failed because of my iniquity, and my body has wasted away.

22 As for me, I said in my alarm, "I am cut off from before Your eyes"; Nevertheless You heard the voice of my supplications When I cried to You.
23 O love the Lord, all you His godly ones! The Lord preserves the faithful and fully recompenses the proud doer.
24 Be strong and let your heart take courage, All you who hope in the Lord.

Psalm 32

This is a penitential Psalm. It includes words of grace and shows how our spiritual and physical life can change with the acknowledgment of sin. It reveals how God preserves us from trouble.

1 How blessed is he whose transgression is forgiven, whose sin is covered!
2 How blessed is the man to whom the Lord does not impute iniquity, and in whose spirit there is no deceit!
3 When I kept silent about my sin, my body wasted away Through my groaning all day long.
4 For day and night Your hand was heavy upon me; My vitality was drained away as with the fever heat of summer. Selah.
5 I acknowledged my sin to You, and my iniquity I did not hide; I said, "I will confess my transgressions to the Lord"; And You forgave the guilt of my sin. Selah.
6 Therefore, let everyone who is godly pray to You in a time when You may be found; Surely in a flood of great waters they will not reach him.
7 You are my hiding place; You preserve me from trouble; You surround me with songs

of deliverance. Selah.
8 I will instruct you and teach you in the way which you should go; I will counsel you with My eye upon you.

Psalm 33

This is a Psalm of confidence and supplication. It shows God's formula for fear and deliverance. It focuses on the need to trust God.

18 Behold, the eye of the Lord is on those who fear Him, on those who hope for His lovingkindness,
19 To deliver their soul from death and to keep them alive in famine.
20 Our soul waits for the Lord; He is our help and our shield.
21 For our heart rejoices in Him, because we trust in His holy name.
22 Let Your lovingkindness, O Lord, be upon us, According as we have hoped in You.

Psalm 34

This is a prayer of confidence, supplication, and thanksgiving. It shows that God protects those who fear Him. It describes a relationship between righteousness and deliverance.

4 I sought the Lord, and He answered me, and delivered me from all my fears.
5 They looked to Him and were radiant, and their faces will never be ashamed.
6 This poor man cried, and the Lord heard him and saved him out of all his troubles.
7 The angel of the Lord encamps around those who fear Him, and rescues them.
8 O taste and see that the Lord is good; How blessed is the man who takes refuge in Him!
9 O fear the Lord, you His saints; For to those who fear Him there is no want.
10 The young lions do lack and suffer hunger; But they who seek the Lord shall not be in want of any good thing.
11 Come, you children, listen to me; I will teach you the fear of the Lord.
12 Who is the man who desires life and loves length of days that he may see good?
13 Keep your tongue from evil and your lips from speaking deceit.
14 Depart from evil and do good; Seek peace and pursue it.
15 The eyes of the Lord are toward the righteous and His ears are open to their cry.
16 The face of the Lord is against evildoers, to cut off the memory of them from the earth.
17 The righteous cry, and the Lord hears and delivers them out of all their troubles.
18 The Lord is near to the brokenhearted and saves those who are crushed in spirit.
19 Many are the afflictions of the righteous, But the Lord delivers him out of them all.

22 The Lord redeems the soul of His servants, and none of those who take refuge in Him will be condemned.

Psalm 37

This Psalm includes words of confidence and supplication. It calls on you to commit to the Lord and He "will give you the desires of your heart."

3 Trust in the Lord and do good; Dwell in the land and cultivate faithfulness.
4 Delight yourself in the Lord; And He will give you the desires of your heart.
5 Commit your way to the Lord, trust also in Him, and He will do it.
6 He will bring forth your righteousness as the light and your judgment as the noonday.

Psalm 38

This is a penitential Psalm. It includes a recital of physical pain and distress caused by sin and emotional isolation. Pleads for God's protection and hopes for His deliverance.

1 O Lord, rebuke me not in Your wrath, and chasten me not in Your burning anger.
2 For Your arrows have sunk deep into me, and Your hand has pressed down on me.
3 There is no soundness in my flesh because of Your indignation; There is no health in my bones because of my sin.
4 For my iniquities are gone over my head; As a heavy burden they weigh too much for me.
5 My wounds grow foul and fester Because of my folly.
6 I am bent over and greatly bowed down; I go mourning all day long.
7 For my loins are filled with burning, and there is no soundness in my flesh.
8 I am benumbed and badly crushed; I groan because of the agitation of my heart.
9 Lord, all my desire is before You; And my sighing is not hidden from You.
10 My heart throbs, my strength fails me; And the light of my eyes, even that has gone from me.
11 My loved ones and my friends stand aloof from my plague; And my kinsmen stand afar off.
12 Those who seek my life lay snares for me; And those who seek to injure me have threatened destruction, and they devise treachery all day long.
13 But I, like a deaf man, do not hear; And I am like a mute man who does not open his mouth.
14 Yes, I am like a man who does not hear, and in whose mouth are no arguments.

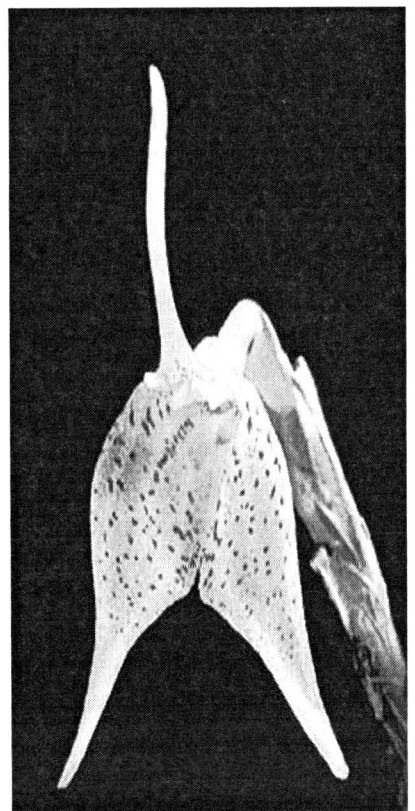

15 For I hope in You, O Lord; You will answer, O Lord my God.
16 For I said, "May they not rejoice over me, who, when my foot slips, would magnify themselves against me."
17 For I am ready to fall, and my sorrow is continually before me.
18 For I confess my iniquity; I am full of anxiety because of my sin.

21 Do not forsake me, O Lord; O my God, do not be far from me!
22 Make haste to help me, O Lord, my salvation!

Psalm 40

This is a prayer of thanksgiving and supplication. Although going through a dark period, the petitioner "waits patiently" for the Lord. It urges God to give compassion and protection.

1 I waited patiently for the Lord; And He inclined to me and heard my cry.
2 He brought me up out of the pit of destruction, out of the miry clay, and He set my feet upon a rock making my footsteps firm.
3 He put a new song in my mouth, a song of praise to our God; Many will see and fear and will trust in the Lord.

11 You, O Lord, will not withhold Your compassion from me; Your lovingkindness and Your truth will continually preserve me.
12 For evils beyond number have surrounded me; My iniquities have overtaken me, so that I am not able to see; They are more numerous than the hairs of my head, and my heart has failed me.
13 Be pleased, O Lord, to deliver me; Make haste, O Lord, to help me.

17 Since I am afflicted and needy, let the Lord be mindful of me. You are my help and my deliverer; Do not delay, O my God.

Psalm 42

This is a beautiful prayer of supplication. The petitioner expresses sadness, fear, personal abandonment, and thirst for God. It shows great hope for God's deliverance.

1 As the deer pants for the water brooks, so my soul pants for You, O God.
2 My soul thirsts for God, for the living God; When shall I come and appear before God?
3 My tears have been my food day and night, while they say to me all day long, "Where is your God?"

5 Why are you in despair, O my soul? And why have you become disturbed within me? Hope in God, for I shall again praise Him for the help of His presence.

7 Deep calls to deep at the sound of Your waterfalls; All Your breakers and Your waves have rolled over me.
8 The Lord will command His lovingkindness in the daytime; And His song will be with me in the night, a prayer to the God of my life.

11 Why are you in despair, O my soul? And why have you become disturbed within me? Hope in God, for I shall yet praise Him, the help of my countenance and my God.

Psalm 43

This Psalm includes words of confidence and supplication. The Psalmist questions God's rejection but hopes to gain His favor and deliverance.

2 For You are the God of my strength; Why have You rejected me? Why do I go mourning because of the oppression of the enemy?
3 O send out Your light and Your truth, let them lead me; Let them bring me to Your holy hill and to Your dwelling places.
4 Then I will go to the altar of God, to God my exceeding joy; And upon the lyre I shall praise You, O God, my God.
5 Why are you in despair, O my soul? And why

are you disturbed within me? Hope in God, for I shall again praise Him, the help of my countenance and my God.

Psalm 46

This Psalm includes words of assurance showing that God is our refuge and that we should not fear in times of trouble.

1 God is our refuge and strength, a very present help in trouble.
2 Therefore we will not fear, though the earth should change and though the mountains slip into the heart of the sea;
3 Though its waters roar and foam, though the mountains quake at its swelling pride. Selah.

11 The Lord of hosts is with us; The God of Jacob is our stronghold. Selah.

Psalm 51

This is a beautiful prayer of supplication and contrition for our sins. It includes words of hope and redemption. It announces the possibility of new beginnings.

1 Be gracious to me, O God, according to Your lovingkindness; According to the greatness of Your compassion blot out my transgressions.
2 Wash me thoroughly from my iniquity and cleanse me from my sin.
3 For I know my transgressions, and my sin is ever before me.
4 Against You, You only, I have sinned and done what is evil in Your sight, so that You are justified when You speak and blameless when You judge.
5 Behold, I was brought forth in iniquity, and in sin my mother conceived me.
6 Behold, You desire truth in the innermost being, and in the hidden part You will make me know wisdom.
7 Purify me with hyssop, and I shall be clean; Wash me, and I shall be whiter than snow.

8 Make me to hear joy and gladness, let the bones which You have broken rejoice.
9 Hide Your face from my sins and blot out all my iniquities.
10 Create in me a clean heart, O God, and renew a steadfast spirit within me.
11 Do not cast me away from Your presence and do not take Your Holy Spirit from me.
12 Restore to me the joy of Your salvation and sustain me with a willing spirit.
13 Then I will teach transgressors Your ways, and sinners will be converted to You.

Psalm 55

This is a prayer for supplication and confidence. It teaches us to place our burdens upon the Lord to alleviate our sorrows.

1 Give ear to my prayer, O God; And do not hide Yourself from my supplication.

22 Cast your burden upon the Lord and He will sustain you; He will never allow the righteous to be shaken.

Psalm 61

This is a prayer for supplication. It calls for God's protection when "our heart is faint."

1 Hear my cry, O God; Give heed to my prayer.
2 From the end of the earth I call to You when my heart is faint; Lead me to the rock that is higher than I.

4 Let me dwell in Your tent forever; Let me take refuge in the shelter of Your wings. Selah.

Psalm 62

This is prayer of confidence and supplication. It urges us to "wait in silence" for God's salvation.

1 My soul waits in silence for God only; From Him is my salvation.

Psalms I-13 Petition

2 He only is my rock and my salvation, my stronghold; I shall not be greatly shaken.

5 My soul, wait in silence for God only, for my hope is from Him.
6 He only is my rock and my salvation, my stronghold; I shall not be shaken.
7 On God my salvation and my glory rest; The rock of my strength, my refuge is in God.

𝒫salm 69

This is a lament from an individual experiencing great sorrows and awaiting deliverance. It pleads for God's compassion.

1 Save me, O God, for the waters have threatened my life.
2 I have sunk in deep mire, and there is no foothold; I have come into deep waters, and a flood overflows me.
3 I am weary with my crying; My throat is parched; My eyes fail while I wait for my God.

13 But as for me, my prayer is to You, O Lord, at an acceptable time; O God, in the greatness of Your lovingkindness, Answer me with Your saving truth.
14 Deliver me from the mire and do not let me sink; May I be delivered from my foes and from the deep waters.
15 May the flood of water not overflow me Nor the deep swallow me up, nor the pit shut its mouth on me.
16 Answer me, O Lord, for Your lovingkindness is good; According to the greatness of Your compassion, turn to me,
17 And do not hide Your face from Your servant, for I am in distress; Answer me quickly.

29 But I am afflicted and in pain; May Your salvation, O God, set me securely on high.
30 I will praise the name of God with song and magnify Him with thanksgiving.

𝒫salm 70

This is a Psalm of supplication. It urges God to provide deliverance and salvation.

1 O God, hasten to deliver me; O Lord, hasten to my help!

4 Let all who seek You rejoice and be glad in You; And let those who love Your salvation say continually, "Let God be magnified."
5 But I am afflicted and needy; Hasten to me, O God! You are my help and my deliverer; O Lord, do not delay.

Psalm 71

This Psalm includes words of supplication. It anticipates deliverance while experiencing a period of darkness and failing strength.

1 In You, O Lord, I have taken refuge; Let me never be ashamed.
2 In Your righteousness deliver me and rescue me; Incline Your ear to me and save me.
3 Be to me a rock of habitation to which I may continually come; You have given commandment to save me, for You are my rock and my fortress.

5 For You are my hope; O Lord God, You are my confidence from my youth.
6 By You I have been sustained from my birth; You are He who took me from my mother's womb; My praise is continually of You.
7 I have become a marvel to many, for You are my strong refuge.
8 My mouth is filled with Your praise and with Your glory all day long.
9 Do not cast me off in the time of old age; Do not forsake me when my strength fails.

19 For Your righteousness, O God, reaches to the heavens, You who have done great things; O God, Who is like You?
20 You who have shown me many troubles and distresses Will revive me again, and will bring me up again from the depths of the earth.
21 May You increase my greatness and turn to comfort me.

Psalm 77

This Psalm includes a call for help. It shows a desire to regain God's favor. A good night prayer.

1 My voice rises to God, and I will cry aloud; My voice rises to God, and He will hear me.
2 In the day of my trouble I sought the Lord; In the night my hand was stretched out without weariness; My soul refused to be comforted.
3 When I remember God, then I am disturbed; When I sigh, then my spirit grows faint. Selah.
4 You have held my eyelids open; I am so troubled that I cannot speak.
5 I have considered the days of old, the years of long ago.
6 I will remember my song in the night; I will meditate with my heart, and my spirit ponders.
7 Will the Lord reject forever? And will He never be favorable again?

8 Has His lovingkindness ceased forever? Has His promise come to an end forever?
9 Has God forgotten to be gracious, or has He in anger withdrawn His compassion? Selah.
10 Then I said, "It is my grief, that the right hand of the Most High has changed."

Psalm 86

This Psalm calls for help while experiencing great sorrows. The Psalm evokes God's extraordinary kindness, forgiveness, and thanksgiving.

1 Incline Your ear, O Lord, and answer me; For I am afflicted and needy.
2 Preserve my soul, for I am a godly man; O You my God, save Your servant who trusts in You.
3 Be gracious to me, O Lord, for to You I cry all day long.
4 Make glad the soul of Your servant, for to You, O Lord, I lift up my soul.
5 For You, Lord, are good, and ready to forgive, and abundant in lovingkindness to all who call upon You.
6 Give ear, O Lord, to my prayer; And give heed to the voice of my supplications!
7 In the day of my trouble I shall call upon You, for You will answer me.
8 There is no one like You among the gods, O Lord, nor are there any works like Yours.
9 All nations whom You have made shall come and worship before You, O Lord, and they shall glorify Your name.
10 For You are great and do wondrous deeds; You alone are God.
11 Teach me Your way, O Lord; I will walk in Your truth; Unite my heart to fear Your name.
12 I will give thanks to You, O Lord my God, with all my heart, and will glorify Your name forever.
13 For Your lovingkindness toward me is great, and You have delivered my soul from the depths of Sheol.

Psalm 88

This is a Psalm of supplication in times of great affliction and isolation. It shows God's rejection and possible restoration through prayers. A good morning prayer.

1 O Lord, the God of my salvation, I have cried out by day and in the night before You.
2 Let my prayer come before You; Incline Your ear to my cry!
3 For my soul has had enough troubles, and my life has drawn near to Sheol.
4 I am reckoned among those who go down to the pit; I have become like a man without strength,
5 Forsaken among the dead, like the slain who lie in the grave, whom You remember no more, and they are cut off from Your hand.
6 You have put me in the lowest pit, in dark places, in the depths.
7 Your wrath has rested upon me, and You have afflicted me with all Your waves. Selah.
8 You have removed my acquaintances far from me; You have made me an object of loathing to them; I am shut up and cannot go out.
9 My eye has wasted away because of affliction; I have called upon You every day, O Lord; I have spread out my hands to You.
10 Will You perform wonders for the dead? Will the departed spirits rise and praise You? Selah.
11 Will Your lovingkindness be declared in the grave, Your faithfulness in Abaddon?
12 Will Your wonders be made known in the darkness? And Your righteousness in the land of forgetfulness?
13 But I, O Lord, have cried out to You for help, and in the morning my prayer comes before You.
14 O Lord, why do You reject my soul? Why do You hide Your face from me?
15 I was afflicted and about to die from my youth on; I suffer Your terrors; I am overcome.

Petition   *Psalms*

16 Your burning anger has passed over me; Your terrors have destroyed me.
17 They have surrounded me like water all day long; They have encompassed me altogether.
18 You have removed lover and friend far from me; My acquaintances are in darkness.

Psalm 89

This is a Psalm of supplication. It urges God's favor and the end of His wrath.

46 How long, O Lord? Will You hide Yourself forever? Will Your wrath burn like fire?
47 Remember what my span of life is; For what vanity You have created all the sons of men!
48 What man can live and not see death? Can he deliver his soul from the power of Sheol? Selah.
49 Where are Your former lovingkindnesses, O Lord, which You swore to David in Your faithfulness?

52 Blessed be the Lord forever! Amen and Amen.

Psalm 91

This is a great Psalm of supplication and deliverance. It includes words of protection for God's loved ones. It involves Angels in the safeguard of God's people. A good evening prayer.

1 He who dwells in the shelter of the Most High will abide in the shadow of the Almighty.
2 I will say to the Lord, "My refuge and my fortress, my God, in whom I trust!"
3 For it is He who delivers you from the snare of the trapper and from the deadly pestilence.
4 He will cover you with His pinions, and under His wings you may seek refuge; His faithfulness is a shield and bulwark.
5 You will not be afraid of the terror by night, or of the arrow that flies by day;
6 Of the pestilence that stalks in darkness, or of the destruction that lays waste at noon.
7 A thousand may fall at your side and ten thousand at your right hand, But it shall not approach you.

10 No evil will befall you, nor will any plague come near your tent.
11 For He will give His angels charge concerning you, to guard you in all your ways.
12 They will bear you up in their hands, that you do not strike your foot against a stone.
13 You will tread upon the lion and cobra, the young lion and the serpent you will trample down.
14 "Because he has loved Me, therefore I will deliver him; I will set him securely on high, because he has known My name.
15 "He will call upon Me, and I will answer him; I will be with him in trouble; I will rescue him and honor him.
16 "With a long life I will satisfy him and let him see My salvation."

Psalm 102

The opening of this Psalm is a call for help. It urges God to answer our prayers quickly. It includes expressions of sorrow and physical pain. It shows the relationship between God's indignation and our present sorrows.

1 Hear my prayer, O Lord! And let my cry for help come to You.
2 Do not hide Your face from me in the day of my distress; Incline Your ear to me; In the day when I call answer me quickly.
3 For my days have been consumed in smoke, and my bones have been scorched like a hearth.
4 My heart has been smitten like grass and has withered away, indeed, I forget to eat my bread.
5 Because of the loudness of my groaning My bones cling to my flesh.
6 I resemble a pelican of the wilderness; I have become like an owl of the waste places.

7 I lie awake, I have become like a lonely bird on a housetop.

10 Because of Your indignation and Your wrath, for You have lifted me up and cast me away.
11 My days are like a lengthened shadow, and I wither away like grass.

18 This will be written for the generation to come, that a people yet to be created may praise the Lord.
19 For He looked down from His holy height; From heaven the Lord gazed upon the earth,
20 To hear the groaning of the prisoner, to set free those who were doomed to death,
21 That men may tell of the name of the Lord in Zion and His praise in Jerusalem,
22 When the peoples are gathered together, and the kingdoms, to serve the Lord.
23 He has weakened my strength in the way; He has shortened my days.
24 I say, "O my God, do not take me away in the midst of my days, Your years are throughout all generations.
25 "Of old You founded the earth, and the heavens are the work of Your hands.

Psalm 109

This Psalm includes words of lament from an individual experiencing great sorrow and who has been wrongly accused. It ends with words of thanksgiving.

21 But You, O God, the Lord, deal kindly with me for Your name's sake; Because Your lovingkindness is good, deliver me;
22 For I am afflicted and needy, and my heart is wounded within me.
23 I am passing like a shadow when it lengthens; I am shaken off like the locust.
24 My knees are weak from fasting, and my flesh has grown lean, without fatness.

26 Help me, O Lord my God; Save me according to Your lovingkindness.
27 And let them know that this is Your hand; You, Lord, have done it.
28 Let them curse, but You bless; When they arise, they shall be ashamed, But Your servant shall be glad.
29 Let my accusers be clothed with dishonor, and let them cover themselves with their own shame as with a robe.
30 With my mouth I will give thanks abundantly to the Lord; And in the midst of many I will praise Him.
31 For He stands at the right hand of the needy, to save him from those who judge his soul.

Psalm 115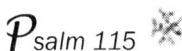

This prayer includes multiple blessings, especially for our children. It asks God to deliver us from a premature death and concludes with words of praise and confidence.

14 May the Lord give you increase, you and your children.
15 May you be blessed of the Lord, Maker of heaven and earth.
16 The heavens are the heavens of the Lord, But the earth He has given to the sons of men.
17 The dead do not praise the Lord, nor do any who go down into silence;
18 But as for us, we will bless the Lord From this time forth and forever. Praise the Lord!

Psalm 119

This prayer for supplication calls for God's comfort in the midst of afflictions. The Psalmist pleads for discernment, knowledge, and has a strong desire to learn the law as a way to achieve God's favor. The Psalm establishes a relationship between righteousness and an end of sorrows. The Psalmist longs for salvation. A good night prayer.

49 Remember the word to Your servant, in which You have made me hope.
50 This is my comfort in my affliction, that Your word has revived me.
51 The arrogant utterly deride me, yet I do not turn aside from Your law.
52 I have remembered Your ordinances from of old, O Lord, and comfort myself.

64 The earth is full of Your lovingkindness, O Lord; Teach me Your statutes.
65 You have dealt well with Your servant, O Lord, according to Your word.
66 Teach me good discernment and knowledge, for I believe in Your commandments.
67 Before I was afflicted I went astray, But now I keep Your word.
68 You are good and do good; Teach me Your statutes.

141 I am small and despised, yet I do not forget Your precepts.
142 Your righteousness is an everlasting righteousness, and Your law is truth.
143 Trouble and anguish have come upon me, yet Your commandments are my delight.
144 Your testimonies are righteous forever; Give me understanding that I may live.

145 I cried with all my heart; Answer me, O Lord!
I will observe Your statutes.
146 I cried to You; Save me and I shall keep Your
testimonies.
147 I rise before dawn and cry for help; I wait for
Your words.
148 My eyes anticipate the night watches, that I
may meditate on Your word.
149 Hear my voice according to Your
lovingkindness; Revive me, O Lord,
according to Your ordinances.

152 Of old I have known from Your testimonies
that You have founded them forever.
153 Look upon my affliction and rescue me, for I
do not forget Your law.
154 Plead my cause and redeem me; Revive me
according to Your word.
155 Salvation is far from the wicked, for they do
not seek Your statutes.
156 Great are Your mercies, O Lord; Revive me
according to Your ordinances.

169 Let my cry come before You, O Lord; Give
me understanding according to Your word.
170 Let my supplication come before You; Deliver
me according to Your word.
171 Let my lips utter praise, for You teach me
Your statutes.
172 Let my tongue sing of Your word, for all Your
commandments are righteousness.
173 Let Your hand be ready to help me, for I have
chosen Your precepts.
174 I long for Your salvation, O Lord, and Your
law is my delight.
175 Let my soul live that it may praise You, and
let Your ordinances help me.
176 I have gone astray like a lost sheep; Seek
Your servant, for I do not forget Your
commandments.

*P*salm 121

*This is a lovely Psalm that asks God for help
and intervention in times of trouble. It is a plea
for protection for God's loved ones.*

1 I will lift up my eyes to the mountains; From
where shall my help come?
2 My help comes from the Lord, Who made
heaven and earth.
3 He will not allow your foot to slip; He who
keeps you will not slumber.

5 The Lord is your keeper; The Lord is your
shade on your right hand.
6 The sun will not smite you by day, nor the
moon by night.
7 The Lord will protect you from all evil; He will
keep your soul.
8 The Lord will guard your going out and your
coming in From this time forth and forever.

*P*salm 127

*This Psalm shows that only God is in
control of our lives and that He watches over
us even as we "sleep".*

1 Unless the Lord builds the house, they labor
in vain who build it; Unless the Lord
guards the city, the watchman keeps
awake in vain.
2 It is vain for you to rise up early, to retire late,
to eat the bread of painful labors; For He
gives to His beloved even in his sleep.

*P*salm 130

*This Psalm includes words of supplication
and confidence, and provides assurance of
God's forgiveness. It urges us to "wait" for the
Lord.*

1 Out of the depths I have cried to You, O Lord.
2 Lord, hear my voice! Let Your ears be
attentive To the voice of my supplications.
3 If You, Lord, should mark iniquities, O Lord,
who could stand?
4 But there is forgiveness with You, that You
may be feared.
5 I wait for the Lord, my soul does wait, and in
His word do I hope.
6 My soul waits for the Lord More than the
watchmen for the morning; Indeed, more
than the watchmen for the morning.

Psalm 141

This is an invocation for help. It urges God's deliverance. A good evening prayer.

1 O Lord, I call upon You; Hasten to me! Give ear to my voice when I call to You!
2 May my prayer be counted as incense before You; The lifting up of my hands as the evening offering.

Psalm 142

This Psalm is a personal lament of expressions of sorrow. It calls for God's protection in times of affliction.

1 I cry aloud with my voice to the Lord; I make supplication with my voice to the Lord.
2 I pour out my complaint before Him; I declare my trouble before Him.
3 When my spirit was overwhelmed within me, You knew my path. In the way where I walk They have hidden a trap for me.
4 Look to the right and see; For there is no one who regards me; There is no escape for me; No one cares for my soul.
5 I cried out to You, O Lord; I said, "You are my refuge, my portion in the land of the living.
6 "Give heed to my cry, for I am brought very low; Deliver me from my persecutors, for they are too strong for me.
7 "Bring my soul out of prison, so that I may give thanks to Your name; The righteous will surround me, for You will deal bountifully with me."

Psalm 143

This is a penitential Psalm. It urges God for grace and quick deliverance while keeping our souls "out of trouble."

1 Hear my prayer, O Lord, give ear to my supplications! Answer me in Your faithfulness, in Your righteousness!
2 And do not enter into judgment with Your servant, for in Your sight no man living is righteous.
7 Answer me quickly, O Lord, my spirit fails; Do not hide Your face from me, or I will become like those who go down to the pit.
8 Let me hear Your lovingkindness in the morning; For I trust in You; Teach me the way in which I should walk; For to You I lift up my soul.
10 Teach me to do Your will, for You are my God; Let Your good Spirit lead me on level ground.
11 For the sake of Your name, O Lord, revive me. In Your righteousness bring my soul out of trouble.

Psalm 145

This is a prayer for help and confidence in God's deliverance. It shows that God is near to us and will fulfill the desire of those who call upon and fear Him.

14 The Lord sustains all who fall and raises up all who are bowed down.
15 The eyes of all look to You, and You give them their food in due time.
16 You open Your hand and satisfy the desire of every living thing.
17 The Lord is righteous in all His ways and kind in all His deeds.
18 The Lord is near to all who call upon Him, to all who call upon Him in truth.
19 He will fulfill the desire of those who fear Him; He will also hear their cry and will save them.
20 The Lord keeps all who love Him, But all the wicked He will destroy.
21 My mouth will speak the praise of the Lord, and all flesh will bless His holy name forever and ever.

Praise

Psalm 8

This is a Psalm of praise. It shows the majestic nature of God as the Creator of heaven and earth.

1 O Lord, our Lord, how majestic is Your name in all the earth, Who have displayed Your splendor above the heavens!

3 When I consider Your heavens, the work of Your fingers, the moon and the stars, which You have ordained;
4 What is man that You take thought of him, and the son of man that You care for him?
5 Yet You have made him a little lower than God, and You crown him with glory and majesty!
6 You make him to rule over the works of Your hands; You have put all things under his feet,
7 All sheep and oxen, and also the beasts of the field,
8 The birds of the heavens and the fish of the sea, whatever passes through the paths of the seas.
9 O Lord, our Lord, how majestic is Your name in all the earth!.

Psalm 16

This Psalm includes words of praise and assurance that God will not abandon the righteous. A good night prayer.

7 I will bless the Lord who has counseled me; Indeed, my mind instructs me in the night.
8 I have set the Lord continually before me; Because He is at my right hand, I will not be shaken.
9 Therefore my heart is glad and my glory rejoices; My flesh also will dwell securely.
10 For You will not abandon my soul to Sheol; Nor will You allow Your Holy One to undergo decay.
11 You will make known to me the path of life; In Your presence is fullness of joy; In Your right hand there are pleasures forever.

Psalm 19 ✳

This Psalm opens with a description of God's glory. It expresses the relationship among the Law, fear of God, and judgment. It asks for God's grace.

1 The heavens are telling of the glory of God; And their expanse is declaring the work of His hands.

7 The law of the Lord is perfect, restoring the soul; The testimony of the Lord is sure, making wise the simple.
8 The precepts of the Lord are right, rejoicing the heart; The commandment of the Lord is pure, enlightening the eyes.
9 The fear of the Lord is clean, enduring forever; The judgments of the Lord are true; They are righteous altogether.
10 They are more desirable than gold, yes, than much fine gold; Sweeter also than honey and the drippings of the honeycomb.
11 Moreover, by them Your servant is warned; In keeping them there is great reward.

14 Let the words of my mouth and the meditation of my heart be acceptable in Your sight, O Lord, my rock and my Redeemer.

Psalm 24 ✝

This is a Psalm of praise and indicates that all the earth and its contents are of God's. It shows the relationship between a pure heart and God's blessings.

1 The earth is the Lord's, and all it contains, the world, and those who dwell in it.
2 For He has founded it upon the seas and established it upon the rivers.
3 Who may ascend into the hill of the Lord? And who may stand in His holy place?
4 He who has clean hands and a pure heart, who has not lifted up his soul to falsehood and has not sworn deceitfully.
5 He shall receive a blessing from the Lord and righteousness from the God of his salvation.
6 This is the generation of those who seek Him, who seek Your face-- even Jacob. Selah.
7 Lift up your heads, O gates, and be lifted up, O ancient doors, that the King of glory may come in!
8 Who is the King of glory? The Lord strong and mighty, the Lord mighty in battle.
9 Lift up your heads, O gates, and lift them up, O

ancient doors, that the King of glory may come in!
10 Who is this King of glory? The Lord of hosts, He is the King of glory. Selah.

Psalm 29 ✝

This Psalm praises God and describes His glory as the Creator who overcame the chaotic forces of nature.

1 Ascribe to the Lord, O sons of the mighty, ascribe to the Lord glory and strength.
2 Ascribe to the Lord the glory due to His name; Worship the Lord in holy array.
3 The voice of the Lord is upon the waters; The God of glory thunders, the Lord is over many waters.
4 The voice of the Lord is powerful, the voice of the Lord is majestic.
5 The voice of the Lord breaks the cedars; Yes, the Lord breaks in pieces the cedars of Lebanon.
6 He makes Lebanon skip like a calf, and Sirion like a young wild ox.
7 The voice of the Lord hews out flames of fire.
8 The voice of the Lord shakes the wilderness; The Lord shakes the wilderness of Kadesh.
9 The voice of the Lord makes the deer to calve and strips the forests bare; And in His temple everything says, "Glory!"
10 The Lord sat as King at the flood; Yes, the Lord sits as King forever.
11 The Lord will give strength to His people; The Lord will bless His people with peace.

Psalm 33

This Psalm stresses the joy of glorifying God. It makes references to the theology of the divine word. It shows that God controls and intervenes in human plans.

1 Sing for joy in the Lord, O you righteous ones; Praise is becoming to the upright.
2 Give thanks to the Lord with the lyre; Sing praises to Him with a harp of ten strings.
3 Sing to Him a new song; Play skillfully with a shout of joy.
4 For the word of the Lord is upright, and all His work is done in faithfulness.
5 He loves righteousness and justice; The earth is full of the lovingkindness of the Lord.
6 By the word of the Lord the heavens were made, and by the breath of His mouth all their host.
7 He gathers the waters of the sea together as a heap; He lays up the deeps in storehouses.
8 Let all the earth fear the Lord; Let all the inhabitants of the world stand in awe of Him.
9 For He spoke, and it was done; He commanded, and it stood fast.
10 The Lord nullifies the counsel of the nations; He frustrates the plans of the peoples.
11 The counsel of the Lord stands forever, the plans of His heart from generation to generation.
12 Blessed is the nation whose God is the Lord, the people whom He has chosen for His own inheritance.
13 The Lord looks from heaven; He sees all the sons of men;
14 From His dwelling place He looks out On all the inhabitants of the earth,
15 He who fashions the hearts of them all, He who understands all their works.

Psalm 34

This Psalm invites us to praise God at all times and exalt His name.

1 I will bless the Lord at all times; His praise shall continually be in my mouth.
2 My soul will make its boast in the Lord; The humble will hear it and rejoice.
3 O magnify the Lord with me, and let us exalt His name together.
8 O taste and see that the Lord is good; How blessed is the man who takes refuge in Him!

Psalm 36

This Psalm praises God and recognizes His presence in heaven and earth. It states that His children can take refuge "in the shadow of His wings."

5 Your lovingkindness, O Lord, extends to the heavens, Your faithfulness reaches to the skies.
6 Your righteousness is like the mountains of God; Your judgments are like a great deep. O Lord, You preserve man and beast.
7 How precious is Your lovingkindness, O God! And the children of men take refuge in the shadow of Your wings.
8 They drink their fill of the abundance of Your house; And You give them to drink of the river of Your delights.
9 For with You is the fountain of life; In Your light we see light.
10 O continue Your lovingkindness to those who know You, and Your righteousness to the upright in heart.

Psalm 47

This Psalm calls and praises God through shouts and claps. When the Ark of the Lord was brought to Jerusalem, 2 Samuel 6 tells us that David was "dancing before the Lord with all his might" and that all the house of Israel were bringing up the ark with "shouting and the sound of the trumpet."

1 O clap your hands, all peoples; Shout to God with the voice of joy.
2 For the Lord Most High is to be feared, a great King over all the earth.
3 He subdues peoples under us and nations under our feet.
4 He chooses our inheritance for us, the glory of Jacob whom He loves. Selah.
5 God has ascended with a shout, the Lord, with the sound of a trumpet.
6 Sing praises to God, sing praises; Sing praises to our King, sing praises.
7 For God is the King of all the earth; Sing praises with a skillful psalm.

Psalm 57

This Psalm includes praises and words of thanksgiving. It indicates that God is exalted in the heavens and earth.

7 My heart is steadfast, O God, my heart is steadfast; I will sing, yes, I will sing praises!
8 Awake, my glory! Awake, harp and lyre! I will awaken the dawn.
9 I will give thanks to You, O Lord, among the peoples; I will sing praises to You among the nations.
10 For Your lovingkindness is great to the heavens and Your truth to the clouds.
11 Be exalted above the heavens, O God; Let Your glory be above all the earth.

Psalm 59

This Psalm includes words of joy and praises to the Lord. A good morning prayer.

16 But as for me, I shall sing of Your strength; Yes, I shall joyfully sing of Your lovingkindness in the morning, for You have been my stronghold and a refuge in the day of my distress.
17 O my strength, I will sing praises to You; For God is my stronghold, the God who shows me lovingkindness.

Psalm 63

This Psalm includes words of praise. The Psalmist yearns and meditates on God "in the night watches." A good night prayer.

1 O God, You are my God; I shall seek You earnestly; My soul thirsts for You, my flesh yearns for You, in a dry and weary land where there is no water.
2 Thus I have seen You in the sanctuary, to see Your power and Your glory.
3 Because Your lovingkindness is better than life, my lips will praise You.
4 So I will bless You as long as I live; I will lift up my hands in Your name.

5 My soul is satisfied as with marrow and fatness, and my mouth offers praises with joyful lips.
6 When I remember You on my bed, I meditate on You in the night watches,
7 For You have been my help, and in the shadow of Your wings I sing for joy.
8 My soul clings to You; Your right hand upholds me.

Psalm 66

This Psalm includes praises to an "awesome" God and His divine work.

1 Shout joyfully to God, all the earth;
2 Sing the glory of His name; Make His praise glorious.
3 Say to God, "How awesome are Your works! Because of the greatness of Your power Your enemies will give feigned obedience to You.
4 "All the earth will worship You, and will sing praises to You; They will sing praises to Your name." Selah.
5 Come and see the works of God, Who is awesome in His deeds toward the sons of men.
6 He turned the sea into dry land; They passed through the river on foot; There let us rejoice in Him!
7 He rules by His might forever; His eyes keep watch on the nations; Let not the rebellious exalt themselves. Selah.
8 Bless our God, O peoples, and sound His praise abroad,
9 Who keeps us in life and does not allow our feet to slip.

Psalm 67

This Psalm of praise shows the providential care of God upon His people and nations.

1 God be gracious to us and bless us, and cause His face to shine upon us-- Selah.
2 That Your way may be known on the earth, Your salvation among all nations.
3 Let the peoples praise You, O God; Let all the peoples praise You.
4 Let the nations be glad and sing for joy; For You will judge the peoples with uprightness and guide the nations on the earth. Selah.
5 Let the peoples praise You, O God; Let all the peoples praise You.
6 The earth has yielded its produce; God, our God, blesses us.
7 God blesses us, that all the ends of the earth may fear Him.

Psalm 68

This Psalm includes praises to God. It speaks of His strength and majesty.

32 Sing to God, O kingdoms of the earth, sing praises to the Lord, Selah.
33 To Him who rides upon the highest heavens, which are from ancient times; Behold, He speaks forth with His voice, a mighty voice.
34 Ascribe strength to God; His majesty is over Israel and His strength is in the skies.
35 O God, You are awesome from Your sanctuary. The God of Israel Himself gives strength and power to the people. Blessed be God!

Psalm 71

This Psalm includes words of praise. It requests protection and speaks of the righteousness of God.

14 But as for me, I will hope continually, and will praise You yet more and more.
15 My mouth shall tell of Your righteousness and of Your salvation all day long; For I do not know the sum of them.
16 I will come with the mighty deeds of the Lord God; I will make mention of Your righteousness, Yours alone.
17 O God, You have taught me from my youth, and I still declare Your wondrous deeds.
18 And even when I am old and gray, O God, do not forsake me, until I declare Your strength to this generation, Your power to all who are to come.
19 For Your righteousness, O God, reaches to the heavens, You Who have done great things; O God, who is like You?

22 I will also praise You with a harp, even Your truth, O my God; To You I will sing praises with the lyre, O Holy One of Israel.
23 My lips will shout for joy when I sing praises to You; And my soul, which You have redeemed.

Psalm 77

This Psalm includes words of praise. God's power is associated with nature and how He can bring order from chaos.

11 I shall remember the deeds of the Lord;
Surely I will remember Your wonders of
old.
12 I will meditate on all Your work and muse on
Your deeds.
13 Your way, O God, is holy; What god is great
like our God?
14 You are the God who works wonders; You
have made known Your strength among
the peoples.
15 You have by Your power redeemed Your
people, the sons of Jacob and Joseph.
Selah.
16 The waters saw You, O God; The waters saw
You, they were in anguish; The deeps also
trembled.
17 The clouds poured out water; The skies gave
forth a sound; Your arrows flashed here
and there.
18 The sound of Your thunder was in the
whirlwind; The lightnings lit up the world;
The earth trembled and shook.
19 Your way was in the sea and Your paths in
the mighty waters, and Your footprints may
not be known.

Psalm 89

*This Psalm includes words of loving
kindness and praise. The mighty power of
God is associated with the forces of nature. It
invites us to rejoice.*

1 I will sing of the lovingkindness of the Lord
forever; To all generations I will make
known Your faithfulness with my mouth.
2 For I have said, "Lovingkindness will be
built up forever; In the heavens You will
establish Your faithfulness."

5 The heavens will praise Your wonders, O Lord;
Your faithfulness also in the assembly of
the holy ones.
6 For who in the skies is comparable to the
Lord? Who among the sons of the mighty
is like the Lord,
7 A God greatly feared in the council of the holy
ones, and awesome above all those who
are around Him?
8 O Lord God of hosts, Who is like You, O
mighty Lord? Your faithfulness also
surrounds You.
9 You rule the swelling of the sea; When its
waves rise, You still them.
10 You Yourself crushed Rahab like one who
is slain; You scattered Your enemies with
Your mighty arm.
11 The heavens are Yours, the earth also is
Yours; The world and all it contains, You
have founded them.
12 The north and the south, You have created
them; Tabor and Hermon shout for joy at
Your name.
13 You have a strong arm; Your hand is mighty,
Your right hand is exalted.
14 Righteousness and justice are the foundation
of Your throne; Lovingkindness and truth
go before You.
15 How blessed are the people who know the
joyful sound! O Lord, they walk in the light
of Your countenance.
16 In Your name they rejoice all the day, and by
Your righteousness they are exalted.
17 For You are the glory of their strength, and by
Your favor our horn is exalted.
18 For our shield belongs to the Lord, and our
king to the Holy One of Israel.

Psalm 92

*This Psalm includes words of praise and
thanksgiving. It declares the loving kindness
of God. A good morning prayer.*

1 It is good to give thanks to the Lord and to sing
praises to Your name, O Most High;
2 To declare Your lovingkindness in the morning
and Your faithfulness by night,
3 With the ten-stringed lute and with the harp,
with resounding music upon the lyre.
4 For You, O Lord, have made me glad by what
You have done, I will sing for joy at the
works of Your hands.

Psalm 93 ✝

This is a beautiful Psalm of praise. It was assigned to the Sabbath to commemorate the creation and God's completed work.

1 The Lord reigns, He is clothed with majesty; The Lord has clothed and girded Himself with strength; Indeed, the world is firmly established, it will not be moved.
2 Your throne is established from of old; You are from everlasting.
3 The floods have lifted up, O Lord, the floods have lifted up their voice, the floods lift up their pounding waves.
4 More than the sounds of many waters, than the mighty breakers of the sea, the Lord on high is mighty.
5 Your testimonies are fully confirmed; Holiness befits Your house, O Lord, forevermore.

Psalm 95

This Psalm includes words of praise and was assigned to the Sabbath and, later, to the New Year Festivals. It calls upon the people to worship, submit and bow down before God.

1 O come, let us sing for joy to the Lord, let us shout joyfully to the rock of our salvation.
2 Let us come before His presence with thanksgiving, let us shout joyfully to Him with psalms.
3 For the Lord is a great God and a great King above all gods,
4 In whose hand are the depths of the earth, the peaks of the mountains are His also.
5 The sea is His, for it was He who made it, and His hands formed the dry land.
6 Come, let us worship and bow down, let us kneel before the Lord our Maker.
7 For He is our God, and we are the people of His pasture and the sheep of His hand. Today, if you would hear His voice,

Psalm 96 ✝

This Psalm became part of a new hymn in 1 Chronicles. Its original intention was to worship during the Feast of Tabernacles. It is a Psalm of praise and motivation. It states that God's Kingship is exercised for the sake of divine justice.

1 Sing to the Lord a new song; Sing to the Lord, all the earth.
2 Sing to the Lord, bless His name; Proclaim good tidings of His salvation from day to day.
3 Tell of His glory among the nations, His wonderful deeds among all the peoples.
4 For great is the Lord and greatly to be praised; He is to be feared above all gods.
5 For all the gods of the peoples are idols, But the Lord made the heavens.
6 Splendor and majesty are before Him, strength and beauty are in His sanctuary.
7 Ascribe to the Lord, O families of the peoples, ascribe to the Lord glory and strength.
8 Ascribe to the Lord the glory of His name; Bring an offering and come into His courts.
9 Worship the Lord in holy attire; Tremble before Him, all the earth.
10 Say among the nations, "The Lord reigns; Indeed, the world is firmly established, it will not be moved; He will judge the peoples with equity."
11 Let the heavens be glad, and let the earth rejoice; Let the sea roar, and all it contains;
12 Let the field exult, and all that is in it. Then all the trees of the forest will sing for joy
13 Before the Lord, for He is coming, for He is coming to judge the earth. He will judge the world in righteousness and the peoples in His faithfulness.

Psalm 98

This Psalm calls for all God's creation to praise Him with joy. It anticipates final judgment.

1 O sing to the Lord a new song, for He has done wonderful things, His right hand and His holy arm have gained the victory for Him.

4 Shout joyfully to the Lord, all the earth; Break forth and sing for joy and sing praises.
5 Sing praises to the Lord with the lyre, with the lyre and the sound of melody.
6 With trumpets and the sound of the horn Shout joyfully before the King, the Lord.
7 Let the sea roar and all it contains, the world and those who dwell in it.
8 Let the rivers clap their hands, let the mountains sing together for joy
9 Before the Lord, for He is coming to judge the earth; He will judge the world with righteousness and the peoples with equity.

*P*salm 99 ✝

This Psalm focuses on the enthronement of God. It includes themes from Exodus and shows how "in a pillar of cloud" God talked and conveyed justice to His people.

1 The Lord reigns, let the peoples tremble; He is enthroned above the cherubim, let the earth shake!
2 The Lord is great in Zion, and He is exalted above all the peoples.
3 Let them praise Your great and awesome name; Holy is He.
4 The strength of the King loves justice; You have established equity; You have executed justice and righteousness in Jacob.
5 Exalt the Lord our God and worship at His footstool; Holy is He.
6 Moses and Aaron were among His priests, and Samuel was among those who called on His name; They called upon the Lord and He answered them.
7 He spoke to them in the pillar of cloud; They kept His testimonies and the statute that He gave them.
8 O Lord our God, You answered them; You were a forgiving God to them, and yet an avenger of their evil deeds.
9 Exalt the Lord our God and worship at His holy hill, for holy is the Lord our God.

*P*salm 100 ✝

This is a Psalm of praise and joy. It calls us to serve the Lord. It shows that He is a merciful God and that His loving kindness is everlasting.

1 Shout joyfully to the Lord, all the earth.
2 Serve the Lord with gladness; Come before Him with joyful singing.
3 Know that the Lord Himself is God; It is He who has made us, and not we ourselves; We are His people and the sheep of His pasture.
4 Enter His gates with thanksgiving and His courts with praise. Give thanks to Him, bless His name.
5 For the Lord is good; His lovingkindness is everlasting and His faithfulness to all generations.

*P*salm 103

This Psalm is a traditional poem. It shows God's grace and power in providing physical and spiritual healing.

1 Bless the Lord, O my soul, and all that is within me, bless His holy name.
2 Bless the Lord, O my soul, and forget none of His benefits;
3 Who pardons all your iniquities, Who heals all your diseases;
4 Who redeems your life from the pit, Who crowns you with lovingkindness and compassion;
5 Who satisfies your years with good things, so that your youth is renewed like the eagle.

8 The Lord is compassionate and gracious, slow to anger and abounding in lovingkindness.
9 He will not always strive with us, nor will He keep His anger forever.
10 He has not dealt with us according to our sins, nor rewarded us according to our iniquities.
11 For as high as the heavens are above the earth, so great is His lovingkindness toward those who fear Him.
12 As far as the east is from the west, so far has He removed our transgressions from us.
13 Just as a father has compassion on his children, so the Lord has compassion on those who fear Him.
14 For He Himself knows our frame; He is mindful that we are but dust.
15 As for man, his days are like grass; As a flower of the field, so he flourishes.
16 When the wind has passed over it, it is no

more, and its place acknowledges it no longer.

17 But the lovingkindness of the Lord is from everlasting to everlasting on those who fear Him, and His righteousness to children's children,
18 To those who keep His covenant and remember His precepts to do them.
19 The Lord has established His throne in the heavens, and His sovereignty rules over all.
20 Bless the Lord, you His angels, Mighty in strength, who perform His word, obeying the voice of His word!
21 Bless the Lord, all you His hosts, you who serve Him, doing His will.
22 Bless the Lord, all you works of His, in all places of His dominion; Bless the Lord, O my soul!

Psalm 104

This Psalm provides a magnificent praise. God appears full of mercy. It acclaims God as a Royal Creator of a world where even "the lion's roar" becomes a prayer.

1 Bless the Lord, O my soul! O Lord my God, You are very great; You are clothed with splendor and majesty,
2 Covering Yourself with light as with a cloak, stretching out heaven like a tent curtain.
3 He lays the beams of His upper chambers in the waters; He makes the clouds His chariot; He walks upon the wings of the wind;
4 He makes the winds His messengers, flaming fire His ministers.
5 He established the earth upon its foundations, so that it will not totter forever and ever.
6 You covered it with the deep as with a garment; The waters were standing above the mountains.
7 At Your rebuke they fled, At the sound of Your thunder they hurried away.
8 The mountains rose; The valleys sank down To the place which You established for them.

9 You set a boundary that they may not pass over, so that they will not return to cover the earth.
10 He sends forth springs in the valleys; They flow between the mountains;
11 They give drink to every beast of the field; The wild donkeys quench their thirst.
12 Beside them the birds of the heavens dwell; They lift up their voices among the branches.
13 He waters the mountains from His upper chambers; The earth is satisfied with the fruit of His works.
14 He causes the grass to grow for the cattle, and vegetation for the labor of man, so that he may bring forth food from the earth,
15 And wine which makes man's heart glad, so that he may make his face glisten with oil, and food which sustains man's heart.
16 The trees of the Lord drink their fill, the cedars of Lebanon which He planted,
17 Where the birds build their nests, and the stork, whose home is the fir trees.
18 The high mountains are for the wild goats; The cliffs are a refuge for the shephanim.
19 He made the moon for the seasons; The sun knows the place of its setting.
20 You appoint darkness and it becomes night, in which all the beasts of the forest prowl about.
21 The young lions roar after their prey and seek their food from God.
22 When the sun rises they withdraw and lie down in their dens.
23 Man goes forth to his work and to his labor until evening.
24 O Lord, how many are Your works! In wisdom You have made them all; The earth is full of Your possessions.
25 There is the sea, great and broad, in which are swarms without number, Animals both small and great.
26 There the ships move along, and Leviathan, which You have formed to sport in it.
27 They all wait for You To give them their food in due season.
28 You give to them, they gather it up; You open

Your hand, they are satisfied with good.
29 You hide Your face, they are dismayed; You take away their spirit, they expire and return to their dust.
30 You send forth Your Spirit, they are created; And You renew the face of the ground.
31 Let the glory of the Lord endure forever; Let the Lord be glad in His works;
32 He looks at the earth, and it trembles; He touches the mountains, and they smoke.
33 I will sing to the Lord as long as I live; I will sing praise to my God while I have my being.
34 Let my meditation be pleasing to Him; As for me, I shall be glad in the Lord.
35 Let sinners be consumed from the earth and let the wicked be no more. Bless the Lord, O my soul. Praise the Lord!

*P*salm 105

This Psalm includes words of invitation to seek God's presence and reminds us of His wonders and judgment.

2 Sing to Him, sing praises to Him; Speak of all His wonders.
3 Glory in His holy name; Let the heart of those who seek the Lord be glad.
4 Seek the Lord and His strength; Seek His face continually.
5 Remember His wonders which He has done, His marvels and the judgments uttered by His mouth,
6 O seed of Abraham, His servant, O sons of Jacob, His chosen ones!
7 He is the Lord our God; His judgments are in all the earth.

*P*salm 111 †

This Psalm celebrates the glory and righteousness of God. It reminds us that the fear of God is the beginning of wisdom.

1 Praise the Lord! I will give thanks to the Lord with all my heart, in the company of the upright and in the assembly.
2 Great are the works of the Lord; They are studied by all who delight in them.
3 Splendid and majestic is His work, and His righteousness endures forever.
4 He has made His wonders to be remembered; The Lord is gracious and compassionate.
5 He has given food to those who fear Him; He will remember His covenant forever.
6 He has made known to His people the power of His works, in giving them the heritage of the nations.
7 The works of His hands are truth and justice; All His precepts are sure.
8 They are upheld forever and ever; They are performed in truth and uprightness.
9 He has sent redemption to His people; He has ordained His covenant forever; Holy and awesome is His name.
10 The fear of the Lord is the beginning of wisdom; A good understanding have all those who do His commandments; His praise endures forever.

*P*salm 113 †

This is an ancient canticle. It reminds us of God's glory and His care for the humble and those in need. He makes the barren woman a joyful mother.

1 Praise the Lord! Praise, O servants of the Lord, Praise the name of the Lord.
2 Blessed be the name of the Lord From this time forth and forever.
3 From the rising of the sun to its setting The name of the Lord is to be praised.
4 The Lord is high above all nations; His glory is above the heavens.
5 Who is like the Lord our God, Who is enthroned on high,
6 Who humbles Himself to behold The things that are in heaven and in the earth?
7 He raises the poor from the dust and lifts the needy from the ash heap,
8 To make them sit with princes, with the princes of His people.

Psalms   *Praise*

9 He makes the barren woman abide in the house As a joyful mother of children. Praise the Lord!

Psalm 117 ✝

This is the shortest Psalm in the Psalter. It is a hymn of praise and shows God's loving kindness for us.

1 Praise the Lord, all nations; Laud Him, all peoples!
2 For His lovingkindness is great toward us, and the truth of the Lord is everlasting. Praise the Lord!

Psalm 119 ✳

These verses are part of the longest Psalm in the Psalter. It includes praises to the Lord who is the center of the Psalmist's life. The words of the Lord are shown to be "sweeter than honey." A good night prayer.

55 O Lord, I remember Your name in the night, and keep Your law.
56 This has become mine, that I observe Your precepts.
57 The Lord is my portion; I have promised to keep Your words.
58 I sought Your favor with all my heart; Be gracious to me according to Your word.
59 I considered my ways and turned my feet to Your testimonies.
60 I hastened and did not delay To keep Your commandments.

89 Forever, O Lord, Your word is settled in heaven.
90 Your faithfulness continues throughout all generations; You established the earth, and it stands.
91 They stand this day according to Your ordinances, for all things are Your servants.
92 If Your law had not been my delight, then I would have perished in my affliction.
93 I will never forget Your precepts, for by them You have revived me.
94 I am Yours, save me; For I have sought Your precepts.

97 O how I love Your law! It is my meditation all the day.
98 Your commandments make me wiser than my enemies, for they are ever mine.
99 I have more insight than all my teachers, for Your testimonies are my meditation.
100 I understand more than the aged, because I have observed Your precepts.
101 I have restrained my feet from every evil way, that I may keep Your word.
102 I have not turned aside from Your ordinances, for You Yourself have taught me.
103 How sweet are Your words to my taste! Yes, sweeter than honey to my mouth!
104 From Your precepts I get understanding; Therefore I hate every false way.
105 Your word is a lamp to my feet and a light to my path.
106 I have sworn and I will confirm it, that I will keep Your righteous ordinances.

123 My eyes fail with longing for Your salvation and for Your righteous word.
124 Deal with Your servant according to Your lovingkindness and teach me Your statutes.
125 I am Your servant; Give me understanding, that I may know Your testimonies.
126 It is time for the Lord to act, for they have broken Your law.
127 Therefore I love Your commandments Above gold, yes, above fine gold.
128 Therefore I esteem right all Your precepts concerning everything, I hate every false way.
129 Your testimonies are wonderful; Therefore my soul observes them.
130 The unfolding of Your words gives light; It gives understanding to the simple.
131 I opened my mouth wide and panted, for I longed for Your commandments.
132 Turn to me and be gracious to me, After Your manner with those who love Your name.

164 Seven times a day I praise You, because of Your righteous ordinances.
165 Those who love Your law have great peace, and nothing causes them to stumble.
166 I hope for Your salvation, O Lord, and do Your commandments.
167 My soul keeps Your testimonies, and I love them exceedingly.
168 I keep Your precepts and Your testimonies, for all my ways are before You.

*P*salm 135

This Psalm includes words of praise. It tells us how lovely God's name is.

1 Praise the Lord! Praise the name of the Lord; Praise Him, O servants of the Lord,
2 You who stand in the house of the Lord, in the courts of the house of our God!
3 Praise the Lord, for the Lord is good; Sing praises to His name, for it is lovely.

*P*salm 136

This Psalm uses words showing God as the creator of the universe.

4 To Him who alone does great wonders, for His lovingkindness is everlasting;
5 To Him who made the heavens with skill, for His lovingkindness is everlasting;
6 To Him who spread out the earth above the waters, for His lovingkindness is everlasting;
7 To Him who made the great lights, for His lovingkindness is everlasting:
8 The sun to rule by day, for His lovingkindness is everlasting,
9 The moon and stars to rule by night, for His lovingkindness is everlasting.

Psalm 139

This is one of the most beautiful Psalms in the Psalter. In these verses, the Psalmist peers into the heavens, into mysteries of God, and invites the Lord to search his heart.

17 How precious also are Your thoughts to me, O God! How vast is the sum of them!
18 If I should count them, they would outnumber the sand. When I awake, I am still with You.

23 Search me, O God, and know my heart; Try me and know my anxious thoughts;
24 And see if there be any hurtful way in me, and lead me in the everlasting way.

Psalm 145

This Psalm refers to God's great deeds and shows God's grace and mercy. It tells us that God is "Slow to anger and great in kindness."

1 I will extol You, my God, O King, and I will bless Your name forever and ever.
2 Every day I will bless You, and I will praise Your name forever and ever.
3 Great is the Lord, and highly to be praised, and His greatness is unsearchable.
4 One generation shall praise Your works to another, and shall declare Your mighty acts.
5 On the glorious splendor of Your majesty and on Your wonderful works, I will meditate.
6 Men shall speak of the power of Your awesome acts, and I will tell of Your greatness.
7 They shall eagerly utter the memory of Your abundant goodness and will shout joyfully of Your righteousness.
8 The Lord is gracious and merciful; Slow to anger and great in kindness.
9 The Lord is good to all, and His mercies are over all His works.
10 All Your works shall give thanks to You, O Lord, and Your godly ones shall bless You.
11 They shall speak of the glory of Your kingdom and talk of Your power;
12 To make known to the sons of men Your mighty acts and the glory of the majesty of Your kingdom.
13 Your kingdom is an everlasting kingdom, and Your dominion endures throughout all generations.

Psalm 146

This Psalm of praise tells us to trust only in God. It speaks of the power of God, His protection, and glory.

1 Praise the Lord! Praise the Lord, O my soul!
2 I will praise the Lord while I live; I will sing praises to my God while I have my being.
3 Do not trust in princes, in mortal man, in whom there is no salvation.
4 His spirit departs, he returns to the earth; In that very day his thoughts perish.
5 How blessed is he whose help is the God of Jacob, whose hope is in the Lord his God,
6 Who made heaven and earth, the sea and all that is in them; Who keeps faith forever;
7 Who executes justice for the oppressed; Who gives food to the hungry. The Lord sets the prisoners free.
8 The Lord opens the eyes of the blind; The Lord raises up those who are bowed down; The Lord loves the righteous;
9 The Lord protects the strangers; He supports the fatherless and the widow, But He thwarts the way of the wicked.
10 The Lord will reign forever, Your God, O Zion, to all generations. Praise the Lord!

Psalm 147

This Psalm shows God's care for the poor and the outcast. It shows that He controls the instruments of war and peace and heaven and earth. It shows that God is gracious and merciful.

1 Praise the Lord! For it is good to sing praises to our God; For it is pleasant and praise is becoming.
2 The Lord builds up Jerusalem; He gathers the outcasts of Israel.

3 He heals the brokenhearted and binds up their wounds.
4 He counts the number of the stars; He gives names to all of them.
5 Great is our Lord and abundant in strength; His understanding is infinite.
6 The Lord supports the afflicted; He brings down the wicked to the ground.
7 Sing to the Lord with thanksgiving; Sing praises to our God on the lyre,
8 Who covers the heavens with clouds, Who provides rain for the earth, Who makes grass to grow on the mountains.
9 He gives to the beast its food, and to the young ravens which cry.
10 He does not delight in the strength of the horse; He does not take pleasure in the legs of a man.
11 The Lord favors those who fear Him, those who wait for His lovingkindness.

15 He sends forth His command to the earth; His word runs very swiftly.
16 He gives snow like wool; He scatters the frost like ashes.
17 He casts forth His ice as fragments; Who can stand before His cold?
18 He sends forth His word and melts them; He causes His wind to blow and the waters to flow.
19 He declares His words to Jacob, His statutes and His ordinances to Israel.
20 He has not dealt thus with any nation; And as for His ordinances, they have not known them. Praise the Lord!

Psalm 148 ✝

This Psalm consists of an invitation to the heavens and their inhabitants to praise God. It makes reference to God's throne in heaven surrounded by His heavenly court.

1 Praise the Lord! Praise the Lord from the heavens; Praise Him in the heights!
2 Praise Him, all His angels; Praise Him, all His hosts!
3 Praise Him, sun and moon; Praise Him, all stars of light!
4 Praise Him, highest heavens, and the waters that are above the heavens!
5 Let them praise the name of the Lord, for He commanded and they were created.
6 He has also established them forever and ever; He has made a decree which will not pass away.
7 Praise the Lord from the earth, sea monsters and all deeps;
8 Fire and hail, snow and clouds; Stormy wind, fulfilling His word;
9 Mountains and all hills; Fruit trees and all cedars;
10 Beasts and all cattle; Creeping things and winged fowl;
11 Kings of the earth and all peoples; Princes and all judges of the earth;
12 Both young men and virgins; Old men and children.
13 Let them praise the name of the Lord, for His name alone is exalted; His glory is above earth and heaven.
14 And He has lifted up a horn for His people, Praise for all His godly ones; Even for the sons of Israel, a people near to Him. Praise the Lord!

Psalm 149

This Psalm includes words of praise and shows that God "takes pleasure in His people."

1 Praise the Lord! Sing to the Lord a new song, and His praise in the congregation of the godly ones.
2 Let Israel be glad in his Maker; Let the sons of Zion rejoice in their King.
3 Let them praise His name with dancing; Let them sing praises to Him with timbrel and lyre.
4 For the Lord takes pleasure in His people; He will beautify the afflicted ones with salvation.
5 Let the godly ones exult in glory; Let them sing for joy on their beds.

Psalm 150 ✝

This Psalm is a magnificent conclusion of the Psalter. It is of exuberant praise. The Lord is praised in the heavenly sanctuary and in the firmament. It encourages the use of instruments when praising and glorifying God.

1 Praise the Lord! Praise God in His sanctuary; Praise Him in His mighty expanse.
2 Praise Him for His mighty deeds; Praise Him according to His excellent greatness.
3 Praise Him with trumpet sound; Praise Him with harp and lyre.
4 Praise Him with timbrel and dancing; Praise Him with stringed instruments and pipe.
5 Praise Him with loud cymbals; Praise Him with resounding cymbals.
6 Let everything that has breath praise the Lord. Praise the Lord!

Thanksgiving

Psalm 7

Verse of thanksgiving and praise.

17 I will give thanks to the Lord according to His righteousness and will sing praise to the name of the Lord Most High.

Psalm 9

Verses of thanksgiving and praise.

1 I will give thanks to the Lord with all my heart; I will tell of all Your wonders.
2 I will be glad and exult in You; I will sing praise to Your name, O Most High.

Psalm 52

Verses of thanksgiving calling to trust the Lord.

8 But as for me, I am like a green olive tree in the house of God; I trust in the loving kindness of God forever and ever.
9 I will give You thanks forever, because You have done it, and I will wait on Your name, for it is good, in the presence of Your godly ones.

Psalm 54
Verse of thanksgiving and sacrifice.

6 Willingly I will sacrifice to You; I will give thanks to Your name, O Lord, for it is good.

Psalm 66
Verses of thanksgiving for a prayer that has been answered.

19 But certainly God has heard; He has given heed to the voice of my prayer.
20 Blessed be God, Who has not turned away my prayer Nor His lovingkindness from me.

Psalm 75
Verse of thanksgiving and praise.

1 We give thanks to You, O God, we give thanks, for Your name is near; Men declare Your wondrous works.

Psalm 86
Verse of thanksgiving and glorification of God's name.

12 I will give thanks to You, O Lord my God, with all my heart, and will glorify Your name forever.

Psalm 92
A joyful hymn of thanksgiving for answering our prayers. It includes words of praise and deliverance.

1 It is good to give thanks to the Lord and to sing praises to Your name, O Most High;
2 To declare Your lovingkindness in the morning and Your faithfulness by night,
3 With the ten-stringed lute and with the harp, with resounding music upon the lyre.
4 For You, O Lord, have made me glad by what You have done, I will sing for joy at the works of Your hands.

Psalm 105

This Psalm includes words of thanksgiving followed by praises. It assures that the heart of those that seek the Lord will be full of gladness and that He will judge the earth.

1 Oh give thanks to the Lord, call upon His name; Make known His deeds among the peoples.
2 Sing to Him, sing praises to Him; Speak of all His wonders.
3 Glory in His holy name; Let the heart of those who seek the Lord be glad.
4 Seek the Lord and His strength; Seek His face continually.
5 Remember His wonders which He has done, His marvels and the judgments uttered by His mouth,
6 O seed of Abraham, His servant, O sons of Jacob, His chosen ones!
7 He is the Lord our God; His judgments are in all the earth.

Psalm 107

This Psalm includes words of thanksgiving. It shows that God blesses the needy and punishes the unrighteousness. It speaks of God's loving kindness.

31 Let them give thanks to the Lord for His lovingkindness, and for His wonders to the sons of men!
32 Let them extol Him also in the congregation of the people, and praise Him at the seat of the elders.
33 He changes rivers into a wilderness and springs of water into a thirsty ground;
34 A fruitful land into a salt waste, because of the wickedness of those who dwell in it.
35 He changes a wilderness into a pool of water and a dry land into springs of water;
36 And there He makes the hungry to dwell, so that they may establish an inhabited city,
37 And sow fields and plant vineyards, and gather a fruitful harvest.
38 Also He blesses them and they multiply greatly, and He does not let their cattle decrease.
39 When they are diminished and bowed down through oppression, misery and sorrow,
40 He pours contempt upon princes and makes them wander in a pathless waste.
41 But He sets the needy securely on high away from affliction, and makes his families like a flock.
42 The upright see it and are glad; But all unrighteousness shuts its mouth.
43 Who is wise? Let him give heed to these things, and consider the lovingkindnesses of the Lord.

Psalm 108

This Psalm includes words of thanksgiving and praise. It anticipates deliverance and answers to prayers. It includes words of exaltation.

1 My heart is steadfast, O God; I will sing, I will sing praises, even with my soul.
2 Awake, harp and lyre; I will awaken the dawn!
3 I will give thanks to You, O Lord, among the peoples, and I will sing praises to You among the nations.
4 For Your lovingkindness is great above the heavens, and Your truth reaches to the skies.
5 Be exalted, O God, above the heavens, and Your glory above all the earth.
6 That Your beloved may be delivered, save with Your right hand, and answer me!

Psalm 116

This is a Psalm of praise and thanksgiving. It includes a confession of sorrow and faith. It shows that God answers the prayers of those in need.

1 I love the Lord, because He hears My voice and my supplications.
2 Because He has inclined His ear to me, therefore I shall call upon Him as long as I live.

3 The cords of death encompassed me and the terrors of Sheol came upon me; I found distress and sorrow.
4 Then I called upon the name of the Lord: "O Lord, I beseech You, save my life!"
5 Gracious is the Lord, and righteous; Yes, our God is compassionate.
6 The Lord preserves the simple; I was brought low, and He saved me.
7 Return to your rest, O my soul, for the Lord has dealt bountifully with you.
8 For You have rescued my soul from death, my eyes from tears, my feet from stumbling.
9 I shall walk before the Lord In the land of the living.
10 I believed when I said, "I am greatly afflicted."
11 I said in my alarm, "All men are liars."
12 What shall I render to the Lord For all His benefits toward me?
13 I shall lift up the cup of salvation and call upon the name of the Lord.
14 I shall pay my vows to the Lord, Oh may it be in the presence of all His people.
15 Precious in the sight of the Lord Is the death of His godly ones.
16 O Lord, surely I am your servant, I am your servant, the son of your handmaid, You have loosed my bonds.
17 To You I shall offer a sacrifice of thanksgiving, and call upon the name of the Lord.
18 I shall pay my vows to the Lord, Oh may it be in the presence of all His people,
19 In the courts of the LORD'S house, in the midst of you, O Jerusalem. Praise the Lord!

Psalm 118 ✝

This Psalm was quoted by our Lord Jesus in the parable of the "landowner who planted a vineyard" (Matthew 21:33-41): "The stone which the builders rejected Has become the chief corner stone." (Matthew 21:42). This Psalm of thanksgiving includes words of praise and deliverance. The Psalmist faced great distress and the "Lord answered." It shows the Lord as strength and salvation. The Psalm asks us to rejoice and be glad.

1 Give thanks to the Lord, for He is good; For His lovingkindness is everlasting.
2 Oh let Israel say, "His lovingkindness is everlasting."
3 Oh let the house of Aaron say, "His lovingkindness is everlasting."
4 Oh let those who fear the Lord say, "His lovingkindness is everlasting."
5 From my distress I called upon the Lord; The Lord answered me and set me in a large place.
6 The Lord is for me; I will not fear; What can man do to me?
7 The Lord is for me among those who help me; Therefore I will look with satisfaction on those who hate me.
8 It is better to take refuge in the Lord Than to trust in man.
9 It is better to take refuge in the Lord Than to trust in princes.
10 All nations surrounded me; In the name of the Lord I will surely cut them off.
11 They surrounded me, yes, they surrounded me; In the name of the Lord I will surely cut them off.
12 They surrounded me like bees; They were extinguished as a fire of thorns; In the name of the Lord I will surely cut them off.
13 You pushed me violently so that I was falling, But the Lord helped me.
14 The Lord is my strength and song, and He has become my salvation.
15 The sound of joyful shouting and salvation is in the tents of the righteous; The right hand of the Lord does valiantly.
16 The right hand of the Lord is exalted; The right hand of the Lord does valiantly.
17 I will not die, but live, and tell of the works of the Lord.
18 The Lord has disciplined me severely, But He has not given me over to death.
19 Open to me the gates of righteousness; I shall enter through them, I shall give thanks to the Lord.
20 This is the gate of the Lord; The righteous will enter through it.

21 I shall give thanks to You, for You have answered me, and You have become my salvation.
22 The stone which the builders rejected Has become the chief corner stone.
23 This is the Lord's doing; It is marvelous in our eyes.
24 This is the day which the Lord has made; Let us rejoice and be glad in it.
25 O Lord, do save, we beseech You; O Lord, we beseech You, do send prosperity!
26 Blessed is the one who comes in the name of the Lord; We have blessed you from the house of the Lord.
27 The Lord is God, and He has given us light; Bind the festival sacrifice with cords to the horns of the altar.
28 You are my God, and I give thanks to You; You are my God, I extol You.
29 Give thanks to the Lord, for He is good; For His lovingkindness is everlasting.

Psalm 119

This Psalm includes words of thanksgiving and loving kindness. It shows a correlation between righteous and deliverance.

7 I shall give thanks to You with uprightness of heart, when I learn Your righteous judgments.
8 I shall keep Your statutes; Do not forsake me utterly!

64 The earth is full of Your lovingkindness, O Lord; Teach me Your statutes.
65 You have dealt well with Your servant, O Lord, according to Your word.
66 Teach me good discernment and knowledge, for I believe in Your commandments.
67 Before I was afflicted I went astray, But now I keep Your word.
68 You are good and do good; Teach me Your statutes.

132 Turn to me and be gracious to me, After Your manner with those who love Your name.
133 Establish my footsteps in Your word, and do not let any iniquity have dominion over me.

Psalm 136

This is a hymn of thanksgiving and loving kindness. Throughout the Psalm, God is acclaimed for His great deeds. It tells us that God's love is everlasting.

1 Give thanks to the Lord, for He is good, for His lovingkindness is everlasting.
2 Give thanks to the God of gods, for His lovingkindness is everlasting.

3 Give thanks to the Lord of Lords, for His lovingkindness is everlasting.
4 To Him who alone does great wonders, for His lovingkindness is everlasting;
5 To Him who made the heavens with skill, for His lovingkindness is everlasting;
6 To Him who spread out the earth above the waters, for His lovingkindness is everlasting;
7 To Him who made the great lights, for His lovingkindness is everlasting:
8 The sun to rule by day, for His lovingkindness is everlasting,
9 The moon and stars to rule by night, for His lovingkindness is everlasting.
10 To Him who smote the Egyptians in their firstborn, for His lovingkindness is everlasting,
11 And brought Israel out from their midst, for His lovingkindness is everlasting,
12 With a strong hand and an outstretched arm, for His lovingkindness is everlasting.
13 To Him who divided the Red Sea asunder, for His lovingkindness is everlasting,
14 And made Israel pass through the midst of it, for His lovingkindness is everlasting;
15 But He overthrew Pharaoh and his army in the Red Sea, for His lovingkindness is everlasting.
16 To Him who led His people through the wilderness, for His lovingkindness is everlasting;
17 To Him who smote great kings, for His lovingkindness is everlasting,
18 And slew mighty kings, for His lovingkindness is everlasting:
19 Sihon, king of the Amorites, for His lovingkindness is everlasting,
20 And Og, king of Bashan, for His lovingkindness is everlasting,
21 And gave their land as a heritage, for His lovingkindness is everlasting,
22 Even a heritage to Israel His servant, for His lovingkindness is everlasting.
23 Who remembered us in our low estate, for His lovingkindness is everlasting,
24 And has rescued us from our adversaries, for His lovingkindness is everlasting;
25 Who gives food to all flesh, for His lovingkindness is everlasting.
26 Give thanks to the God of heaven, for His lovingkindness is everlasting.

Psalm 138 ✝

This is a hymn of thanksgiving completed by a song of confidence. It tells us that the Lord answers our prayers.

1 I will give You thanks with all my heart; I will sing praises to You before the gods.
2 I will bow down toward Your holy temple and give thanks to Your name for Your lovingkindness and Your truth; For You have magnified Your word according to all Your name.
3 On the day I called, You answered me; You made me bold with strength in my soul.

4 All the kings of the earth will give thanks to You, O Lord, when they have heard the words of Your mouth.
5 And they will sing of the ways of the Lord, for great is the glory of the Lord.
6 For though the Lord is exalted, yet He regards the lowly, But the haughty He knows from afar.
7 Though I walk in the midst of trouble, You will revive me; You will stretch forth Your hand against the wrath of my enemies, and Your right hand will save me.
8 The Lord will accomplish what concerns me; Your lovingkindness, O Lord, is everlasting; Do not forsake the works of Your hands.

Recovery

Psalm 6

This Psalm includes words of healing and is a prayer to God to save our lives and souls. It anticipates thanksgiving.

1 O Lord, do not rebuke me in Your anger, nor chasten me in Your wrath.
2 Be gracious to me, O Lord, for I am pining away; Heal me, O Lord, for my bones are dismayed.
3 And my soul is greatly dismayed; But You, O Lord-- how long?
4 Return, O Lord, rescue my soul; Save me because of Your lovingkindness.
5 For there is no mention of You in death; In Sheol who will give You thanks?
6 I am weary with my sighing; Every night I make my bed swim, I dissolve my couch with my tears.

9 The Lord has heard my supplication, the Lord receives my prayer.

Psalm 18

This Psalm declares our love and trust in God. It tells of a sick person who has been healed by the grace of God.

1 "I love You, O Lord, my strength."
2 The Lord is my rock and my fortress and my deliverer, my God, my rock, in whom I take refuge; My shield and the horn of my salvation, my stronghold.

4 The cords of death encompassed me, and the torrents of ungodliness terrified me.
5 The cords of Sheol surrounded me; The snares of death confronted me.
6 In my distress I called upon the Lord, and cried to my God for help; He heard my voice out of His temple, and my cry for help before Him came into His ears.

Psalm 30

This Psalm tells of somebody that, once seriously sick, has recovered.

2 O Lord my God, I cried to You for help, and You healed me.
3 O Lord, You have brought up my soul from Sheol; You have kept me alive, that I would not go down to the pit.
4 Sing praise to the Lord, you His godly ones, and give thanks to His holy name.

Psalm 39

This Psalm tells of hope in God to heal while on the verge of death.

4 "Lord, make me to know my end and what is the extent of my days; Let me know how transient I am.
5 "Behold, You have made my days as handbreadths, and my lifetime as nothing in Your sight; Surely every man at his best is a mere breath. Selah.
6 "Surely every man walks about as a phantom;

Surely they make an uproar for nothing; He amasses riches and does not know who will gather them.
7 "And now, Lord, for what do I wait? My hope is in You.
8 "Deliver me from all my transgressions; Make me not the reproach of the foolish.
9 "I have become mute, I do not open my mouth, because it is You who have done it.
10 "Remove Your plague from me; Because of the opposition of Your hand I am perishing.
11 "With reproofs You chasten a man for iniquity; You consume as a moth what is precious to him; Surely every man is a mere breath. Selah.
12 "Hear my prayer, O Lord, and give ear to my cry; Do not be silent at my tears; For I am a stranger with You, a sojourner like all my fathers.
13 "Turn Your gaze away from me, that I may smile again Before I depart and am no more."

Psalm 41

This Psalm includes a petition for healing. It asks for the forgiveness of our sins.

2 The Lord will protect him and keep him alive, and he shall be called blessed upon the earth; And do not give him over to the desire of his enemies.
3 The Lord will sustain him upon his sickbed; In his illness, You restore him to health.
4 As for me, I said, "O Lord, be gracious to me; Heal my soul, for I have sinned against You."

Psalm 69

This Psalm accounts for personal agony as a result of sickness and isolation. It ends with words of praise.

20 Reproach has broken my heart and I am so sick. And I looked for sympathy, but there was none, and for comforters, but I found none.

29 But I am afflicted and in pain; May Your salvation, O God, set me securely on high.
30 I will praise the name of God with song and magnify Him with thanksgiving.

Psalm 86

Verses include words of lovingkindness and healing.

13 For Your lovingkindness toward me is great, and You have delivered my soul from the depths of Sheol.

Psalm 91

This Psalm includes words of assurance. It declares that God is our refuge and, thus, we should not be afraid of sickness and other afflictions. It shows that God does not remove perils but assists us in time of troubles.

1 He who dwells in the shelter of the Most High Will abide in the shadow of the Almighty.
2 I will say to the Lord, "My refuge and my fortress, my God, in whom I trust!"
3 For it is He who delivers you from the snare of the trapper and from the deadly pestilence.
4 He will cover you with His pinions, and under His wings you may seek refuge; His faithfulness is a shield and bulwark.
5 You will not be afraid of the terror by night, or of the arrow that flies by day;
6 Of the pestilence that stalks in darkness, or of the destruction that lays waste at noon.
7 A thousand may fall at your side and ten thousand at your right hand, But it shall not approach you.
9 For you have made the Lord, my refuge, even the Most High, your dwelling place.
10 No evil will befall you, nor will any plague come near your tent.
11 For He will give His angels charge concerning you, to guard you in all your ways.
12 They will bear you up in their hands, that you do not strike your foot against a stone.

13 You will tread upon the lion and cobra, the young lion and the serpent you will trample down.
14 "Because he has loved Me, therefore I will deliver him; I will set him securely on high, because he has known My name.
15 "He will call upon Me, and I will answer him; I will be with him in trouble; I will rescue him and honor him.
16 "With a long life I will satisfy him and let him see My salvation."

Psalm 103

This Psalm includes words of gratitude for physical healing.

1 Bless the Lord, O my soul, and all that is within me, bless His holy name.
2 Bless the Lord, O my soul, and forget none of His benefits;
3 Who pardons all your iniquities, Who heals all your diseases;
4 Who redeems your life from the pit, Who crowns you with lovingkindness and compassion;
5 Who satisfies your years with good things, so that your youth is renewed like the eagle.

Protection (against enemies)

Psalm 3

This is a Psalm of protection. It anticipates deliverance and pleads for God's vengeance.

1 O Lord, how my adversaries have increased! Many are rising up against me.
2 Many are saying of my soul, "There is no deliverance for him in God." Selah.
3 But You, O Lord, are a shield about me, my glory, and the One who lifts my head.
4 I was crying to the Lord with my voice, and He answered me from His holy mountain. Selah.
5 I lay down and slept; I awoke, for the Lord sustains me.
6 I will not be afraid of ten thousands of people Who have set themselves against me round about.
7 Arise, O Lord; Save me, O my God! For You have smitten all my enemies on the cheek; You have shattered the teeth of the wicked.
8 Salvation belongs to the Lord; Your blessing be upon Your people! Selah.

Psalm 7 ✝

This Psalm includes a plea for God's protection and His rage for our adversaries. The Psalmist declares innocence and anticipates deliverance.

1 O Lord my God, in You I have taken refuge; Save me from all those who pursue me, and deliver me,
2 Or he will tear my soul like a lion, dragging me away, while there is none to deliver.
3 O Lord my God, if I have done this, if there is injustice in my hands,
4 If I have rewarded evil to my friend, or have plundered him who without cause was my adversary,
5 Let the enemy pursue my soul and overtake it; And let him trample my life down to the ground and lay my glory in the dust. Selah.
6 Arise, O Lord, in Your anger; Lift up Yourself against the rage of my adversaries, and arouse Yourself for me; You have appointed judgment.
7 Let the assembly of the peoples encompass You, and over them return on high.
8 The Lord judges the peoples; Vindicate me, O Lord, according to my righteousness and my integrity that is in me.
9 O let the evil of the wicked come to an end, but establish the righteous; For the righteous God tries the hearts and minds.
10 My shield is with God, Who saves the upright in heart.
11 God is a righteous judge, and a God who has indignation every day.
12 If a man does not repent, He will sharpen His sword; He has bent His bow and made it ready.
13 He has also prepared for Himself deadly weapons; He makes His arrows fiery shafts.
14 Behold, he travails with wickedness, and he conceives mischief and brings forth falsehood.
15 He has dug a pit and hollowed it out, and has fallen into the hole which he made.
16 His mischief will return upon his own head, and his violence will descend upon his own pate.
17 I will give thanks to the Lord according to His righteousness and will sing praise to the name of the Lord Most High.

Psalm 10

This Psalm includes words that call for the punishment of our adversaries. It declares that the afflicted can be wrongly perceived to be forgotten by God.

1 Why do You stand afar off, O Lord? Why do You hide Yourself in times of trouble?
2 In pride the wicked hotly pursue the afflicted; Let them be caught in the

plots which they have devised.
3 For the wicked boasts of his heart's desire, and the greedy man curses and spurns the Lord.

11 He says to himself, "God has forgotten; He has hidden His face; He will never see it."
12 Arise, O Lord; O God, lift up Your hand. Do not forget the afflicted.
13 Why has the wicked spurned God? He has said to himself, "You will not require it."
14 You have seen it, for You have beheld mischief and vexation to take it into Your hand. The unfortunate commits himself to You; You have been the helper of the orphan.
15 Break the arm of the wicked and the evildoer, seek out his wickedness until You find none.

Psalm 11 ✝

This Psalm calls for protection against the wicked. It teaches us that God hates those who use violence but loves the righteous.

1 In the Lord I take refuge; How can you say to my soul, "Flee as a bird to your mountain;
2 For, behold, the wicked bend the bow, they make ready their arrow upon the string To shoot in darkness at the upright in heart.
3 If the foundations are destroyed, what can the righteous do?"
4 The Lord is in His holy temple; The Lord's throne is in heaven; His eyes behold, His eyelids test the sons of men.
5 The Lord tests the righteous and the wicked, and the one who loves violence His soul hates.
6 Upon the wicked He will rain snares; Fire and brimstone and burning wind will be the portion of their cup.
7 For the Lord is righteous, He loves righteousness; The upright will behold His face.

Psalm 13 ✝

This Psalm asks for God's favor and the punishment of the wicked. It assures us that the wicked will finally be subjected to the anger of the Lord.

1 How long, O Lord? Will You forget me forever? How long will You hide Your face from me?
2 How long shall I take counsel in my soul, having sorrow in my heart all the day? How long will my enemy be exalted over me?
3 Consider and answer me, O Lord my God; Enlighten my eyes, or I will sleep the sleep of death,
4 And my enemy will say, "I have overcome him," and my adversaries will rejoice when I am shaken.
5 But I have trusted in Your lovingkindness; My heart shall rejoice in Your salvation.
6 I will sing to the Lord, because He has dealt bountifully with me.

Psalm 17

This Psalm includes words of outrage that plead for God to arise against deadly enemies.

6 I have called upon You, for You will answer me, O God; Incline Your ear to me, hear my speech.
7 Wondrously show Your lovingkindness, O Savior of those who take refuge at Your right hand from those who rise up against them.
8 Keep me as the apple of the eye; Hide me in the shadow of Your wings
9 From the wicked who despoil me, my deadly enemies who surround me.
10 They have closed their unfeeling heart, with their mouth they speak proudly.
11 They have now surrounded us in our steps; They set their eyes to cast us down to the ground.
12 He is like a lion that is eager to tear, and as a young lion lurking in hiding places.
13 Arise, O Lord, confront him, bring him low; Deliver my soul from the wicked with Your sword,

Protection   *Psalms*

Psalm 18

This Psalm includes a calling for God's protection against enemies and calamities. It assures us that with God's will all enemies will be defeated.

3 I call upon the Lord, Who is worthy to be praised, and I am saved from my enemies.
4 The cords of death encompassed me, and the torrents of ungodliness terrified me.
5 The cords of Sheol surrounded me; The snares of death confronted me.
6 In my distress I called upon the Lord, and cried to my God for help; He heard my voice out of His temple, and my cry for help before Him came into His ears.

16 He sent from on high, He took me; He drew me out of many waters.
17 He delivered me from my strong enemy, and from those who hated me, for they were too mighty for me.
18 They confronted me in the day of my calamity, But the Lord was my stay.
19 He brought me forth also into a broad place; He rescued me, because He delighted in me.

36 You enlarge my steps under me, and my feet have not slipped.
37 I pursued my enemies and overtook them, and I did not turn back until they were consumed.
38 I shattered them, so that they were not able to rise; They fell under my feet.
39 For You have girded me with strength for battle; You have subdued under me those who rose up against me.
40 You have also made my enemies turn their backs to me, and I destroyed those who hated me.
41 They cried for help, but there was none to save, even to the Lord, but He did not answer them.
42 Then I beat them fine as the dust before the wind; I emptied them out as the mire of the streets.

46 The Lord lives, and blessed be my rock; And exalted be the God of my salvation,
47 The God who executes vengeance for me, and subdues peoples under me.
48 He delivers me from my enemies; Surely You lift me above those who rise up against me; You rescue me from the violent man.
49 Therefore I will give thanks to You among the nations, O Lord, and I will sing praises to Your name.

Psalm 25

This Psalm tells us to wait for God's intervention to defeat our enemies.

1 To You, O Lord, I lift up my soul.
2 O my God, in You I trust, do not let me be ashamed; Do not let my enemies exult over me.
3 Indeed, none of those who wait for You will be ashamed; Those who deal treacherously without cause will be ashamed.

Psalm 27

This Psalm includes words of pleading and anticipates God's intervention to defeat the enemies.

1 The Lord is my light and my salvation; Whom shall I fear? The Lord is the defense of my life; Whom shall I dread?
2 When evildoers came upon me to devour my flesh, my adversaries and my enemies, they stumbled and fell.
3 Though a host encamp against me, my heart will not fear; Though war arise against me, in spite of this I shall be confident.
4 One thing I have asked from the Lord, that I shall seek: That I may dwell in the house of the Lord all the days of my life, to behold the beauty of the Lord and to meditate in His temple.
5 For in the day of trouble He will conceal me in His tabernacle; In the secret place of His tent He will hide me; He will lift me up on

a rock.
6 And now my head will be lifted up above my enemies around me, and I will offer in His tent sacrifices with shouts of joy; I will sing, yes, I will sing praises to the Lord.

Psalm 31

This Psalm includes a deep feeling of isolation. It shows someone that has been deeply hurt by the snare of adversaries. It calls on us to trust the Lord.

11 Because of all my adversaries, I have become a reproach, especially to my neighbors, and an object of dread to my acquaintances; Those who see me in the street flee from me.
12 I am forgotten as a dead man, out of mind; I am like a broken vessel.
13 For I have heard the slander of many, terror is on every side; While they took counsel together against me, they schemed to take away my life.
14 But as for me, I trust in You, O Lord, I say, "You are my God."
15 My times are in Your hand; Deliver me from the hand of my enemies and from those who persecute me.
16 Make Your face to shine upon Your servant; Save me in Your lovingkindness.
17 Let me not be put to shame, O Lord, for I call upon You; Let the wicked be put to shame, let them be silent in Sheol.
18 Let the lying lips be mute, which speak arrogantly against the righteous With pride and contempt.
19 How great is Your goodness, which You have stored up for those who fear You, which You have wrought for those who take refuge in You, before the sons of men!
20 You hide them in the secret place of Your presence from the conspiracies of man; You keep them secretly in a shelter from the strife of tongues.

Psalm 35 †

This Psalm oscillates from sorrow, anger and revenge. It includes words of punishment for the enemy.

1 Contend, O Lord, with those who contend with me; Fight against those who fight against me.
2 Take hold of buckler and shield and rise up for my help.
3 Draw also the spear and the battle-axe to meet those who pursue me; Say to my soul, "I am your salvation."
4 Let those be ashamed and dishonored who seek my life; Let those be turned back and humiliated who devise evil against me.
5 Let them be like chaff before the wind, with the angel of the Lord driving them on.
6 Let their way be dark and slippery, with the angel of the Lord pursuing them.
7 For without cause they hid their net for me; Without cause they dug a pit for my soul.
8 Let destruction come upon him unawares, and let the net which he hid catch himself; Into that very destruction let him fall.

9 And my soul shall rejoice in the Lord; It shall exult in His salvation.
10 All my bones will say, "Lord, Who is like You, Who delivers the afflicted from him who is too strong for him, and the afflicted and the needy from him who robs him?"
11 Malicious witnesses rise up; They ask me of things that I do not know.
12 They repay me evil for good, to the bereavement of my soul.
13 But as for me, when they were sick, my clothing was sackcloth; I humbled my soul with fasting, and my prayer kept returning to my bosom.
14 I went about as though it were my friend or brother; I bowed down mourning, as one who sorrows for a mother.
15 But at my stumbling they rejoiced and gathered themselves together; The smiters whom I did not know gathered together against me, they slandered me without ceasing.
16 Like godless jesters at a feast, they gnashed at me with their teeth.
17 Lord, how long will You look on? Rescue my soul from their ravages, my only life from the lions.
18 I will give You thanks in the great congregation; I will praise You among a mighty throng.
19 Do not let those who are wrongfully my enemies rejoice over me; Nor let those who hate me without cause wink maliciously.
20 For they do not speak peace, But they devise deceitful words against those who are quiet in the land.
21 They opened their mouth wide against me; They said, "Aha, aha, our eyes have seen it!"
22 You have seen it, O Lord, do not keep silent; O Lord, do not be far from me.
23 Stir up Yourself, and awake to my right and to my cause, my God and my Lord.
24 Judge me, O Lord my God, according to Your righteousness, and do not let them rejoice over me.
25 Do not let them say in their heart, "Aha, our desire!" Do not let them say, "We have swallowed him up!"
26 Let those be ashamed and humiliated altogether who rejoice at my distress; Let those be clothed with shame and dishonor who magnify themselves over me.
27 Let them shout for joy and rejoice, who favor my vindication; And let them say continually, "The Lord be magnified, Who delights in the prosperity of His servant."
28 And my tongue shall declare Your righteousness and Your praise all day long.

Psalm 37

This Psalm shows God will take revenge against the wicked. It shows that in the final account, the virtuous will be blessed and the wicked reduced to disgrace.

1 Do not fret because of evildoers, be not envious toward wrongdoers.
2 For they will wither quickly like the grass and fade like the green herb.
3 Trust in the Lord and do good; Dwell in the land and cultivate faithfulness.
4 Delight yourself in the Lord; And He will give you the desires of your heart.
5 Commit your way to the Lord, trust also in Him, and He will do it.
6 He will bring forth your righteousness as the light and your judgment as the noonday.
7 Rest in the Lord and wait patiently for Him; Do not fret because of him who prospers in his way, because of the man who carries out wicked schemes.
8 Cease from anger and forsake wrath; Do not fret; It leads only to evildoing.
9 For evildoers will be cut off, But those who wait for the Lord, they will inherit the land.
10 Yet a little while and the wicked man will be no more; And you will look carefully for his place and he will not be there.
11 But the humble will inherit the land and will delight themselves in abundant prosperity.
12 The wicked plots against the righteous and gnashes at him with his teeth.
13 The Lord laughs at him, for He sees his day is coming.
14 The wicked have drawn the sword and bent their bow To cast down the afflicted and the needy, to slay those who are upright in conduct.
15 Their sword will enter their own heart, and their bows will be broken.
16 Better is the little of the righteous Than the abundance of many wicked.
17 For the arms of the wicked will be broken, But the Lord sustains the righteous.
18 The Lord knows the days of the blameless, and their inheritance will be forever.
19 They will not be ashamed in the time of evil, and in the days of famine they will have abundance.

30 The mouth of the righteous utters wisdom, and his tongue speaks justice.
31 The law of his God is in his heart; His steps do not slip.
32 The wicked spies upon the righteous and seeks to kill him.
33 The Lord will not leave him in his hand Or let him be condemned when he is judged.
34 Wait for the Lord and keep His way, and He will exalt you to inherit the land; When the wicked are cut off, you will see it.

Psalm 41

This Psalm includes words that shows the betrayal of close friends. It declares confidence that God will protect us against our enemies.

4 As for me, I said, "O Lord, be gracious to me; Heal my soul, for I have sinned against You."
5 My enemies speak evil against me, "When will he die, and his name perish?"
6 And when he comes to see me, he speaks falsehood; His heart gathers wickedness to itself; When he goes outside, he tells it.
7 All who hate me whisper together against me; Against me they devise my hurt, saying,
8 "A wicked thing is poured out upon him, that when he lies down, he will not rise up again."
9 Even my close friend in whom I trusted, who ate my bread, has lifted up his heel against me.
10 But You, O Lord, be gracious to me and raise me up, that I may repay them.
11 By this I know that You are pleased with me, because my enemy does not shout in triumph over me.
12 As for me, You uphold me in my integrity, and You set me in Your presence forever.
13 Blessed be the Lord, the God of Israel, from everlasting to everlasting. Amen and Amen.

Psalm 42

This Psalm includes words of confidence. God will bring joy and defeat the enemies.

9 I will say to God my rock, "Why have You forgotten me? Why do I go mourning because of the oppression of the enemy?"
10 As a shattering of my bones, my adversaries revile me, while they say to me all day long, "Where is your God?"
11 Why are you in despair, O my soul? And why have you become disturbed within me? Hope in God, for I shall yet praise Him, the help of my countenance and my God.

Psalm 52

In this Psalm, the wicked are addressed with strong words. It anticipates the defeat of the enemies.

1 Why do you boast in evil, O mighty man? The lovingkindness of God endures all day long.
2 Your tongue devises destruction, like a sharp razor, O worker of deceit.
3 You love evil more than good, falsehood more than speaking what is right. Selah.
4 You love all words that devour, O deceitful tongue.
5 But God will break you down forever; He will snatch you up and tear you away from your tent, and uproot you from the land of the living. Selah.
6 The righteous will see and fear, and will laugh at him, saying,
7 "Behold, the man who would not make God his refuge, But trusted in the abundance of his riches and was strong in his evil desire."
8 But as for me, I am like a green olive tree in the house of God; I trust in the lovingkindness of God forever and ever.
9 I will give You thanks forever, because You have done it, and I will wait on Your name, for it is good, in the presence of Your godly ones.

Psalm 54

This Psalm declares that God is our helper and will sustain us in spite of the violence of our enemies.

1 Save me, O God, by Your name, and vindicate me by Your power.
2 Hear my prayer, O God; Give ear to the words of my mouth.
3 For strangers have risen against me and violent men have sought my life; They have not set God before them. Selah.
4 Behold, God is my helper; The Lord is the sustainer of my soul.
5 He will recompense the evil to my foes; Destroy them in Your faithfulness.
6 Willingly I will sacrifice to You; I will give thanks to Your name, O Lord, for it is good.
7 For He has delivered me from all trouble, and my eye has looked with satisfaction upon my enemies.

Psalm 55

This is a prayer of supplication against our enemies. It shows the betrayal of close friends. It includes words of revenge for the evil ones and deliverance for the righteous.

1 Give ear to my prayer, O God; And do not hide Yourself from my supplication.
2 Give heed to me and answer me; I am restless in my complaint and am surely distracted,
3 Because of the voice of the enemy, because of the pressure of the wicked; For they bring down trouble upon me and in anger they bear a grudge against me.
4 My heart is in anguish within me, and the terrors of death have fallen upon me.
5 Fear and trembling come upon me, and horror has overwhelmed me.
6 I said, "Oh, that I had wings like a dove! I would fly away and be at rest.
7 "Behold, I would wander far away, I would lodge in the wilderness. Selah.
8 "I would hasten to my place of refuge From the stormy wind and tempest."

9 Confuse, O Lord, divide their tongues, for I have seen violence and strife in the city.
10 Day and night they go around her upon her walls, and iniquity and mischief are in her midst.
11 Destruction is in her midst; Oppression and deceit do not depart from her streets.
12 For it is not an enemy who reproaches me, then I could bear it; Nor is it one who hates me who has exalted himself against me, then I could hide myself from him.
13 But it is you, a man my equal, my companion and my familiar friend;
14 We who had sweet fellowship together Walked in the house of God in the throng.
15 Let death come deceitfully upon them; Let them go down alive to Sheol, for evil is in their dwelling, in their midst.
16 As for me, I shall call upon God, and the Lord will save me.
17 Evening and morning and at noon, I will complain and murmur, and He will hear my voice.
18 He will redeem my soul in peace from the battle which is against me, for they are many who strive with me.
19 God will hear and answer them-- Even the one who sits enthroned from of old-- Selah. With whom there is no change, and who do not fear God.
20 He has put forth his hands against those who were at peace with him; He has violated his covenant.
21 His speech was smoother than butter, But his heart was war; His words were softer than oil, yet they were drawn swords.
22 Cast your burden upon the Lord and He will sustain you; He will never allow the righteous to be shaken.
23 But You, O God, will bring them down to the pit of destruction; Men of bloodshed and deceit will not live out half their days. But I will trust in You.

*P*salm 56 ✝

This Psalm shows someone oppressed by the attack of their enemies. It declares deliverance and trust in God.

1 Be gracious to me, O God, for man has trampled upon me; Fighting all day long he oppresses me.
2 My foes have trampled upon me all day long, for they are many who fight proudly against me.
3 When I am afraid, I will put my trust in You.
4 In God, Whose word I praise, in God I have put my trust; I shall not be afraid. What can mere man do to me?
5 All day long they distort my words; All their thoughts are against me for evil.

6 They attack, they lurk, they watch my steps, As they have waited to take my life.
7 Because of wickedness, cast them forth, in anger put down the peoples, O God!
8 You have taken account of my wanderings; Put my tears in Your bottle. Are they not in Your book?
9 Then my enemies will turn back in the day when I call; This I know, that God is for me.
10 In God, Whose word I praise, in the Lord, Whose word I praise,
11 In God I have put my trust, I shall not be afraid. What can man do to me?
12 Your vows are binding upon me, O God; I will render thank offerings to You.
13 For You have delivered my soul from death, indeed my feet from stumbling, so that I may walk before God In the light of the living.

Psalm 57

This Psalm includes a plea for God's deliverance against adverse circumstances.

4 My soul is among lions; I must lie among those who breathe forth fire, even the sons of men, Whose teeth are spears and arrows and their tongue a sharp sword.
5 Be exalted above the heavens, O God; Let Your glory be above all the earth.
6 They have prepared a net for my steps; My soul is bowed down; They dug a pit before me; They themselves have fallen into the midst of it. Selah.

Psalm 58

This Psalm includes some of the most violent images of the Psalter. It includes seven curses against the enemies which intensify with each statement.

1 Do you indeed speak righteousness, O gods? Do you judge uprightly, O sons of men?
2 No, in heart you work unrighteousness; On earth you weigh out the violence of your hands.
3 The wicked are estranged from the womb; These who speak lies go astray from birth.
4 They have venom like the venom of a serpent; Like a deaf cobra that stops up its ear,
5 So that it does not hear the voice of charmers, or a skillful caster of spells.
6 O God, shatter their teeth in their mouth; Break out the fangs of the young lions, O Lord.
7 Let them flow away like water that runs off; When he aims his arrows, let them be as headless shafts.

Psalms   *Protection*

8 Let them be as a snail which melts away as it goes along, like the miscarriages of a woman which never see the sun.
9 Before your pots can feel the fire of thorns He will sweep them away with a whirlwind, the green and the burning alike.
10 The righteous will rejoice when he sees the vengeance; He will wash his feet in the blood of the wicked.
11 And men will say, "Surely there is a reward for the righteous; Surely there is a God who judges on earth!"

Psalm 59

This Psalm includes a plea for deliverance from our enemies.

1 Deliver me from my enemies, O my God; Set me securely on high away from those who rise up against me.
2 Deliver me from those who do iniquity and save me from men of bloodshed.
3 For behold, they have set an ambush for my life; Fierce men launch an attack against me, not for my transgression nor for my sin, O Lord,
4 For no guilt of mine, they run and set themselves against me. Arouse Yourself to help me, and see!

Psalm 61

This Psalm pleads for God's protection against our enemies. It asks for God to be our refuge and urges us to give Him praises.

1 Hear my cry, O God; Give heed to my prayer.
2 From the end of the earth I call to You when my heart is faint; Lead me to the rock that is higher than I.
3 For You have been a refuge for me, a tower of strength against the enemy.
4 Let me dwell in Your tent forever; Let me take refuge in the shelter of Your wings. Selah.
5 For You have heard my vows, O God; You have given me the inheritance of those who fear Your name.

8 So I will sing praise to Your name forever, that I may pay my vows day by day.

Psalm 64 ✝

This Psalm is a lament over intrigue. It anticipates deliverance since the opponents will be subdued by God's intervention.

1 Hear my voice, O God, in my complaint; Preserve my life from dread of the enemy.
2 Hide me from the secret counsel of evildoers, from the tumult of those who do iniquity,
3 Who have sharpened their tongue like a sword. They aimed bitter speech as their arrow,
4 To shoot from concealment at the blameless; Suddenly they shoot at him, and do not fear.
5 They hold fast to themselves an evil purpose; They talk of laying snares secretly; They say, "Who can see them?"
6 They devise injustices, saying, "We are ready with a well-conceived plot"; For the inward thought and the heart of a man are deep.
7 But God will shoot at them with an arrow; Suddenly they will be wounded.
8 So they will make him stumble; Their own tongue is against them; All who see them will shake the head.
9 Then all men will fear, and they will declare the work of God, and will consider what He has done.
10 The righteous man will be glad in the Lord and will take refuge in Him; And all the upright in heart will glory.

Psalm 69

This is one of the most quoted Psalms in the New Testament. It is a prophetic Psalm since it narrates some of the events of the death of Christ (verses 21-22). This Psalm includes a recitation of personal agony and isolation.

1 Save me, O God, for the waters have threatened my life.

Protection   Psalms

2 I have sunk in deep mire, and there is no foothold; I have come into deep waters, and a flood overflows me.
3 I am weary with my crying; My throat is parched; My eyes fail while I wait for my God.
4 Those who hate me without a cause are more than the hairs of my head; Those who would destroy me are powerful, being wrongfully my enemies; What I did not steal, I then have to restore.
5 O God, it is You who knows my folly, and my wrongs are not hidden from You.
6 May those who wait for You not be ashamed through me, O Lord God of hosts; May those who seek You not be dishonored through me, O God of Israel,
7 Because for Your sake I have borne reproach; Dishonor has covered my face.
8 I have become estranged from my brothers and an alien to my mother's sons.
9 For zeal for Your house has consumed me, and the reproaches of those who reproach You have fallen on me.
10 When I wept in my soul with fasting, It became my reproach.
11 When I made sackcloth my clothing, I became a byword to them.
12 Those who sit in the gate talk about me, and I am the song of the drunkards.
13 But as for me, my prayer is to You, O Lord, at an acceptable time; O God, in the greatness of Your lovingkindness, Answer me with Your saving truth.
14 Deliver me from the mire and do not let me sink; May I be delivered from my foes and from the deep waters.
15 May the flood of water not overflow me Nor the deep swallow me up, nor the pit shut its mouth on me.
16 Answer me, O Lord, for Your lovingkindness is good; According to the greatness of Your compassion, turn to me,
17 And do not hide Your face from Your servant, for I am in distress; Answer me quickly.
18 Oh draw near to my soul and redeem it; Ransom me because of my enemies!
19 You know my reproach and my shame and my dishonor; All my adversaries are before You.
20 Reproach has broken my heart and I am so sick. And I looked for sympathy, but there was none, and for comforters, but I found none.
21 They also gave me gall for my food and for my thirst they gave me vinegar to drink.
22 May their table before them become a snare; And when they are in peace, may it become a trap.
23 May their eyes grow dim so that they cannot see, and make their loins shake continually.
24 Pour out Your indignation on them, and may Your burning anger overtake them.
25 May their camp be desolate; May none dwell in their tents.
26 For they have persecuted him whom You Yourself have smitten, and they tell of the pain of those whom You have wounded.
27 Add iniquity to their iniquity, and may they not come into Your righteousness.
28 May they be blotted out of the book of life and may they not be recorded with the righteous.
29 But I am afflicted and in pain; May Your salvation, O God, set me securely on high.

Psalm 70 ✝

This Psalm urges God to deliver and punish adversaries who are seeking our lives.

1 O God, hasten to deliver me; O Lord, hasten to my help!
2 Let those be ashamed and humiliated Who seek my life; Let those be turned back and dishonored Who delight in my hurt.
3 Let those be turned back because of their shame Who say, "Aha, aha!"
4 Let all who seek You rejoice and be glad in You; And let those who love Your salvation say continually, "Let God be magnified."
5 But I am afflicted and needy; Hasten to me, O God! You are my help and my deliverer; O Lord, do not delay.

Psalm 71

This Psalm includes words that invoke God's help to withstand persecution or rejection. It proclaims faith and anticipates deliverance.

10 For my enemies have spoken against me; And those who watch for my life have consulted together,
11 Saying, "God has forsaken him; Pursue and seize him, for there is no one to deliver."
12 O God, do not be far from me; O my God, hasten to my help!
13 Let those who are adversaries of my soul be ashamed and consumed; Let them be covered with reproach and dishonor, who seek to injure me.
14 But as for me, I will hope continually, and will praise You yet more and more.
15 My mouth shall tell of Your righteousness and of Your salvation all day long; For I do not know the sum of them.
16 I will come with the mighty deeds of the Lord God; I will make mention of Your righteousness, Yours alone.

Psalm 86

This Psalm includes words that plead for God's protection from our enemies. It states that God's deliverance will shame the enemies and will serve His glorification.

14 O God, arrogant men have risen up against me, and a band of violent men have sought my life, and they have not set You before them.
15 But You, O Lord, are a God merciful and gracious, slow to anger and abundant in lovingkindness and truth.
16 Turn to me, and be gracious to me; Oh grant Your strength to Your servant, and save the son of Your handmaid.
17 Show me a sign for good, that those who hate me may see it and be ashamed, because You, O Lord, have helped me and comforted me.

Psalm 94

This Psalm includes words that show that God cares for the persecuted and will act out vengeance. It reveals that God provides comfort to those who are oppressed.

1 O Lord, God of vengeance, God of vengeance, shine forth!
2 Rise up, O Judge of the earth, render recompense to the proud.
3 How long shall the wicked, O Lord, how long shall the wicked exult?
4 They pour forth words, they speak arrogantly; All who do wickedness vaunt themselves.
5 They crush Your people, O Lord, and afflict Your heritage.
6 They slay the widow and the stranger and murder the orphans.
7 They have said, "The Lord does not see, nor does the God of Jacob pay heed."
8 Pay heed, you senseless among the people; And when will you understand, stupid ones?
9 He who planted the ear, does He not hear? He who formed the eye, does He not see?
10 He who chastens the nations, will He not rebuke, even He who teaches man knowledge?

16 Who will stand up for me against evildoers? Who will take his stand for me against those who do wickedness?
17 If the Lord had not been my help, my soul would soon have dwelt in the abode of silence.
18 If I should say, "My foot has slipped," Your lovingkindness, O Lord, will hold me up.
19 When my anxious thoughts multiply within me, Your consolations delight my soul.

Psalm 109

This Psalm shows an individual who has been slandered, falsely judged, and betrayed by close friends. It introduces the strongest curses in the Psalter.

1 O God of my praise, do not be silent!
2 For they have opened the wicked and deceitful mouth against me; They have spoken against me with a lying tongue.
3 They have also surrounded me with words of hatred, and fought against me without cause.
4 In return for my love they act as my accusers; But I am in prayer.
5 Thus they have repaid me evil for good and hatred for my love.
6 Appoint a wicked man over him, and let an accuser stand at his right hand.
7 When he is judged, let him come forth guilty, and let his prayer become sin.
8 Let his days be few; Let another take his office.

9 Let his children be fatherless and his wife a widow.
10 Let his children wander about and beg; And let them seek sustenance far from their ruined homes.
11 Let the creditor seize all that he has, and let strangers plunder the product of his labor.
12 Let there be none to extend lovingkindness to him, nor any to be gracious to his fatherless children.
13 Let his posterity be cut off; In a following generation let their name be blotted out.
14 Let the iniquity of his fathers be remembered before the Lord, and do not let the sin of his mother be blotted out.
15 Let them be before the Lord continually, that He may cut off their memory from the earth;
16 Because he did not remember to show lovingkindness, But persecuted the afflicted and needy man, and the despondent in heart, to put them to death.
17 He also loved cursing, so it came to him; And he did not delight in blessing, so it was far from him.
18 But he clothed himself with cursing as with his garment, and it entered into his body like water and like oil into his bones.
19 Let it be to him as a garment with which he covers himself, and for a belt with which he constantly girds himself.
20 Let this be the reward of my accusers from the Lord, and of those who speak evil against my soul.

Psalm 140 ✝

This Psalm asks for God's rescue and protection from our enemies. It includes curses followed by words of deliverance.

1 Rescue me, O Lord, from evil men; Preserve me from violent men
2 Who devise evil things in their hearts; They continually stir up wars.
3 They sharpen their tongues as a serpent; Poison of a viper is under their lips. Selah.
4 Keep me, O Lord, from the hands of the wicked; Preserve me from violent men Who have purposed to trip up my feet.
5 The proud have hidden a trap for me, and cords; They have spread a net by the wayside; They have set snares for me. Selah.
6 I said to the Lord, "You are my God; Give ear, O Lord, to the voice of my supplications.
7 "O God the Lord, the strength of my salvation, You have covered my head in the day of battle.
8 "Do not grant, O Lord, the desires of the wicked; Do not promote his evil device, that they not be exalted. Selah.
9 "As for the head of those who surround me, may the mischief of their lips cover them.
10 "May burning coals fall upon them; May they be cast into the fire, into deep pits from which they cannot rise.
11 "May a slanderer not be established in the earth; May evil hunt the violent man speedily."
12 I know that the Lord will maintain the cause of the afflicted and justice for the poor.
13 Surely the righteous will give thanks to Your name; The upright will dwell in Your presence.

Psalm 143

This Psalm includes words that plead for God's intervention to defeat our enemies. The Psalmist is overwhelmed by the oppression of opponents.

1 Hear my prayer, O Lord, give ear to my supplications! Answer me in Your faithfulness, in Your righteousness!
2 And do not enter into judgment with Your servant, for in Your sight no man living is righteous.
3 For the enemy has persecuted my soul; He has crushed my life to the ground; He has made me dwell in dark places, like those who have long been dead.
4 Therefore my spirit is overwhelmed within me; My heart is appalled within me.

5 I remember the days of old; I meditate on all Your doings; I muse on the work of Your hands.
6 I stretch out my hands to You; My soul longs for You, as a parched land. Selah.

9 Deliver me, O Lord, from my enemies; I take refuge in You.
10 Teach me to do Your will, for You are my God; Let Your good Spirit lead me on level ground.
11 For the sake of Your name, O Lord, revive me. In Your righteousness bring my soul out of trouble.
12 And in Your lovingkindness, cut off my enemies and destroy all those who afflict my soul, for I am Your servant.

Nations

Psalm 9

This Psalm includes words of judgment against unfaithful nations. It asks God to instill His fear on these nations.

4 For You have maintained my just cause; You have sat on the throne judging righteously.
5 You have rebuked the nations, You have destroyed the wicked; You have blotted out their name forever and ever.
6 The enemy has come to an end in perpetual ruins, and You have uprooted the cities; The very memory of them has perished.
7 But the Lord abides forever; He has established His throne for judgment,
8 And He will judge the world in righteousness; He will execute judgment for the peoples with equity.

15 The nations have sunk down in the pit which they have made; In the net which they hid, their own foot has been caught.
16 The Lord has made Himself known; He has executed judgment. In the work of his own hands the wicked is snared. Higgaion Selah.
17 The wicked will return to Sheol, even all the nations who forget God.
18 For the needy will not always be forgotten, nor the hope of the afflicted perish forever.
19 Arise, O Lord, do not let man prevail; Let the nations be judged before You.
20 Put them in fear, O Lord; Let the nations know that they are but men. Selah.

Psalm 33

This Psalm includes words showing God above all nations. It shows a theology of the divine word. It states that God blesses all faithful nations.

9 For He spoke, and it was done; He commanded, and it stood fast.
10 The Lord nullifies the counsel of the nations; He frustrates the plans of the peoples.
11 The counsel of the Lord stands forever, the plans of His heart from generation to generation.
12 Blessed is the nation whose God is the Lord, the people whom He has chosen for His own inheritance.

Psalm 46

This Psalm includes verses that show God's control over nations, governments, and wars. It assures us that God controls the forces that bring and keep peace.

4 There is a river whose streams make glad the city of God, the holy dwelling places of the Most High.
5 God is in the midst of her, she will not be moved; God will help her when morning dawns.
6 The nations made an uproar, the kingdoms tottered; He raised His voice, the earth melted.
7 The Lord of hosts is with us; The God of Jacob is our stronghold. Selah.

8 Come, behold the works of the Lord, Who has wrought desolations in the earth.
9 He makes wars to cease to the end of the earth; He breaks the bow and cuts the spear in two; He burns the chariots with fire.
10 "Cease striving and know that I am God; I will be exalted among the nations, I will be exalted in the earth."
11 The Lord of hosts is with us; The God of Jacob is our stronghold. Selah.

Psalm 47

This Psalm shows God as the King of the earth. It assures us that God reigns over nations.

1 O clap your hands, all peoples; Shout to God with the voice of joy.
2 For the Lord Most High is to be feared, a great King over all the earth.
3 He subdues peoples under us and nations under our feet.
4 He chooses our inheritance for us, the glory of Jacob whom He loves. Selah.

7 For God is the King of all the earth; Sing praises with a skillful psalm.
8 God reigns over the nations, God sits on His holy throne.
9 The princes of the people have assembled themselves as the people of the God of Abraham, for the shields of the earth belong to God; He is highly exalted.

Psalm 48

This Psalm contains words honoring God and the City of God. It shows that the nations stand in awe at what God has done for Israel. It contains narratives related to the victories of Israel.

1 Great is the Lord, and greatly to be praised, in the city of our God, His holy mountain.
2 Beautiful in elevation, the joy of the whole earth, is Mount Zion in the far north, the city of the great King.
3 God, in her palaces, has made Himself known as a stronghold.
4 For, lo, the kings assembled themselves, they passed by together.
5 They saw it, then they were amazed; They were terrified, they fled in alarm.
6 Panic seized them there, anguish, as of a woman in childbirth.
7 With the east wind You break the ships of Tarshish.
8 As we have heard, so have we seen In the city of the Lord of hosts, in the city of our God; God

Nations   *Psalms*

will establish her forever. Selah.
9 We have thought on Your lovingkindness, O God, in the midst of Your temple.
10 As is Your name, O God, so is Your praise to the ends of the earth; Your right hand is full of righteousness.

Psalm 59

This Psalm includes a calling for the destruction of nations that abide in iniquity.

5 You, O Lord God of hosts, the God of Israel, Awake to punish all the nations; Do not be gracious to any who are treacherous in iniquity. Selah.
6 They return at evening, they howl like a dog, and go around the city.
7 Behold, they belch forth with their mouth; Swords are in their lips, for, they say, "Who hears?"
8 But You, O Lord, laugh at them; You scoff at all the nations.
9 Because of his strength I will watch for You, for God is my stronghold.
10 My God in His lovingkindness will meet me; God will let me look triumphantly upon my foes.
11 Do not slay them, or my people will forget; Scatter them by Your power, and bring them down, O Lord, our shield.
12 On account of the sin of their mouth and the words of their lips, let them even be caught in their pride, and on account of curses and lies which they utter.
13 Destroy them in wrath, destroy them that they may be no more; That men may know that God rules in Jacob To the ends of the earth. Selah.
14 They return at evening, they howl like a dog, and go around the city.
15 They wander about for food and growl if they are not satisfied.
16 But as for me, I shall sing of Your strength; Yes, I shall joyfully sing of Your lovingkindness in the morning, for You have been my stronghold and a refuge in the day of my distress.
17 O my strength, I will sing praises to You; For God is my stronghold, the God who shows me lovingkindness.

Psalm 60

This Psalm includes words showing God's mysterious presence in Israel's history. It pleads for help against adversarial nations. It assures us that God is in control and that only faith in Him can restore Israel's hope.

1 O God, You have rejected us. You have broken us; You have been angry; O, restore us.
2 You have made the land quake, You have split it open; Heal its breaches, for it totters.
3 You have made Your people experience hardship; You have given us wine to drink that makes us stagger.
4 You have given a banner to those who fear You, that it may be displayed because of the truth. Selah.
5 That Your beloved may be delivered, save with Your right hand, and answer us!

9 Who will bring me into the besieged city? Who will lead me to Edom?
10 Have not You Yourself, O God, rejected us? And will You not go forth with our armies, O God?
11 O give us help against the adversary, for deliverance by man is in vain.
12 Through God we shall do valiantly, and it is He who will tread down our adversaries.

Psalm 67 ✝

The centerpiece of this Psalm is the announcement of God's providential care for the nations of the world. The image of the harvest announces the final Glory of God.

1 God be gracious to us and bless us, and cause His face to shine upon us-- Selah.
2 That Your way may be known on the earth, Your salvation among all nations.
3 Let the peoples praise You, O God; Let all the peoples praise You.
4 Let the nations be glad and sing for joy; For You will judge the peoples with uprightness and guide the nations on the earth. Selah.
5 Let the peoples praise You, O God; Let all the peoples praise You.
6 The earth has yielded its produce; God, our God, blesses us.
7 God blesses us, that all the ends of the earth may fear Him.

Psalm 79 ✝

This Psalm discusses the destruction of the Holy City and concludes that these painful events do not break the continuity of God's plan for His chosen people. It pleads with God to bring His wrath on nations that do not know Him.

1 O God, the nations have invaded Your inheritance; They have defiled Your holy temple; They have laid Jerusalem in ruins.
2 They have given the dead bodies of Your servants for food to the birds of the heavens, the flesh of Your godly ones to the beasts of the earth.
3 They have poured out their blood like water round about Jerusalem; And there was no one to bury them.
4 We have become a reproach to our neighbors, a scoffing and derision to those around us.
5 How long, O Lord? Will You be angry forever? Will Your jealousy burn like fire?
6 Pour out Your wrath upon the nations which do not know You, and upon the kingdoms which do not call upon Your name.
7 For they have devoured Jacob and laid waste his habitation.
8 Do not remember the iniquities of our forefathers against us; Let Your compassion come quickly to meet us, for we are brought very low.
9 Help us, O God of our salvation, for the glory of Your name; And deliver us and forgive our sins for Your name's sake.
10 Why should the nations say, "Where is their God?" Let there be known among the nations in our sight, vengeance for the blood of Your servants which has been shed.
11 Let the groaning of the prisoner come before You; According to the greatness of Your power preserve those who are doomed to die.
12 And return to our neighbors sevenfold into their bosom The reproach with which they have reproached You, O Lord.

13 So we Your people and the sheep of Your pasture Will give thanks to You forever; To all generations we will tell of Your praise.

Psalm 81

This Psalm shows that Israel's sorrows are related to disobedience. It announces God's final reconciliation with Israel.

1 Sing for joy to God our strength; Shout joyfully to the God of Jacob.
2 Raise a song, strike the timbrel, the sweet sounding lyre with the harp.
3 Blow the trumpet at the new moon, At the full moon, on our feast day.
4 For it is a statute for Israel, An ordinance of the God of Jacob.

8 "Hear, O My people, and I will admonish you; O Israel, if you would listen to Me!
9 "Let there be no strange god among you; Nor shall you worship any foreign god.
10 "I, the Lord, am your God, Who brought you up from the land of Egypt; Open your mouth wide and I will fill it.
11 "But My people did not listen to My voice, and Israel did not obey Me.
12 "So I gave them over to the stubbornness of their heart, to walk in their own devices.
13 "Oh that My people would listen to Me, that Israel would walk in My ways!
14 "I would quickly subdue their enemies and turn My hand against their adversaries.
15 "Those who hate the Lord would pretend obedience to Him, and their time of punishment would be forever.
16 "But I would feed you with the finest of the wheat, and with honey from the rock I would satisfy you."

Psalm 83

This Psalm includes words showing hostile nations surrounding Israel. It reveals that God controls the outcome of war.

1 O God, do not remain quiet; Do not be silent and, O God, do not be still.
2 For behold, Your enemies make an uproar, and those who hate You have exalted themselves.
3 They make shrewd plans against Your people, and conspire together against Your treasured ones.
4 They have said, "Come, and let us wipe them out as a nation, that the name of Israel be remembered no more."
5 For they have conspired together with one mind; Against You they make a covenant:

12 Who said, "Let us possess for ourselves The pastures of God."
13 O my God, make them like the whirling dust, like chaff before the wind.
14 Like fire that burns the forest and like a flame that sets the mountains on fire,
15 So pursue them with Your tempest and terrify them with Your storm.
16 Fill their faces with dishonor, that they may seek Your name, O Lord.
17 Let them be ashamed and dismayed forever, and let them be humiliated and perish,
18 That they may know that You alone, Whose name is the Lord, Are the Most High over all the earth.

Psalm 94

This Psalm is a national lament. It shows God cares for His people and what might be the pretension of the lawless.

14 For the Lord will not abandon His people, nor will He forsake His inheritance.
15 For judgment will again be righteous, and all the upright in heart will follow it.
16 Who will stand up for me against evildoers? Who will take his stand for me against those who do wickedness?

20 Can a throne of destruction be allied with You, One which devises mischief by decree?

21 They band themselves together against the life of the righteous and condemn the innocent to death.
22 But the Lord has been my stronghold, and my God the rock of my refuge.
23 He has brought back their wickedness upon them and will destroy them in their evil; The Lord our God will destroy them.

Psalm 102

This Psalm includes a national mourning over fallen Jerusalem. It pleads for God's compassion. It shows that Israel's redemption will serve God's glory.

12 But You, O Lord, abide forever, and Your name to all generations.
13 You will arise and have compassion on Zion; For it is time to be gracious to her, for the appointed time has come.
14 Surely Your servants find pleasure in her stones and feel pity for her dust.
15 So the nations will fear the name of the Lord and all the kings of the earth Your glory.
16 For the Lord has built up Zion; He has appeared in His glory.

Psalm 115

This Psalm introduces the pretension of unfaithful nations. It pleads for God's favor toward Israel.

1 Not to us, O Lord, not to us, But to Your name give glory Because of Your lovingkindness, because of Your truth.
2 Why should the nations say, "Where, now, is their God?"
3 But our God is in the heavens; He does whatever He pleases.
4 Their idols are silver and gold, the work of man's hands.
5 They have mouths, but they cannot speak; They have eyes, but they cannot see;
6 They have ears, but they cannot hear; They have noses, but they cannot smell;
7 They have hands, but they cannot feel; They have feet, but they cannot walk; They cannot make a sound with their throat.
8 Those who make them will become like them, everyone who trusts in them.
9 O Israel, trust in the Lord; He is their help and their shield.
10 O house of Aaron, trust in the Lord; He is their help and their shield.
11 You who fear the Lord, trust in the Lord; He is their help and their shield.

12 The Lord has been mindful of us; He will bless us; He will bless the house of Israel; He will bless the house of Aaron.
13 He will bless those who fear the Lord, the small together with the great.

Psalm 118

This Psalm includes prayers of thanksgiving. It assures that God will provide the means to defend Israel.

1 Give thanks to the Lord, for He is good; For His lovingkindness is everlasting.
2 Oh let Israel say, "His lovingkindness is everlasting."
3 Oh let the house of Aaron say, "His lovingkindness is everlasting."
4 Oh let those who fear the Lord say, "His lovingkindness is everlasting."

10 All nations surrounded me; In the name of the Lord I will surely cut them off.
11 They surrounded me, yes, they surrounded me; In the name of the Lord I will surely cut them off.
12 They surrounded me like bees; They were extinguished as a fire of thorns; In the name of the Lord I will surely cut them off.

Psalm 122

This Psalm shows the joy of going to Jerusalem, the City of the Lord. It encourages us to pray for Israel's peace.

1 I was glad when they said to me, "Let us go to the house of the Lord."
2 Our feet are standing Within your gates, O Jerusalem,
3 Jerusalem, that is built As a city that is compact together;
4 To which the tribes go up, even the tribes of the Lord-- An ordinance for Israel-- To give thanks to the name of the Lord.
5 For there thrones were set for judgment, the thrones of the house of David.
6 Pray for the peace of Jerusalem: "May they prosper who love you.
7 "May peace be within your walls, and prosperity within your palaces."
8 For the sake of my brothers and my friends, I will now say, "May peace be within you."
9 For the sake of the house of the Lord our God, I will seek your good.

Psalms   I - 67   Nations

Psalm 124 ✝

This Psalm shows that the Lord intervenes to favor Israel.

1 "Had it not been the Lord who was on our side," Let Israel now say,
2 "Had it not been the Lord who was on our side when men rose up against us,
3 Then they would have swallowed us alive, when their anger was kindled against us;
4 Then the waters would have engulfed us, the stream would have swept over our soul;
5 Then the raging waters would have swept over our soul."
6 Blessed be the Lord, Who has not given us to be torn by their teeth.
7 Our soul has escaped as a bird out of the snare of the trapper; The snare is broken and we have escaped.
8 Our help is in the name of the Lord, Who made heaven and earth.

Psalm 128 ✹

This Psalm includes a plea for the prosperity of Israel.

4 Behold, for thus shall the man be blessed Who fears the Lord.
5 The Lord bless you from Zion, and may you see the prosperity of Jerusalem all the days of your life.
6 Indeed, may you see your children's children. Peace be upon Israel!

Psalm 129 ✝

This Psalm asserts that those who hate Zion will be put to shame and destroyed.

1 "Many times they have persecuted me from my youth up," Let Israel now say,
2 "Many times they have persecuted me from my youth up; Yet they have not prevailed against me.
3 "The plowers plowed upon my back; They lengthened their furrows."
4 The Lord is righteous; He has cut in two the cords of the wicked.
5 May all who hate Zion Be put to shame and turned backward;
6 Let them be like grass upon the housetops, which withers before it grows up;
7 With which the reaper does not fill his hand, or the binder of sheaves his bosom;
8 Nor do those who pass by say, "The blessing of the Lord be upon you; We bless you in the name of the Lord."

Psalm 137 ✝

This Psalm laments the impossibility of chanting songs for Jerusalem in enemy lands. It laments the destruction of the Holy City.

1 By the rivers of Babylon, there we sat down and wept, when we remembered Zion.
2 Upon the willows in the midst of it We hung our harps.
3 For there our captors demanded of us songs, and our tormentors mirth, saying, "Sing us one of the songs of Zion."
4 How can we sing the Lord's song In a foreign land?
5 If I forget you, O Jerusalem, may my right hand forget her skill.
6 May my tongue cling to the roof of my mouth if I do not remember you, if I do not exalt Jerusalem Above my chief joy.
7 Remember, O Lord, against the sons of Edom the day of Jerusalem, who said, "Raze it, raze it To its very foundation."
8 O daughter of Babylon, you devastated one, how blessed will be the one who repays you With the recompense with which you have repaid us.
9 How blessed will be the one who seizes and dashes your little ones Against the rock.

Psalm 144 ✝

This Psalm shows that God is in control during times of war and peace. It supplicates peaceful prosperity for Israel.

1 Blessed be the Lord, my rock, Who trains my hands for war, and my fingers for battle;
2 My lovingkindness and my fortress, my stronghold and my deliverer, my shield and He in Whom I take refuge, Who subdues my people under me.
3 O Lord, what is man, that You take knowledge of him? Or the son of man, that You think of him?
4 Man is like a mere breath; His days are like a passing shadow.
5 Bow Your heavens, O Lord, and come down; Touch the mountains, that they may smoke.
6 Flash forth lightning and scatter them; Send out Your arrows and confuse them.
7 Stretch forth Your hand from on high; Rescue me and deliver me out of great waters, out of the hand of aliens
8 Whose mouths speak deceit, and whose right hand is a right hand of falsehood.
9 I will sing a new song to You, O God; Upon a harp of ten strings I will sing praises to You,
10 Who gives salvation to kings, Who rescues David His servant from the evil sword.
11 Rescue me and deliver me out of the hand of aliens, whose mouth speaks deceit and whose right hand is a right hand of falsehood.
12 Let our sons in their youth be as grown-up plants, and our daughters as corner pillars fashioned as for a palace;
13 Let our garners be full, furnishing every kind of produce, and our flocks bring forth thousands and ten thousands in our fields;
14 Let our cattle bear Without mishap and without loss, let there be no outcry in our streets!
15 How blessed are the people who are so situated; How blessed are the people whose God is the Lord!

Psalm 147

This Psalm includes words indicating that God is the architect of Jerusalem. It shows that God controls war and peace and the prospering of Israel.

1 Praise the Lord! For it is good to sing praises to our God; For it is pleasant and praise is becoming.
2 The Lord builds up Jerusalem; He gathers the outcasts of Israel.

12 Praise the Lord, O Jerusalem! Praise your God, O Zion!
13 For He has strengthened the bars of your gates; He has blessed your sons within you.
14 He makes peace in your borders; He satisfies you with the finest of the wheat.
15 He sends forth His command to the earth; His word runs very swiftly.

Psalm 149

This is a Psalm of praise to the creator of Israel. It shows that, for the sake of Israel, God enters into battle with other nations to achieve victory and peace.

1 Praise the Lord! Sing to the Lord a new song, and His praise in the congregation of the godly ones.
2 Let Israel be glad in his Maker; Let the sons of Zion rejoice in their King.
3 Let them praise His name with dancing; Let them sing praises to Him with timbrel and lyre.
4 For the Lord takes pleasure in His people; He will beautify the afflicted ones with salvation.
5 Let the godly ones exult in glory; Let them sing for joy on their beds.
6 Let the high praises of God be in their mouth, and a two-edged sword in their hand,
7 To execute vengeance on the nations and punishment on the peoples,
8 To bind their kings with chains and their nobles with fetters of iron,
9 To execute on them the judgment written; This is an honor for all His godly ones. Praise the Lord!

Psalms   Nations

Favorites

Psalm 22 ✝

This Psalm of supplication and thanksgiving shows Israel's faith in times of distress. After a long ordeal of sickness and/or imprisonment, the sufferer realizes that God is truly listening and anticipates a liturgy of thanksgiving in the Temple. This is a Psalm of exquisite beauty. This Psalm was consecrated by the dying breath of Jesus on the cross. It is cited frequently in the New Testament.

1 My God, my God, why have You forsaken me? Far from my deliverance are the words of my groaning.
2 O my God, I cry by day, but You do not answer; And by night, but I have no rest.
3 Yet You are holy, O You who are enthroned upon the praises of Israel.
4 In You our fathers trusted; They trusted and You delivered them.
5 To You they cried out and were delivered; In You they trusted and were not disappointed.
6 But I am a worm and not a man, a reproach of men and despised by the people.
7 All who see me sneer at me; They separate with the lip, they wag the head, saying,
8 "Commit yourself to the Lord; Let Him deliver him; Let Him rescue him, because He delights in him."
9 Yet You are He who brought me forth from the womb; You made me trust when upon my mother's breasts.
10 Upon You I was cast from birth; You have been my God from my mother's womb.
11 Be not far from me, for trouble is near; For there is none to help.
12 Many bulls have surrounded me; Strong bulls of Bashan have encircled me.
13 They open wide their mouth at me, As a ravening and a roaring lion.
14 I am poured out like water, and all my bones are out of joint; My heart is like wax; It is melted within me.
15 My strength is dried up like a potsherd, and my tongue cleaves to my jaws; And You lay me in the dust of death.

16 For dogs have surrounded me; A band of evildoers has encompassed me; They pierced my hands and my feet.
17 I can count all my bones. They look, they stare at me;
18 They divide my garments among them, and for my clothing they cast lots.
19 But You, O Lord, be not far off; O You my help, hasten to my assistance.
20 Deliver my soul from the sword, my only life from the power of the dog.
21 Save me from the lion's mouth; From the horns of the wild oxen You answer me.
22 I will tell of Your name to my brethren; In the midst of the assembly I will praise You.
23 You who fear the Lord, praise Him; All you descendants of Jacob, glorify Him, and stand in awe of Him, all you descendants of Israel.
24 For He has not despised nor abhorred the affliction of the afflicted; Nor has He hidden His face from him; But when he cried to Him for help, He heard.
25 From You comes my praise in the great assembly; I shall pay my vows before those who fear Him.
26 The afflicted will eat and be satisfied; Those who seek Him will praise the Lord. Let your heart live forever!
27 All the ends of the earth will remember and turn to the Lord, and all the families of the nations will worship before You.
28 For the kingdom is the Lord's and He rules over the nations.
29 All the prosperous of the earth will eat and worship, All those who go down to the dust will bow before Him, even he who cannot keep his soul alive.
30 Posterity will serve Him; It will be told of the Lord to the coming generation.
31 They will come and will declare His righteousness To a people who will be born, that He has performed it.

*P*salm 23 ✝

This is a prayer of confidence, petition, and thanksgiving. It shows the release of an individual returning from exile. This Psalm of great beauty, uses metaphorical language, such as the "The Lord is my Shepherd" and the "valley of darkness". In the early church this Psalm was sang during baptism.

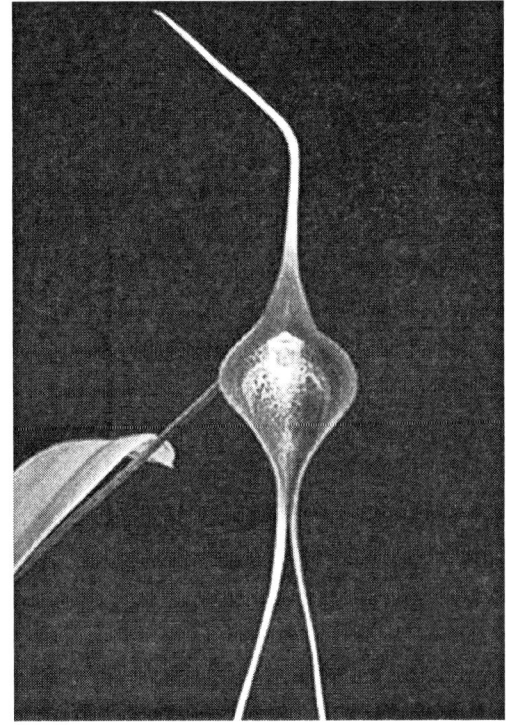

1 The Lord is my shepherd, I shall not want.
2 He makes me lie down in green pastures; He leads me beside quiet waters.
3 He restores my soul; He guides me in the paths of righteousness For His name's sake.
4 Even though I walk through the valley of the shadow of death, I fear no evil, for You are with me; Your rod and Your staff, they comfort me.
5 You prepare a table before me in the presence of my enemies; You have anointed my head with oil; My cup overflows.
6 Surely goodness and lovingkindness will follow me all the days of my life, and I will dwell in the house of the Lord forever.

Psalm 42 ✝

This Psalm is a prayer of supplication for an individual. The pen of the master poet is exhibited in this Psalm: in the intricate structure, the correspondence of imagery and mood, and the play on words and sounds. The Psalmist is timid and afraid, and is saddened by personal exile and memories of Temple worship. He is scorned by enemies and absorbed in suffering. At the end of the Psalm he directs his gaze to future hopes and praises the Lord.

1 As the deer pants for the water brooks, so my soul pants for You, O God.
2 My soul thirsts for God, for the living God; When shall I come and appear before God?
3 My tears have been my food day and night, while they say to me all day long, "Where is your God?"
4 These things I remember and I pour out my soul within me. For I used to go along with the throng and lead them in procession to the house of God, with the voice of joy and thanksgiving, a multitude keeping festival.
5 Why are you in despair, O my soul? And why have you become disturbed within me? Hope in God, for I shall again praise Him For the help of His presence.
6 O my God, my soul is in despair within me; Therefore I remember You from the land of the Jordan and the peaks of Hermon, from Mount Mizar.
7 Deep calls to deep at the sound of Your waterfalls; All Your breakers and Your waves have rolled over me.
8 The Lord will command His lovingkindness in the daytime; And His song will be with me in the night, a prayer to the God of my life.
9 I will say to God my rock, "Why have You forgotten me? Why do I go mourning because of the oppression of the enemy?"
10 As a shattering of my bones, my adversaries revile me, while they say to me all day long, "Where is your God?"
11 Why are you in despair, O my soul? And why have you become disturbed within me? Hope in God, for I shall yet praise Him, the help of my countenance and my God.

Psalm 51 ✝

This is a penitential prayer of supplication for an individual. To write this Psalm, the Psalmist uses prophetic literature, especially the one found in Jeremiah. This Psalm is composed in the first-person singular. The concept of guilt and sin dominate most of the Psalm. This was probably written after David committed his "great sin" when he had Bathsheba's husband killed in order to marry her. The style shows expert balancing and development. Despite the intensity, the Psalm flows easily. Traditionally this has been a classic prayer for Lent and the forgiveness of sin.

1 Be gracious to me, O God, according to Your lovingkindness; According to the greatness of Your compassion blot out my transgressions.
2 Wash me thoroughly from my iniquity and cleanse me from my sin.
3 For I know my transgressions, and my sin is ever before me.
4 Against You, You only, I have sinned and done what is evil in Your sight, so that You are justified when You speak and blameless when You judge.

5 Behold, I was brought forth in iniquity, and in sin my mother conceived me.
6 Behold, You desire truth in the innermost being, and in the hidden part You will make me know wisdom.
7 Purify me with hyssop, and I shall be clean; Wash me, and I shall be whiter than snow.
8 Make me to hear joy and gladness, let the bones which You have broken rejoice.
9 Hide Your face from my sins and blot out all my iniquities.
10 Create in me a clean heart, O God, and renew a steadfast spirit within me.
11 Do not cast me away from Your presence and do not take Your Holy Spirit from me.
12 Restore to me the joy of Your salvation and sustain me with a willing spirit.
13 Then I will teach transgressors Your ways, and sinners will be converted to You.
14 Deliver me from blood guiltiness, O God, the God of my salvation; Then my tongue will joyfully sing of Your righteousness.
15 O Lord, open my lips, that my mouth may declare Your praise.
16 For You do not delight in sacrifice, otherwise I would give it; You are not pleased with burnt offering.
17 The sacrifices of God are a broken spirit; A broken and a contrite heart, O God, You will not despise.
18 By Your favor do good to Zion; Build the walls of Jerusalem.
19 Then You will delight in righteous sacrifices, in burnt offering and whole burnt offering; Then young bulls will be offered on Your altar.

Psalm 63 †

This Psalm is a prayer of petition and thanksgiving. Through a lament, the Psalmist breathes such tranquility it almost modulates into a prayer of confidence. Most verses call for continuous action, implying completion, praises, and confidence in God. The final section focuses on the king. This Psalm became an early morning prayer for the early church.

1 O God, You are my God; I shall seek You earnestly; My soul thirsts for You, my flesh yearns for You, in a dry and weary land where there is no water.
2 Thus I have seen You in the sanctuary, to see Your power and Your glory.
3 Because Your lovingkindness is better than life, my lips will praise You.
4 So I will bless You as long as I live; I will lift up my hands in Your name.
5 My soul is satisfied as with marrow and fatness, and my mouth offers praises with joyful lips.
6 When I remember You on my bed, I meditate on You in the night watches,
7 For You have been my help, and in the shadow of Your wings I sing for joy.
8 My soul clings to You; Your right hand upholds me.
9 But those who seek my life to destroy it, will go into the depths of the earth.
10 They will be delivered over to the power of the sword; They will be a prey for foxes.
11 But the king will rejoice in God; Everyone who swears by Him will glory, for the mouths of those who speak lies will be stopped.

Psalm 70 †

This is a Psalm of supplication and protection against our enemies. From the viewpoint of literary excellence, this Psalm is one of the finest. The Psalmist urges God to punish and shame those who seek his life. It anticipates deliverance from God. This Psalm was employed during memorial offerings. The opening of the Psalm became the traditional way for beginning the divine office of Psalms. It became a traditional reading in Christian monastic communities.

1 O God, hasten to deliver me; O Lord, hasten to my help!
2 Let those be ashamed and humiliated Who seek my life; Let those be turned back and dishonored Who delight in my hurt.
3 Let those be turned back because of their shame Who say, "Aha, aha!"

4 Let all who seek You rejoice and be glad in You; And let those who love Your salvation say continually, "Let God be magnified."
5 But I am afflicted and needy; Hasten to me, O God! You are my help and my deliverer; O Lord, do not delay.

Psalm 84 ✝

This Psalm begins with a melancholic and peaceful tone. It focuses on prayers and reflections regarding the Temple. The desire for God touches every side of the Psalmist: soul, heart, and flesh. The bird implies glorification of God and adds a touch of gentleness and sensitivity. It may have been sung during pilgrimage to the sanctuary.

1 How lovely are Your dwelling places, O Lord of hosts!
2 My soul longed and even yearned for the courts of the Lord; My heart and my flesh sing for joy to the living God.
3 The bird also has found a house, and the swallow a nest for herself, where she may lay her young, even Your altars, O Lord of hosts, my King and my God.
4 How blessed are those who dwell in Your house! They are ever praising You. Selah.
5 How blessed is the man whose strength is in You, in whose heart are the highways to Zion!
6 Passing through the valley of Baca they make it a spring; The early rain also covers it with blessings.
7 They go from strength to strength, every one of them appears before God in Zion.
8 O Lord God of hosts, hear my prayer; Give ear, O God of Jacob! Selah.
9 Behold our shield, O God, and look upon the face of Your anointed.
10 For a day in Your courts is better than a thousand outside. I would rather stand at the threshold of the house of my God Than dwell in the tents of wickedness.
11 For the Lord God is a sun and shield; The Lord gives grace and glory; No good thing does He withhold from those who walk uprightly.
12 O Lord of hosts, how blessed is the man who trusts in You!

Psalm 91 ✝

This is a prayer of petition and confidence. It implores God for protection from adversaries and affliction. The Psalmist makes references to the darkness of the night which contrasts with the strength and glory of God. It suggests that God does not remove the danger but provides strength in times of struggles. The words "He will give His angels charge concerning you" brings it to the reader's personal life. The Psalm concludes with the promise of a long, peaceful life, and God's assurance for salvation. This Psalm was used as entrance and departure liturgy at the Temple.

1 He who dwells in the shelter of the Most High Will abide in the shadow of the Almighty.
2 I will say to the Lord, "My refuge and my fortress, my God, in whom I trust!"
3 For it is He who delivers you from the snare of the trapper and from the deadly pestilence.
4 He will cover you with His pinions, and under His wings you may seek refuge; His faithfulness is a shield and bulwark.
5 You will not be afraid of the terror by night, or of the arrow that flies by day;
6 Of the pestilence that stalks in darkness, or of the destruction that lays waste at noon.
7 A thousand may fall at your side and ten thousand at your right hand, But it shall not approach you.
8 You will only look on with your eyes and see the recompense of the wicked.
9 For you have made the Lord, my refuge, even the Most High, your dwelling place.
10 No evil will befall you, nor will any plague come near your tent.
11 For He will give His angels charge concerning you, to guard you in all your ways.
12 They will bear you up in their hands, that you do not strike your foot against a stone.
13 You will tread upon the lion and cobra, the young lion and the serpent you will trample down.
14 "Because he has loved Me, therefore I will deliver him; I will set him securely on high, because he has known My name.
15 "He will call upon Me, and I will answer him; I will be with him in trouble; I will rescue him and honor him.
16 "With a long life I will satisfy him and let him see My salvation."

Psalm 103

This Psalm is a traditional poem. The first part thanks God for return to health. The second part is a Psalm of praise. The Psalmist expresses gratitude for both, physical and spiritual healing. Sickness and sin are linked. Pardon is begged due to His promise in the ancient covenant. The Psalmist reveals important attributes of God. He is a God "slow to anger and abounding in loving kindness" and "He is mindful that we are but dust". Tradition shows that this Psalm was sung on the Day of Atonement by Jews and each morning by Greek Christians.

1 Bless the Lord, O my soul, and all that is within me, bless His holy name.
2 Bless the Lord, O my soul, and forget none of His benefits;
3 Who pardons all your iniquities, Who heals all your diseases;
4 Who redeems your life from the pit, Who crowns you with lovingkindness and compassion;
5 Who satisfies your years with good things, so that your youth is renewed like the eagle.
6 The Lord performs righteous deeds and judgments for all who are oppressed.

7 He made known His ways to Moses, His acts to the sons of Israel.
8 The Lord is compassionate and gracious, slow to anger and abounding in lovingkindness.
9 He will not always strive with us, nor will He keep His anger forever.
10 He has not dealt with us according to our sins, nor rewarded us according to our iniquities.
11 For as high as the heavens are above the earth, so great is His lovingkindness toward those who fear Him.
12 As far as the east is from the west, so far has He removed our transgressions from us.
13 Just as a father has compassion on his children, so the Lord has compassion on those who fear Him.
14 For He Himself knows our frame; He is mindful that we are but dust.
15 As for man, his days are like grass; As a flower of the field, so he flourishes.
16 When the wind has passed over it, it is no more, and its place acknowledges it no longer.
17 But the lovingkindness of the Lord is from everlasting to everlasting on those who fear Him, and His righteousness to children's children,
18 To those who keep His covenant and remember His precepts to do them.
19 The Lord has established His throne in the heavens, and His sovereignty rules over all.
20 Bless the Lord, you His angels, Mighty in strength, who perform His word, obeying the voice of His word!
21 Bless the Lord, all you His hosts, You who serve Him, doing His will.
22 Bless the Lord, all you works of His, in all places of His dominion; Bless the Lord, O my soul!

Psalm 104 ✝

This Psalm is a magnificent piece of poetry. In this Psalm, God is shown as all-merciful and caring God. God creates a world where, even, the lion's roar becomes a prayer. This Psalm focuses on God's promises and His constant fidelity to His creation. God is acclaimed as the Royal Creator who "established His throne in the heavens". This Psalm has been traditionally used at the Feast of Pentecost.

1 Bless the Lord, O my soul! O Lord my God, You are very great; You are clothed with splendor and majesty,
2 Covering Yourself with light as with a cloak, stretching out heaven like a tent curtain.
3 He lays the beams of His upper chambers in the waters; He makes the clouds His chariot; He walks upon the wings of the wind;
4 He makes the winds His messengers, flaming fire His ministers.
5 He established the earth upon its foundations, so that it will not totter forever and ever.
6 You covered it with the deep as with a garment; The waters were standing above the mountains.
7 At Your rebuke they fled, At the sound of Your thunder they hurried away.
8 The mountains rose; The valleys sank down To the place which You established for them.
9 You set a boundary that they may not pass over, so that they will not return to cover the earth.
10 He sends forth springs in the valleys; They flow between the mountains;
11 They give drink to every beast of the field; The wild donkeys quench their thirst.
12 Beside them the birds of the heavens dwell; They lift up their voices among the branches.
13 He waters the mountains from His upper chambers; The earth is satisfied with the fruit of His works.
14 He causes the grass to grow for the cattle, and vegetation for the labor of man, so that he may bring forth food from the earth,
15 And wine which makes man's heart glad, so that he may make his face glisten with oil, and food which sustains man's heart.

16 The trees of the Lord drink their fill, the cedars of Lebanon which He planted,
17 Where the birds build their nests, and the stork, whose home is the fir trees.
18 The high mountains are for the wild goats; The cliffs are a refuge for the shephanim.
19 He made the moon for the seasons; The sun knows the place of its setting.
20 You appoint darkness and it becomes night, in which all the beasts of the forest prowl about.
21 The young lions roar after their prey and seek their food from God.
22 When the sun rises they withdraw and lie down in their dens.
23 Man goes forth to his work and to his labor until evening.
24 O Lord, how many are Your works! In wisdom You have made them all; The earth is full of Your possessions.
25 There is the sea, great and broad, in which are swarms without number, Animals both small and great.
26 There the ships move along, and Leviathan, which You have formed to sport in it.
27 They all wait for You To give them their food in due season.
28 You give to them, they gather it up; You open Your hand, they are satisfied with good.
29 You hide Your face, they are dismayed; You take away their spirit, they expire and return to their dust.
30 You send forth Your Spirit, they are created; And You renew the face of the ground.
31 Let the glory of the Lord endure forever; Let the Lord be glad in His works;
32 He looks at the earth, and it trembles; He touches the mountains, and they smoke.
33 I will sing to the Lord as long as I live; I will sing praise to my God while I have my being.
34 Let my meditation be pleasing to Him; As for me, I shall be glad in the Lord.
35 Let sinners be consumed from the earth and let the wicked be no more. Bless the Lord, O my soul. Praise the Lord!

*P*salm 121 ✝

This Psalm is a prayer of confidence. The Psalmist directs our eyes to the mountains, the heavenly house of the Lord and reveals essential aspects of our relationship with God. The Lord "will not allow our foot to slip"; "He will protect you from evil"; He guards "your going out and your coming in". "By night the lord is your keeper, by day your shade at your right hand". It is one of the most beautiful Psalms in the Psalter because of its content, style, and easy flow.

1 I will lift up my eyes to the mountains; From where shall my help come?
2 My help comes from the Lord, Who made heaven and earth.
3 He will not allow your foot to slip; He who keeps you will not slumber.
4 Behold, He who keeps Israel Will neither slumber nor sleep.
5 The Lord is your keeper; The Lord is your shade on your right hand.
6 The sun will not smite you by day, nor the moon by night.
7 The Lord will protect you from all evil; He will keep your soul.
8 The Lord will guard your going out and your coming in From this time forth and forever.

*P*salm 139 ✝

This Psalm is a prayer of supplication and one of the greatest Psalms of the Psalter. A lament controls a great portion of this Psalm. It reveals that God is intimately acquainted with our inner selves and that "such knowledge is too wonderful" to bear. The Psalmist asserts that God has "searched" us to "know us". He stresses the omnipotence of God and how we are and always will be in His wonderful presence. This stretches from the silent moment of conception and birth to the farthest reaches of the universe.

1 O Lord, You have searched me and known me.
2 You know when I sit down and when I rise up; You understand my thought from afar.

3 You scrutinize my path and my lying down, and are intimately acquainted with all my ways.
4 Even before there is a word on my tongue, behold, O Lord, You know it all.
5 You have enclosed me behind and before, and laid Your hand upon me.
6 Such knowledge is too wonderful for me; It is too high, I cannot attain to it.
7 Where can I go from Your Spirit? Or where can I flee from Your presence?
8 If I ascend to heaven, You are there; If I make my bed in Sheol, behold, You are there.
9 If I take the wings of the dawn, if I dwell in the remotest part of the sea,
10 Even there Your hand will lead me, and Your right hand will lay hold of me.
11 If I say, "Surely the darkness will overwhelm me, and the light around me will be night,"
12 Even the darkness is not dark to You, and the night is as bright as the day. Darkness and light are alike to You.
13 For You formed my inward parts; You wove me in my mother's womb.
14 I will give thanks to You, for I am fearfully and wonderfully made; Wonderful are Your works, and my soul knows it very well.
15 My frame was not hidden from You, when I was made in secret, and skillfully wrought in the depths of the earth;
16 Your eyes have seen my unformed substance; and in Your book were all written The days that were ordained for me, when as yet there was not one of them.
17 How precious also are Your thoughts to me, O God! How vast is the sum of them!
18 If I should count them, they would outnumber the sand. When I awake, I am still with You.
19 O that You would slay the wicked, O God; Depart from me, therefore, men of bloodshed.
20 For they speak against You wickedly, and Your enemies take Your name in vain.
21 Do I not hate those who hate You, O Lord? And do I not loathe those who rise up against You?
22 I hate them with the utmost hatred; They have become my enemies.
23 Search me, O God, and know my heart; Try me and know my anxious thoughts;
24 And see if there be any hurtful way in me, and lead me in the everlasting way.

$\mathcal{P}$salm 143 ☦

This Psalm is a prayer of supplication. It includes words of protection against our enemies. This Psalm shows that only through God can one arrive at goodness and preserve it. This is a very popular Psalm used in the Greek church and includes many prayers found across the Psalter.

1 Hear my prayer, O Lord, give ear to my supplications! Answer me in Your faithfulness, in Your righteousness!
2 And do not enter into judgment with Your servant, for in Your sight no man living is righteous.
3 For the enemy has persecuted my soul; He has crushed my life to the ground; He has made me dwell in dark places, like those who have long been dead.
4 Therefore my spirit is overwhelmed within me; My heart is appalled within me.
5 I remember the days of old; I meditate on all Your doings; I muse on the work of Your hands.
6 I stretch out my hands to You; My soul longs for You, as a parched land. Selah.
7 Answer me quickly, O Lord, my spirit fails; Do not hide Your face from me, or I will become like those who go down to the pit.
8 Let me hear Your lovingkindness in the morning; For I trust in You; Teach me the way in which I should walk; For to You I lift up my soul.
9 Deliver me, O Lord, from my enemies; I take refuge in You.
10 Teach me to do Your will, for You are my God; Let Your good Spirit lead me on level ground.
11 For the sake of Your name, O Lord, revive me. In Your righteousness bring my soul out of trouble.
12 And in Your lovingkindness, cut off my enemies and destroy all those who afflict my soul, for I am Your servant.

Psalm 145 ✝

This is a Psalm of petition and motivation. It shows a merciful God. He "sustains all who fall And raises up all who are bowed down"; "You open Your hand And satisfy the desire of every living thing". This Psalm assures us that God's domain is and will be universal. This Psalm includes praises; it refers to God's great deeds; and shows the grace and fidelity of God. Rabbi Leazar ben Abina (fourth century A.D.) assured anyone who recited this Psalm three times daily a place in the world to come. It is recited daily in the synagogue for morning, noonday, and evening prayers. Verse 2 was incorporated into the traditional Christian hymn of praise, "Te Deum" and into grace before meals.

1 I will extol You, my God, O King, and I will bless Your name forever and ever.
2 Every day I will bless You, and I will praise Your name forever and ever.
3 Great is the Lord, and highly to be praised, and His greatness is unsearchable.
4 One generation shall praise Your works to another, and shall declare Your mighty acts.
5 On the glorious splendor of Your majesty and on Your wonderful works, I will meditate.
6 Men shall speak of the power of Your awesome acts, and I will tell of Your greatness.
7 They shall eagerly utter the memory of Your abundant goodness and will shout joyfully of Your righteousness.

8 The Lord is gracious and merciful; Slow to anger and great in lovingkindness.
9 The Lord is good to all, and His mercies are over all His works.
10 All Your works shall give thanks to You, O Lord, and Your godly ones shall bless You.
11 They shall speak of the glory of Your kingdom and talk of Your power;
12 To make known to the sons of men Your mighty acts and the glory of the majesty of Your kingdom.
13 Your kingdom is an everlasting kingdom, and Your dominion endures throughout all generations.
14 The Lord sustains all who fall and raises up all who are bowed down.
15 The eyes of all look to You, and You give them their food in due time.
16 You open Your hand and satisfy the desire of every living thing.
17 The Lord is righteous in all His ways and kind in all His deeds.
18 The Lord is near to all who call upon Him, to all who call upon Him in truth.
19 He will fulfill the desire of those who fear Him; He will also hear their cry and will save them.
20 The Lord keeps all who love Him, But all the wicked He will destroy.
21 My mouth will speak the praise of the Lord, and all flesh will bless His holy name forever and ever.

Psalm 150

This Psalm is a hymn of praise and motivation. This Psalm is a magnificent conclusion for the Psalter. While the Psalter opens with a series of Psalms of David characterized mostly by lament, it concludes with exuberant praise. In this Psalm God is praised in the heavenly sanctuary, in the firmament that upholds the heavenly water, and for mighty deeds in Israel's history, ceremonially enacted.

1 Praise the Lord! Praise God in His sanctuary; Praise Him in His mighty expanse.
2 Praise Him for His mighty deeds; Praise Him according to His excellent greatness.
3 Praise Him with trumpet sound; Praise Him with harp and lyre.
4 Praise Him with timbrel and dancing; Praise Him with stringed instruments and pipe.
5 Praise Him with loud cymbals; Praise Him with resounding cymbals.
6 Let everything that has breath praise the Lord. Praise the Lord!

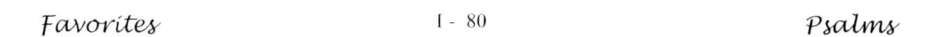

Key for Petition

PSALMS	VERSES
Psalm 4	1-8 C
Psalm 5	1-5 8
Psalm 6	1-9
Psalm 13	1-3 5-6
Psalm 17	1-8 15
Psalm 18	1-2 4-6 20-36
Psalm 20	1-9 C
Psalm 22	1-21
Psalm 23	1-6 C
Psalm 25	1-18 20-21

Psalm 27	1 4-5 7-9 13-14
Psalm 28	1-2 6-9
Psalm 30	2-12
Psalm 31	1-10 22-24
Psalm 32	1-8
Psalm 33	18-22
Psalm 34	4-19 22
Psalm 37	3-6
Psalm 38	1-18 21-22
Psalm 40	1-3 11-13 17
Psalm 42	1-3 5 7-8 11
Psalm 43	2-5
Psalm 46	1-3 11
Psalm 51	1-13
Psalm 55	1 22
Psalm 61	1-2 4
Psalm 62	1-2 5-7

Psalm 69	1-3 13-17 29-30
Psalm 70	1 4-5
Psalm 71	1-3 5-9 19-21
Psalm 77	1-10
Psalm 86	1-13
Psalm 88	1-18 C
Psalm 89	46-49 52
Psalm 91	1-7 10-16
Psalm 102	1-7 10-11 18-25
Psalm 109	21-24 26-31
Psalm 115	14-18
Psalm 119	49-52 64-68 141-149 152-156 169-176
Psalm 121	1-3 5-8
Psalm 127	1-2
Psalm 130	1-6
Psalm 141	1-2
Psalm 142	1-7 C
Psalm 143	1-2 7-8 10-11
Psalm 145	14-21

Psalm of David   C = Psalm Complete

Key for Praise

PSALMS	VERSES
Psalm 8	1 3-9
Psalm 16	7-11
Psalm 19	1 7-11 14
Psalm 24	1-10 C
Psalm 29	1-11 C
Psalm 33	1-15
Psalm 34	1-3 8
Psalm 36	5-10
Psalm 47	1-7

Psalm 57	7-11
Psalm 59	16-17
Psalm 63	1-8
Psalm 66	1-9
Psalm 67	1-7 C
Psalm 68	32-35
Psalm 71	14-19 22-23
Psalm 77	11-19
Psalm 89	1-2 5-18
Psalm 92	1-4
Psalm 93	1-5 C
Psalm 95	1-7
Psalm 96	1-13 C
Psalm 98	1 4-9
Psalm 99	1-9 C
Psalm 100	1-5 C
Psalm 103	1-5 8-22
Psalm 104	1-35 C
Psalm 105	2-7
Psalm 111	1-10 C

Psalm 113	1-9 C
Psalm 117	1-2 C
Psalm 119	55-60 89-94 97-106 123-132 164-168
Psalm 135	1-3
Psalm 136	4-9
Psalm 139	17-18 23-24
Psalm 145	1-13 C
Psalm 146	1-10 C
Psalm 147	1-11 15-20
Psalm 148	1-14 C
Psalm 149	1-5
Psalm 150	1-6 C

C = Psalm Complete

Psalm of David

Key for Thanksgiving

PSALMS	VERSES
Psalm 7	17
Psalm 9	1-2
Psalm 52	8-9
Psalm 54	6
Psalm 66	19-20
Psalm 75	1
Psalm 86	12
Psalm 92	1-4
Psalm 105	1-7
Psalm 107	31-43
Psalm 108	1-6
Psalm 116	1-19 C
Psalm 118	1-29 C
Psalm 119	7-8 64-68 132-133
Psalm 136	1-26 C
Psalm 138	1-8 C

Key for Recovery

PSALMS	VERSES
Psalm 6	1-6 9
Psalm 18	1-2 4-6
Psalm 30	2-4
Psalm 39	4-13
Psalm 41	2-4
Psalm 69	20 29-30
Psalm 86	13
Psalm 91	1-7 9-16
Psalm 103	1-5

Psalm of David

C = Psalm Complete

Key for Protection

PSALMS	VERSES
Psalm 3	1-8 C
Psalm 7	1-17 C
Psalm 10	1-3 11-15
Psalm 11	1-7 C
Psalm 13	1-6 C
Psalm 17	6-13
Psalm 18	3-6 16-19 36-42 46-49
Psalm 25	1-3
Psalm 27	1-6
Psalm 31	11-20
Psalm 35	1-28 C
Psalm 37	1-19 30-34

Psalm 41	4-13
Psalm 42	9-11
Psalm 52	1-9 C
Psalm 54	1-7 C
Psalm 55	1-23 C
Psalm 56	1-13 C
Psalm 57	4-6
Psalm 58	1-11 C
Psalm 59	1-4
Psalm 61	1-5 8
Psalm 64	1-10 C
Psalm 69	1-29
Psalm 70	1-5 C
Psalm 71	10-16
Psalm 86	14-17
Psalm 94	1-10 16-19
Psalm 109	1-20
Psalm 140	1-13 C
Psalm 143	1-6 9-12

C = Psalm Complete   Psalm of David

Key for Nations

PSALMS	VERSES
Psalm 9	4-8 15-20
Psalm 33	9-12
Psalm 46	4-11
Psalm 47	1-4 7-9
Psalm 48	1-10
Psalm 59	5-17
Psalm 60	1-5 9-12
Psalm 67	1-7 C
Psalm 79	1-13 C

Psalm 81	1-4 8-16
Psalm 83	1-5 12-18
Psalm 94	14-16 20-23
Psalm 102	12-16
Psalm 115	1-13
Psalm 118	1-4 10-12
Psalm 122	1-9 C
Psalm 124	1-8 C
Psalm 128	4-6
Psalm 129	1-8 C
Psalm 137	1-9 C
Psalm 144	1-15 C
Psalm 147	1-2 12-15
Psalm 149	1-9 C

Psalm of David

C = Psalm Complete

Key for Favorites

PSALMS
Psalm 22
Psalm 23
Psalm 42
Psalm 51
Psalm 63
Psalm 70
Psalm 84
Psalm 91
Psalm 103

Psalm 104
Psalm 121
Psalm 139
Psalm 143
Psalm 145
Psalm 150

All Psalms are Complete *Psalm of David*

LAYERS from:

- Genesis, Exodus

- Joshua, Judges

- 1 Samuel, 2 Samuel

- 1 Kings

- Daniel, Jonah

Second Collection

The Creation
The Fall of Man
Cain and Abel
Noah
Sodom and Gomorrah
The offering of Issac
Moses
The Passover
Exodus
The Ten Commandments
The Golden Calf
The Conquest of Jericho
Samson and the Philistines
David and Goliath
Bethsheba, David's Great Sin
Solomon's Wisdom
Daniel in the Lion's Den
Jonah's Disobedience

Genesis, Exodus, Joshua, Judges, Samuel, Kings, Daniel, Jonah

The Creation

This narrative provides the foundation for our belief in God the Creator of all living and material things. It provides a timeless picture of God with no beginning and no end. This narrative illustrates the dimension and infiniteness of God. John 1 reveals that our Lord Jesus Christ was the "Word" during the act of Creation. In the beginning was the Word, and the Word was with God, and the Word was God. He was in the beginning with God.

Genesis 1

1 In the beginning God created the heavens and the earth.
2 The earth was formless and void, and darkness was over the surface of the deep, and the Spirit of God was

Bible Stories — *The Creation*

moving over the surface of the waters.
3 Then God said, "Let there be light"; and there was light.
4 God saw that the light was good; and God separated the light from the darkness.
5 God called the light day, and the darkness He called night. And there was evening and there was morning, one day.
6 Then God said, "Let there be an expanse in the midst of the waters, and let it separate the waters from the waters."
7 God made the expanse, and separated the waters which were below the expanse from the waters which were above the expanse; and it was so.
8 God called the expanse heaven. And there was evening and there was morning, a second day.
9 Then God said, "Let the waters below the heavens be gathered into one place, and let the dry land appear"; and it was so.
10 God called the dry land earth, and the gathering of the waters He called seas; and God saw that it was good.
11 Then God said, "Let the earth sprout vegetation, plants yielding seed, and fruit trees on the earth bearing fruit after their kind with seed in them"; and it was so.
12 The earth brought forth vegetation, plants yielding seed after their kind, and trees bearing fruit with seed in them, after their kind; and God saw that it was good.
13 There was evening and there was morning, a third day.
14 Then God said, "Let there be lights in the expanse of the heavens to separate the day from the night, and let them be for signs and for seasons and for days and years;
15 and let them be for lights in the expanse of the heavens to give light on the earth"; and it was so.
16 God made the two great lights, the greater light to govern the day, and the lesser light to govern the night; He made the stars also.
17 God placed them in the expanse of the heavens to give light on the earth,
18 And to govern the day and the night, and to separate the light from the darkness; and God saw that it was good.
19 There was evening and there was morning, a fourth day.
20 Then God said, "Let the waters teem with swarms of living creatures, and let birds fly above the earth in the open expanse of the heavens."
21 God created the great sea monsters and every living creature that moves, with which the waters swarmed after their kind, and every winged bird after its kind; and God saw that it was good.
22 God blessed them, saying, "Be fruitful and multiply, and fill the waters in the seas, and let birds multiply on the earth."
23 There was evening and there was morning, a fifth day.
24 Then God said, "Let the earth bring forth living creatures after their kind: cattle and creeping things and beasts of the earth after their kind"; and it was so.
25 God made the beasts of the earth after their kind, and the cattle after their kind, and everything that creeps on the ground after its kind; and God saw that it was good.
26 Then God said, "Let Us make man in Our image, according to Our likeness; and let them rule over the fish of the sea and over the birds of the sky and over the cattle and over all the earth, and over every creeping thing that creeps on the earth."
27 God created man in His own image, in the image of God He created him; male and female He created them.
28 God blessed them; and God said to them, "Be fruitful and multiply, and fill the earth, and subdue it; and rule over the fish of the sea and over the birds of the sky and over every living thing that moves on the earth."
29 Then God said, "Behold, I have given you every plant yielding seed that is on the surface of all the earth, and every tree which has fruit yielding seed; it shall be food for you;
30 And to every beast of the earth and to every bird of the sky and to every thing that

The Creation   *Bible Stories*

moves on the earth which has life, I have given every green plant for food"; and it was so.
31 God saw all that He had made, and behold, it was very good. And there was evening and there was morning, the sixth day.

The Creation of Adam and Eve

This bible story provides an important perspective of God's divine plan. God meant the world to be a perfect place, the Garden of Eden. It shows mankind as the resident and center of God's creation. It sets a clear dichotomy between God and man: God has an infinite nature; man was made out of dust and became a living being by the will and grace of God.

Genesis 2

7 Then the Lord God formed man of dust from the ground, and breathed into his nostrils the breath of life; and man became a living being.
8 The Lord God planted a garden toward the east, in Eden; and there He placed the man whom He had formed.
9 Out of the ground the Lord God caused to grow every tree that is pleasing to the sight and good for food; the tree of life also in the midst of the garden, and the tree of the knowledge of good and evil.

16 The Lord God commanded the man, saying, "From any tree of the garden you may eat freely;
17 But from the tree of the knowledge of good and evil you shall not eat, for in the day that you eat from it you will surely die."
18 Then the Lord God said, "It is not good for the man to be alone; I will make him a helper suitable for him."
19 Out of the ground the Lord God formed every beast of the field and every bird of the sky, and brought them to the man to see what he would call them; and whatever the man called a living creature, that was its name.
20 The man gave names to all the cattle, and to the birds of the sky, and to every beast of the field, but for Adam there was not found a helper suitable for him.
21 So the Lord God caused a deep sleep to fall upon the man, and he slept; then He took one of his ribs and closed up the flesh at that place.
22 The Lord God fashioned into a woman the rib which He had taken from the man, and brought her to the man.
23 The man said, "This is now bone of my bones, And flesh of my flesh; She shall be called Woman, Because she was taken out of Man."
24 For this reason a man shall leave his father and his mother, and be joined to his wife; and they shall become one flesh.
25 And the man and his wife were both naked and were not ashamed.

The Fall of Man

This bible story unveils how the divine intention of a perfect world was frustrated by human weakness. In this story the boundaries that separate the divine and human world are challenged. It is the first act of disobedience and sin, sin that will be spread to all future generations.

Genesis 3

1 Now the serpent was more crafty than any beast of the field which the Lord God had made. And he said to the woman, "Indeed, has God said, 'You shall not eat from any tree of the garden'?"
2 The woman said to the serpent, "From the fruit of the trees of the garden we may eat;
3 But from the fruit of the tree which is in the middle of the garden, God has said, 'You shall not eat from it or touch it, or you will die.' "
4 The serpent said to the woman, "You surely will not die!
5 "For God knows that in the day you eat from it your eyes will be opened, and you will be like God, knowing good and evil."

6 When the woman saw that the tree was good for food, and that it was a delight to the eyes, and that the tree was desirable to make one wise, she took from its fruit and ate; and she gave also to her husband with her, and he ate.

7 Then the eyes of both of them were opened, and they knew that they were naked; and they sewed fig leaves together and made themselves loin coverings.

8 They heard the sound of the Lord God walking in the garden in the cool of the day, and the man and his wife hid themselves from the presence of the Lord God among the trees of the garden.

9 Then the Lord God called to the man, and said to him, "Where are you?"

10 He said, "I heard the sound of You in the garden, and I was afraid because I was naked; so I hid myself."

11 And He said, "Who told you that you were naked? Have you eaten from the tree of which I commanded you not to eat?"

12 The man said, "The woman whom You gave to be with me, she gave me from the tree, and I ate."

13 Then the Lord God said to the woman, "What is this you have done?" And the woman said, "The serpent deceived me, and I ate."

14 The Lord God said to the serpent, "Because you have done this, Cursed are you more than all cattle, And more than every beast of the field; On your belly you will go, And dust you will eat All the days of your life;

15 And I will put enmity Between you and the woman, And between your seed and her seed; He shall bruise you on the head, And you shall bruise him on the heel."

16 To the woman He said, "I will greatly multiply Your pain in childbirth, In pain you will bring forth children; Yet your desire will be for your husband, And he will rule over you."

17 Then to Adam He said, "Because you have listened to the voice of your wife, and have eaten from the tree about which I commanded you, saying, 'You shall not eat from it'; Cursed is the ground because of you; In toil you will eat of it All the days of your life.

18 "Both thorns and thistles it shall grow for you; And you will eat the plants of the field;

19 By the sweat of your face You will eat bread, Till you return to the ground, Because from it you were taken; For you are dust, And to dust you shall return."

20 Now the man called his wife's name Eve, because she was the mother of all the living.

21 The Lord God made garments of skin for Adam and his wife, and clothed them.

22 Then the Lord God said, "Behold, the man has become like one of Us, knowing good and evil; and now, he might stretch out his hand, and take also from the tree of life, and eat, and live forever"--

23 Therefore the Lord God sent him out from the garden of Eden, to cultivate the ground from which he was taken.

24 So He drove the man out; and at the east of the garden of Eden He stationed the

The Creation of Adam and Eve/The Fall of Man

cherubim and the flaming sword which turned every direction to guard the way to the tree of life.

Cain and Abel

This is the second sinful act committed by man since the Act of Creation. Jealousy and envy are characterized in this story. The narrative effectively demonstrates the contrast between good and evil and how God has the divine right to elect and reject among His Creation. The story shows God exerting judgment and how men can plead with Him to influence His Divine decisions. This is the first time that human blood is spilled and "cursed" the earth.

Genesis 4

1 Now the man had relations with his wife Eve, and she conceived and gave birth to Cain, and she said, "I have gotten a manchild with the help of the Lord."
2 Again, she gave birth to his brother Abel. And Abel was a keeper of flocks, but Cain was a tiller of the ground.
3 So it came about in the course of time that Cain brought an offering to the Lord of the fruit of the ground.
4 Abel, on his part also brought of the firstlings of his flock and of their fat portions. And the Lord had regard for Abel and for his offering;
5 But for Cain and for his offering He had no regard. So Cain became very angry and his countenance fell.
6 Then the Lord said to Cain, "Why are you angry? And why has your countenance fallen?
7 "If you do well, will not your countenance be lifted up? And if you do not do well, sin is crouching at the door; and its desire is for you, but you must master it."
8 Cain told Abel his brother. And it came about when they were in the field, that Cain rose up against Abel his brother and killed him.
9 Then the Lord said to Cain, "Where is Abel your brother?" And he said, "I do not know. Am I my brother's keeper?"
10 He said, "What have you done? The voice of your brother's blood is crying to Me from the ground.
11 "Now you are cursed from the ground, which has opened its mouth to receive your brother's blood from your hand.
12 "When you cultivate the ground, it will no longer yield its strength to you; you will be a vagrant and a wanderer on the earth."
13 Cain said to the Lord, "My punishment is too great to bear!
14 "Behold, You have driven me this day from the face of the ground; and from Your face I will be hidden, and I will be a vagrant and a wanderer on the earth, and whoever finds me will kill me."

15 So the Lord said to him, "Therefore whoever kills Cain, vengeance will be taken on him sevenfold." And the Lord appointed a sign for Cain, so that no one finding him would slay him.

Noah and the Great Flood

This story displays God's wrath and how He chooses to act in the presence of sin. It is a narrative of the growth of sin and evil. It describes improper mating of heavenly beings and earthly women. The Flood story teach us that God, even in the midst of chaos, continues to care for His creation. In the story, God provides Noah with the means to save humanity and all living creatures that populate the world. The story ends with God's command to Noah to bring out "all living things in the ark" to "multiply on the earth." This can be interpreted as a renewal or restoration of God's intended creation.

Genesis 6

1 Now it came about, when men began to multiply on the face of the land, and daughters were born to them,

2 That the sons of God saw that the daughters of men were beautiful; and they took wives for themselves, whomever they chose.

3 Then the LORD said, "My Spirit shall not strive with man forever, because he also is flesh; nevertheless his days shall be one hundred and twenty years."

4 The Nephilim were on the earth in those days, and also afterward, when the sons of God came in to the daughters of men, and they bore children to them. Those were the mighty men who were of old, men of renown.

5 Then the LORD saw that the wickedness of man was great on the earth, and that every intent of the thoughts of his heart was only evil continually.

6 The LORD was sorry that He had made man on the earth, and He was grieved in His heart.

7 The LORD said, "I will blot out man whom I have created from the face of the land, from man to animals to creeping things and to birds of the sky; for I am sorry that I have made them."

8 But Noah found favor in the eyes of the LORD.

9 These are the records of the generations of Noah. Noah was a righteous man, blameless in his time; Noah walked with God.

10 Noah became the father of three sons: Shem, Ham, and Japheth.

11 Now the earth was corrupt in the sight of God, and the earth was filled with violence.

12 God looked on the earth, and behold, it was corrupt; for all flesh had corrupted their way upon the earth.

13 Then God said to Noah, "The end of all flesh has come before Me; for the earth is filled with violence because of them; and behold, I am about to destroy them with the earth.

14 "Make for yourself an ark of gopher wood; you shall make the ark with rooms, and shall cover it inside and out with pitch.

15 "This is how you shall make it: the length of the ark three hundred cubits, its breadth fifty cubits, and its height thirty cubits.

16 "You shall make a window for the ark, and finish it to a cubit from the top; and set the door of the ark in the side of it; you shall make it with lower, second, and third decks.

17 "Behold, I, even I am bringing the flood of water upon the earth, to destroy all flesh in which is the breath of life, from under heaven; everything that is on the earth shall perish.

18 "But I will establish My covenant with you; and you shall enter the ark-- you and your sons and your wife, and your sons' wives with you.

19 "And of every living thing of all flesh, you shall bring two of every kind into the ark, to keep them alive with you; they shall be male and female.

20 "Of the birds after their kind, and of the animals after their kind, of every creeping

thing of the ground after its kind, two of every kind will come to you to keep them alive.
21 "As for you, take for yourself some of all food which is edible, and gather it to yourself; and it shall be for food for you and for them."
22 Thus Noah did; according to all that God had commanded him, so he did.

Genesis 7

1 Then the Lord said to Noah, "Enter the ark, you and all your houschold, for you alone I have seen to be righteous before Me in this time.
2 "You shall take with you of every clean animal by sevens, a male and his female; and of the animals that are not clean two, a male and his female;
3 Also of the birds of the sky, by sevens, male and female, to keep offspring alive on the face of all the earth.
4 "For after seven more days, I will send rain on the earth forty days and forty nights; and I will blot out from the face of the land every living thing that I have made."
5 Noah did according to all that the Lord had commanded him.

17 Then the flood came upon the earth for forty days, and the water increased and lifted up the ark, so that it rose above the earth.
18 The water prevailed and increased greatly upon the earth, and the ark floated on the surface of the water.
19 The water prevailed more and more upon the earth, so that all the high mountains everywhere under the heavens were covered.
20 The water prevailed fifteen cubits higher, and the mountains were covered.
21 All flesh that moved on the earth perished, birds and cattle and beasts and every swarming thing that swarms upon the earth, and all mankind;
22 of all that was on the dry land, all in whose nostrils was the breath of the spirit of life, died.

Genesis 8

1 But God remembered Noah and all the beasts and all the cattle that were with him in the ark; and God caused a wind to pass over the earth, and the water subsided.
2 Also the fountains of the deep and the floodgates of the sky were closed, and the rain from the sky was restrained;
3 and the water receded steadily from the earth, and at the end of one hundred and fifty days the water decreased.
4 In the seventh month, on the seventeenth day of the month, the ark rested upon the mountains of Ararat.
5 The water decreased steadily until the tenth month; in the tenth month, on the first day of the month, the tops of the mountains became visible.
6 Then it came about at the end of forty days, that Noah opened the window of the ark which he had made;
7 and he sent out a raven, and it flew here and there until the water was dried up from the earth.
8 Then he sent out a dove from him, to see if the water was abated from the face of the land;
9 But the dove found no resting place for the sole of her foot, so she returned to him into the ark, for the water was on the surface of all the earth. Then he put out his hand and took her, and brought her into the ark to himself.
10 So he waited yet another seven days; and again he sent out the dove from the ark.
11 The dove came to him toward evening, and behold, in her beak was a freshly picked olive leaf. So Noah knew that the water was abated from the earth.
12 Then he waited yet another seven days, and sent out the dove; but she did not return to him again.
13 Now it came about in the six hundred and first year, in the first month, on the first of the month, the water was dried up from the earth. Then Noah removed the covering of the ark, and looked, and behold, the surface of the ground was dried up.

Bible Stories   II - 9   *Noah and the Great Flood*

14 In the second month, on the twenty-seventh day of the month, the earth was dry.
15 Then God spoke to Noah, saying,
16 "Go out of the ark, you and your wife and your sons and your sons' wives with you.
17 "Bring out with you every living thing of all flesh that is with you, birds and animals and every creeping thing that creeps on the earth, that they may breed abundantly on the earth, and be fruitful and multiply on the earth."
18 So Noah went out, and his sons and his wife and his sons' wives with him.
19 Every beast, every creeping thing, and every bird, everything that moves on the earth, went out by their families from the ark.
20 Then Noah built an altar to the Lord, and took of every clean animal and of every clean bird and offered burnt offerings on the altar.
21 The Lord smelled the soothing aroma; and the Lord said to Himself, "I will never again curse the ground on account of man, for the intent of man's heart is evil from his youth; and I will never again destroy every living thing, as I have done.
22 "While the earth remains, Seedtime and harvest, And cold and heat, And summer and winter, And day and night Shall not cease."

The Doom of Sodom and Gomorrah

This story presents the failure of humankind in spite of God's good intentions for His creation. As in the story of Noah, God is faced with the choice to destroy evil. God gave men freewill but unfortunately, with the right to choose comes the freedom to do evil. In this story, the citizens of Sodom and Gomorrah have become completely corrupted and engaged in all sorts of sexual depravation. Sexual abuse runs counter to the divine command to procreate. God is moved into action: the city must be destroyed through fire. In the story, Angels are appointed to be the executioners of divine judgment. This Bible story teaches us that in time of unspeakable wickedness, the day of doom can be anticipated.

Genesis 19

1 Now the two angels came to Sodom in the evening as Lot was sitting in the gate of Sodom. When Lot saw them, he rose to meet them and bowed down with his face to the ground.
2 And he said, "Now behold, my lords, please turn aside into your servant's house, and spend the night, and wash your feet; then you may rise early and go on your way." They said however, "No, but we shall spend the night in the square."

3 Yet he urged them strongly, so they turned aside to him and entered his house; and he prepared a feast for them, and baked unleavened bread, and they ate.
4 Before they lay down, the men of the city, the men of Sodom, surrounded the house, both young and old, all the people from every quarter;
5 And they called to Lot and said to him, "Where are the men who came to you tonight? Bring them out to us that we may have relations with them."
6 But Lot went out to them at the doorway, and shut the door behind him,
7 And said, "Please, my brothers, do not act wickedly.
8 "Now behold, I have two daughters who have not had relations with man; please let me bring them out to you, and do to them whatever you like; only do nothing to these men, inasmuch as they have come under the shelter of my roof."
9 But they said, "Stand aside." Furthermore, they said, "This one came in as an alien, and already he is acting like a judge; now we will treat you worse than them." So they pressed hard against Lot and came near to break the door.
10 But the men reached out their hands and brought Lot into the house with them, and shut the door.
11 They struck the men who were at the doorway of the house with blindness, both small and great, so that they wearied themselves trying to find the doorway.
12 Then the two men said to Lot, "Whom else have you here? A son-in-law, and your sons, and your daughters, and whomever you have in the city, bring them out of the place;
13 for we are about to destroy this place, because their outcry has become so great before the Lord that the Lord has sent us to destroy it."
14 Lot went out and spoke to his sons-in-law, who were to marry his daughters, and said, "Up, get out of this place, for the Lord will destroy the city." But he appeared to his sons-in-law to be jesting.
15 When morning dawned, the angels urged Lot, saying, "Up, take your wife and your two daughters who are here, or you will be swept away in the punishment of the city."
16 But he hesitated. So the men seized his hand and the hand of his wife and the hands of his two daughters, for the compassion of the Lord was upon him; and they brought him out, and put him outside the city.
17 When they had brought them outside, one said, "Escape for your life! Do not look behind you, and do not stay anywhere in the valley; escape to the mountains, or you will be swept away."
18 But Lot said to them, "Oh no, my lords!

19 "Now behold, your servant has found favor in your sight, and you have magnified your lovingkindness, which you have shown me by saving my life; but I cannot escape to the mountains, for the disaster will overtake me and I will die;
20 Now behold, this town is near enough to flee to, and it is small. Please, let me escape there (is it not small?) that my life may be saved."
21 He said to him, "Behold, I grant you this request also, not to overthrow the town of which you have spoken.
22 "Hurry, escape there, for I cannot do anything until you arrive there." Therefore the name of the town was called Zoar.
23 The sun had risen over the earth when Lot came to Zoar.
24 Then the Lord rained on Sodom and Gomorrah brimstone and fire from the Lord out of heaven,
25 And He overthrew those cities, and all the valley, and all the inhabitants of the cities, and what grew on the ground.
26 But his wife, from behind him, looked back, and she became a pillar of salt.

The Offering of Isaac

This story presents the most compelling act of obedience in the Old Testament. In this story, Abraham receives the divine command to sacrifice his beloved son Isaac. The act of preparation for the sacrifice is carefully described in the story. The tension generated in the narrative is finally resolved by divine intervention. While the story unfolds, Abraham's confidence and obedience to God remained unaltered. He responded to Isaac who asked where was "the lamb for the burnt offering" that "God will provide." As a reward to his obedience, God reiterates His promise that he will become the father of a great nation. This is one of the most important covenants of the Jewish faith.

Genesis 21

2 So Sarah conceived and bore a son to Abraham in his old age, at the appointed time of which God had spoken to him.
3 Abraham called the name of his son who was born to him, whom Sarah bore to him, Isaac.

Genesis 22

1 Now it came about after these things, that God tested Abraham, and said to him, "Abraham!" And he said, "Here I am."
2 He said, "Take now your son, your only son, whom you love, Isaac, and go to the land of Moriah, and offer him there as a burnt offering on one of the mountains of which I will tell you."
3 So Abraham rose early in the morning and saddled his donkey, and took two of his young men with him and Isaac his son; and he split wood for the burnt offering, and arose and went to the place of which God had told him.
4 On the third day Abraham raised his eyes and saw the place from a distance.
5 Abraham said to his young men, "Stay here with the donkey, and I and the lad will go over there; and we will worship and return to you."
6 Abraham took the wood of the burnt offering and laid it on Isaac his son, and he took in his hand the fire and the knife. So the two of them walked on together.
7 Isaac spoke to Abraham his father and said, "My father!" And he said, "Here I am, my son." And he said, "Behold, the fire and the wood, but where is the lamb for the burnt offering?"
8 Abraham said, "God will provide for Himself the lamb for the burnt offering, my son." So the two of them walked on together.
9 Then they came to the place of which God had told him; and Abraham built the altar there and arranged the wood, and bound his son Isaac and laid him on the altar, on top of the wood.
10 Abraham stretched out his hand and took the

knife to slay his son.

11 But the angel of the Lord called to him from heaven and said, "Abraham, Abraham!" And he said, "Here I am."

12 He said, "Do not stretch out your hand against the lad, and do nothing to him; for now I know that you fear God, since you have not withheld your son, your only son, from Me."

13 Then Abraham raised his eyes and looked, and behold, behind him a ram caught in the thicket by his horns; and Abraham went and took the ram and offered him up for a burnt offering in the place of his son.

14 Abraham called the name of that place The Lord Will Provide, as it is said to this day, "In the mount of the Lord it will be provided."

15 Then the angel of the Lord called to Abraham a second time from heaven,

16 And said, "By Myself I have sworn, declares the Lord, because you have done this thing and have not withheld your son, your only son,

17 Indeed I will greatly bless you, and I will greatly multiply your seed as the stars of the heavens and as the sand which is on the seashore; and your seed shall possess the gate of their enemies.

18 "In your seed all the nations of the earth shall be blessed, because you have obeyed My voice."

The Birth of Moses

This story describes the birth of Moses and how he is protected by his mother from Pharaoh's decision to eliminate all male children at childbirth. It is a prelude to Moses' life as one of God's elected.

Exodus 1

15 Then the king of Egypt spoke to the Hebrew midwives, one of whom was named Shiphrah and the other was named Puah;

16 And he said, "When you are helping the Hebrew women to give birth and see them upon the birthstool, if it is a son, then you shall put him to death; but if it is a daughter, then she shall live."

17 But the midwives feared God, and did not do as the king of Egypt had commanded them, but let the boys live.

18 So the king of Egypt called for the midwives and said to them, "Why have you done this thing, and let the boys live?"

19 The midwives said to Pharaoh, "Because the Hebrew women are not as the Egyptian women; for they are vigorous and give birth before the midwife can get to them."

20 So God was good to the midwives, and the people multiplied, and became very mighty.

21 Because the midwives feared God, He established households for them.

22 Then Pharaoh commanded all his people, saying, "Every son who is born you are to cast into the Nile, and every daughter you are to keep alive."

Exodus 2

1 Now a man from the house of Levi went and married a daughter of Levi.

2 The woman conceived and bore a son; and when she saw that he was beautiful, she hid him for three months.

3 But when she could hide him no longer, she got him a wicker basket and covered it over with tar and pitch. Then she put the child into it and set it among the reeds by the bank of the Nile.

4 His sister stood at a distance to find out what would happen to him.

5 The daughter of Pharaoh came down to bathe at the Nile, with her maidens walking alongside the Nile; and she saw the basket among the reeds and sent her maid, and she brought it to her.

6 When she opened it, she saw the child, and behold, the boy was crying. And she had pity on him and said, "This is one of the Hebrews' children."

7 Then his sister said to Pharaoh's daughter, "Shall I go and call a nurse for you from the Hebrew women that she may nurse the

child for you?"
8 Pharaoh's daughter said to her, "Go ahead." So the girl went and called the child's mother.
9 Then Pharaoh's daughter said to her, "Take this child away and nurse him for me and I will give you your wages." So the woman took the child and nursed him.
10 The child grew, and she brought him to Pharaoh's daughter and he became her son. And she named him Moses, and said, "Because I drew him out of the water."

The Passover

The celebration of the Passover is one of the most important festivities of the Jewish calendar. This story shows Israel as the nation of God. After Pharaoh has repeatedly failed to let the Jewish people leave Egypt, God announces his final punishment: all firstborn, family, flock, and field will die. Israelite firstborns are to be spared when covered by sacrificial blood. Rituals of Jewish tradition are introduced in this story.

Exodus 9

1 Then the Lord said to Moses, "Go to Pharaoh and speak to him, 'Thus says the Lord, the God of the Hebrews, "Let My people go, that they may serve Me.
2 "For if you refuse to let them go and continue to hold them,
3 "Behold, the hand of the Lord will come with a very severe pestilence on your livestock which are in the field, on the horses, on the donkeys, on the camels, on the herds, and on the flocks."

Exodus 11

1 Now the Lord said to Moses, "One more plague I will bring on Pharaoh and on Egypt; after that he will let you go from here. When he lets you go, he will surely drive you out from here completely.

4 Moses said, "Thus says the Lord, 'About midnight I am going out into the midst of Egypt,
5 and all the firstborn in the land of Egypt shall die, from the firstborn of the Pharaoh who sits on his throne, even to the firstborn of the slave girl who is behind the millstones; all the firstborn of the cattle as well.
6 'Moreover, there shall be a great cry in all the land of Egypt, such as there has not been before and such as shall never be again.
7 'But against any of the sons of Israel a dog will not even bark, whether against man or beast, that you may understand how the Lord makes a distinction between Egypt and Israel.'
8 "All these your servants will come down to me and bow themselves before me, saying, 'Go out, you and all the people who follow you,' and after that I will go out." And he went out from Pharaoh in hot anger.

9 Then the Lord said to Moses, "Pharaoh will not listen to you, so that My wonders will be multiplied in the land of Egypt."
10 Moses and Aaron performed all these wonders before Pharaoh; yet the Lord hardened Pharaoh's heart, and he did not let the sons of Israel go out of his land.

Exodus 12

21 Then Moses called for all the elders of Israel and said to them, "Go and take for yourselves lambs according to your families, and slay the Passover lamb.
22 "You shall take a bunch of hyssop and dip it in the blood which is in the basin, and apply some of the blood that is in the basin to the lintel and the two doorposts; and none of you shall go outside the door of his house until morning.
23 "For the Lord will pass through to smite the Egyptians; and when He sees the blood on the lintel and on the two doorposts, the Lord will pass over the door and will not allow the destroyer to come in to your houses to smite you.
24 "And you shall observe this event as an ordinance for you and your children forever.
25 "When you enter the land which the Lord will give you, as He has promised, you shall observe this rite.
26 "And when your children say to you, 'What does this rite mean to you?'
27 You shall say, 'It is a Passover sacrifice to the Lord who passed over the houses of the sons of Israel in Egypt when He smote the Egyptians, but spared our homes.' " And the people bowed low and worshiped.
28 Then the sons of Israel went and did so; just as the Lord had commanded Moses and Aaron, so they did.
29 Now it came about at midnight that the Lord struck all the firstborn in the land of Egypt, from the firstborn of Pharaoh who sat on his throne to the firstborn of the captive who was in the dungeon, and all the firstborn of cattle.
30 Pharaoh arose in the night, he and all his servants and all the Egyptians, and there was a great cry in Egypt, for there was no home where there was not someone dead.
31 Then he called for Moses and Aaron at night and said, "Rise up, get out from among my people, both you and the sons of Israel; and go, worship the Lord, as you have said.
32 "Take both your flocks and your herds, as you have said, and go, and bless me also."
33 The Egyptians urged the people, to send them out of

the land in haste, for they said, "We will all be dead."

40 Now the time that the sons of Israel lived in Egypt was four hundred and thirty years.
41 And at the end of four hundred and thirty years, to the very day, all the hosts of the Lord went out from the land of Egypt.
42 It is a night to be observed for the Lord for having brought them out from the land of Egypt; this night is for the Lord, to be observed by all the sons of Israel throughout their generations.

Exodus and the Crossing of the Red Sea

This story describes how Pharaoh pursues the Israelites after granting them permission to leave Egypt. In this narrative, God's intervention is characterized by a "pillar of cloud," which moves between the two armies and allows the Israelite escapade. The most striking part of this story is the parting of the sea which leads to the exodus of the Jewish people. In this story, the delivery of God is questioned by the Israelite themselves; however, the supernatural way in which this story concludes, shows the mighty power of God and his willingness to act in favor of the Jewish people.

Exodus 14

5 When the king of Egypt was told that the people had fled, Pharaoh and his servants had a change of heart toward the people, and they said, "What is this we have done, that we have let Israel go from serving us?"
6 So he made his chariot ready and took his people with him;
7 And he took six hundred select chariots, and all the other chariots of Egypt with officers over all of them.
8 The Lord hardened the heart of Pharaoh, king of Egypt, and he chased after the sons of Israel as the sons of Israel were going out boldly.
9 Then the Egyptians chased after them with all the horses and chariots of Pharaoh, his horsemen and his army, and they overtook them camping by the sea, beside Pi-hahiroth, in front of Baal-zephon.
10 As Pharaoh drew near, the sons of Israel looked, and behold, the Egyptians were marching after them, and they became very frightened; so the sons of Israel cried out to the Lord.
11 Then they said to Moses, "Is it because there were no graves in Egypt that you have taken us away to die in the wilderness? Why have you dealt with us in this way, bringing us out of Egypt?
12 "Is this not the word that we spoke to you in Egypt, saying, 'Leave us alone that we may serve the Egyptians'? For it would have been better for us to serve the Egyptians than to die in the wilderness."
13 But Moses said to the people, "Do not fear! Stand by and see the salvation of the Lord which He will accomplish for you today; for the Egyptians whom you have seen today, you will never see them again forever.
14 "The Lord will fight for you while you keep silent."
15 Then the Lord said to Moses, "Why are you crying out to Me? Tell the sons of Israel to go forward.
16 "As for you, lift up your staff and stretch out your hand over the sea and divide it, and the sons of Israel shall go through the midst of the sea on dry land.
17 "As for Me, behold, I will harden the hearts of the Egyptians so that they will go in after them; and I will be honored through Pharaoh and all his army, through his chariots and his horsemen.
18 "Then the Egyptians will know that I am the Lord, when I am honored through Pharaoh, through his chariots and his horsemen."
19 The angel of God, who had been going before the camp of Israel, moved and went behind them; and the pillar of cloud moved from before them and stood behind them.
20 So it came between the camp of Egypt and the camp of Israel; and there was the cloud

along with the darkness, yet it gave light at night. Thus the one did not come near the other all night.

21 Then Moses stretched out his hand over the sea; and the Lord swept the sea back by a strong east wind all night and turned the sea into dry land, so the waters were divided.

22 The sons of Israel went through the midst of the sea on the dry land, and the waters were like a wall to them on their right hand and on their left.

23 Then the Egyptians took up the pursuit, and all Pharaoh's horses, his chariots and his horsemen went in after them into the midst of the sea.

24 At the morning watch, the Lord looked down on the army of the Egyptians through the pillar of fire and cloud and brought the army of the Egyptians into confusion.

25 He caused their chariot wheels to swerve, and He made them drive with difficulty; so the Egyptians said, "Let us flee from Israel, for the Lord is fighting for them against the Egyptians."

26 Then the Lord said to Moses, "Stretch out your hand over the sea so that the waters may come back over the Egyptians, over their chariots and their horsemen."

27 So Moses stretched out his hand over the sea, and the sea returned to its normal state at daybreak, while the Egyptians were fleeing right into it; then the Lord overthrew the Egyptians in the midst of the sea.

28 The waters returned and covered the chariots and the horsemen, even Pharaoh's entire army that had gone into the sea after them; not even one of them remained.

29 But the sons of Israel walked on dry land through the midst of the sea, and the waters were like a wall to them on their right hand and on their left.

30 Thus the Lord saved Israel that day from the hand of the Egyptians, and Israel saw the Egyptians dead on the seashore.

31 When Israel saw the great power which the Lord had used against the Egyptians, the people feared the Lord, and they believed in the Lord and in His servant Moses.

The Ten Commandments

This narrative presents the most important rules of conduct of human mankind. The Commandments given from the Lord to Moses include both prohibitions and rules for observance. In this narrative, Moses acts as a mediator between God and Israel.

Exodus 20

1 Then God spoke all these words, saying,

2 "I am the Lord your God, who brought you out of the land of Egypt, out of the house of slavery.

3 "You shall have no other gods before Me.

4 "You shall not make for yourself an idol, or any likeness of what is in heaven above or on the earth beneath or in the water under the earth.

5 "You shall not worship them or serve them; for I, the Lord your God, am a jealous God, visiting the iniquity of the fathers on the children, on the third and the fourth generations of those who hate Me,

6 but showing lovingkindness to thousands, to those who love Me and keep My commandments.

7 "You shall not take the name of the Lord your God in vain, for the Lord will not leave him unpunished who takes His name in vain.

8 "Remember the sabbath day, to keep it holy.

9 "Six days you shall labor and do all your work,

10 But the seventh day is a sabbath of the Lord your God; in it you shall not do any work, you or your son or your daughter, your male or your female servant or your cattle or your sojourner who stays with you.

11 "For in six days the Lord made the heavens and the earth, the sea and all that is in them, and rested on the seventh day; therefore the Lord blessed the sabbath day and made it holy.

12 "Honor your father and your mother, that your days may be prolonged in the land which the Lord your God gives you.

13 "You shall not murder.

14 "You shall not commit adultery.
15 "You shall not steal.
16 "You shall not bear false witness against your neighbor.
17 "You shall not covet your neighbor's house; you shall not covet your neighbor's wife or his male servant or his female servant or his ox or his donkey or anything that belongs to your neighbor."
18 All the people perceived the thunder and the lightning flashes and the sound of the trumpet and the mountain smoking; and when the people saw it, they trembled and stood at a distance.
19 Then they said to Moses, "Speak to us yourself and we will listen; but let not God speak to us, or we will die."

The Golden Calf and Moses' Anger

This story vividly describes how, throughout history, Israel has managed to fail God and how He has kept His promise of mercy. This story describes how the Israelites turn their back to God after their miraculous escape from Egypt. While Moses was receiving the tablets of the Ten Commandments, the Israelites demanded the presence of a palpable "god". Moses' frustration reaches its climax when he returns to the camp and sees his people adoring a golden calf. His response was to throw the tablets and "shattered them at the foot of the mountain." The narrative concludes with the decimation of thousands of Israelites as part of God's judgment and Moses cutting a new set of tablets which God reengraves.

Exodus 32

1 Now when the people saw that Moses delayed to come down from the mountain, the people assembled about Aaron and said to him, "Come, make us a god who will go before us; as for this Moses, the man who brought us up from the land of Egypt, we do not know what has become of him."
2 Aaron said to them, "Tear off the gold rings which are in the ears of your wives, your sons, and your daughters, and bring them to me."
3 Then all the people tore off the gold rings which were in their ears and brought them to Aaron.
4 He took this from their hand, and fashioned it with a graving tool and made it into a molten calf; and they said, "This is your god, O Israel, who brought you up from the land of Egypt."
5 Now when Aaron saw this, he built an altar before it; and Aaron made a proclamation and said, "Tomorrow shall be a feast to the Lord."
6 So the next day they rose early and offered burnt offerings, and brought peace offerings; and the people sat down to eat and to drink, and rose up to play.
7 Then the Lord spoke to Moses, "Go down at once, for your people, whom you brought up from the land of Egypt, have corrupted themselves.

8 "They have quickly turned aside from the way which I commanded them. They have made for themselves a molten calf, and have worshiped it and have sacrificed to it and said, 'This is your god, O Israel, who brought you up from the land of Egypt!'
9 The Lord said to Moses, "I have seen this people, and behold, they are an obstinate people.
10 "Now then let Me alone, that My anger may burn against them and that I may destroy them; and I will make of you a great nation."
11 Then Moses entreated the Lord his God, and said, "O Lord, why does Your anger burn against Your people whom You have brought out from the land of Egypt with great power and with a mighty hand?
12 "Why should the Egyptians speak, saying, 'With evil intent He brought them out to kill them in the mountains and to destroy them from the face of the earth'? Turn from Your burning anger and change Your mind about doing harm to Your people.
13 "Remember Abraham, Isaac, and Israel, Your servants to whom You swore by Yourself, and said to them, 'I will multiply your descendants as the stars of the heavens, and all this land of which I have spoken I will give to your descendants, and they shall inherit it forever.'
14 So the Lord changed His mind about the harm which He said He would do to His people.
15 Then Moses turned and went down from the mountain with the two tablets of the testimony in his hand, tablets which were written on both sides; they were written on one side and the other.
16 The tablets were God's work, and the writing was God's writing engraved on the tablets.
17 Now when Joshua heard the sound of the people as they shouted, he said to Moses, "There is a sound of war in the camp."
18 But he said, "It is not the sound of the cry of triumph, Nor is it the sound of the cry of defeat; But the sound of singing I hear."
19 It came about, as soon as Moses came near the camp, that he saw the calf and the dancing; and Moses' anger burned, and he threw the tablets from his hands and shattered them at the foot of the mountain.
20 He took the calf which they had made and burned it with fire, and ground it to powder, and scattered it over the surface of the water and made the sons of Israel drink it.
21 Then Moses said to Aaron, "What did this people do to you, that you have brought such great sin upon them?"
22 Aaron said, "Do not let the anger of my lord burn; you know the people yourself, that they are prone to evil.
23 "For they said to me, 'Make a god for us who will go before us; for this Moses, the man who brought us up from the land of Egypt, we do not know what has become of him.'
24 "I said to them, 'Whoever has any gold, let them tear it off.' So they gave it to me, and I threw it into the fire, and out came this calf."
25 Now when Moses saw that the people were out of control-- for Aaron had

let them get out of control to be a derision among their enemies--
26 Then Moses stood in the gate of the camp, and said, "Whoever is for the Lord, come to me!" And all the sons of Levi gathered together to him.
27 He said to them, "Thus says the Lord, the God of Israel, 'Every man of you put his sword upon his thigh, and go back and forth from gate to gate in the camp, and kill every man his brother, and every man his friend, and every man his neighbor.' "
28 So the sons of Levi did as Moses instructed, and about three thousand men of the people fell that day.
29 Then Moses said, "Dedicate yourselves today to the Lord-- for every man has been against his son and against his brother-- in order that He may bestow a blessing upon you today."
30 On the next day Moses said to the people, "You yourselves have committed a great sin; and now I am going up to the Lord, perhaps I can make atonement for your sin."
31 Then Moses returned to the Lord, and said, "Alas, this people has committed a great sin, and they have made a god of gold for themselves.
32 "But now, if You will, forgive their sin-- and if not, please blot me out from Your book which You have written!"
33 The Lord said to Moses, "Whoever has sinned against Me, I will blot him out of My book.
34 "But go now, lead the people where I told you. Behold, My angel shall go before you; nevertheless in the day when I punish, I will punish them for their sin."
35 Then the Lord smote the people, because of what they did with the calf which Aaron had made.

Exodus 34

1 Now the Lord said to Moses, "Cut out for yourself two stone tablets like the former ones, and I will write on the tablets the words that were on the former tablets which you shattered.
2 "So be ready by morning, and come up in the morning to Mount Sinai, and present yourself there to Me on the top of the mountain.
3 "No man is to come up with you, nor let any man be seen anywhere on the mountain; even the flocks and the herds may not graze in front of that mountain."
4 So he cut out two stone tablets like the former ones, and Moses rose up early in the morning and went up to Mount Sinai, as the Lord had commanded him, and he took two stone tablets in his hand.
5 The Lord descended in the cloud and stood there with him as he called upon the name of the Lord.
6 Then the Lord passed by in front of him and proclaimed, "The Lord, the Lord God, compassionate and gracious, slow to anger, and abounding in lovingkindness and truth;
7 Who keeps lovingkindness for thousands, who forgives iniquity, transgression and sin; yet He will by no means leave the guilty unpunished, visiting the iniquity of fathers on the children and on the grandchildren to the third and fourth generations."
8 Moses made haste to bow low toward the earth and worship.
9 He said, "If now I have found favor in Your sight, O Lord, I pray, let the Lord go along in our midst, even though the people are so obstinate, and pardon our iniquity and our sin, and take us as Your own possession."

The Conquest of Jericho

This story is an important element in the institution of holy wars. It shows that God chooses to intervene in the battles and struggles of man.

This narrative is a powerful expression of faith and deliverance. In this story, all actions leading to triumph are directly prescribed by God.

Joshua 6

1 Now Jericho was tightly shut because of the sons of Israel; no one went out and no one came in.
2 The Lord said to Joshua, "See, I have given Jericho into your hand, with its king and the valiant warriors.
3 "You shall march around the city, all the men of war circling the city once. You shall do so for six days.
4 "Also seven priests shall carry seven trumpets of rams' horns before the ark; then on the seventh day you shall march around the city seven times, and the priests shall blow the trumpets.
5 "It shall be that when they make a long blast with the ram's horn, and when you hear the sound of the trumpet, all the people shall shout with a great shout; and the wall of the city will fall down flat, and the people will go up every man straight ahead."
6 So Joshua the son of Nun called the priests and said to them, "Take up the ark of the covenant, and let seven priests carry seven trumpets of rams' horns before the ark of the Lord."
7 Then he said to the people, "Go forward, and march around the city, and let the armed men go on before the ark of the Lord."
8 And it was so, that when Joshua had spoken to the people, the seven priests carrying the seven trumpets of rams' horns before the Lord went forward and blew the trumpets; and the ark of the covenant of the Lord followed them.
9 The armed men went before the priests who blew the trumpets, and the rear guard came after the ark, while they continued to blow the trumpets.
10 But Joshua commanded the people, saying, "You shall not shout nor let your voice be heard nor let a word proceed out of your mouth, until the day I tell you, 'Shout!' Then you shall shout!"
11 So he had the ark of the Lord taken around the city, circling it once; then they came into the camp and spent the night in the camp.
12 Now Joshua rose early in the morning, and the priests took up the ark of the Lord.
13 The seven priests carrying the seven trumpets of rams' horns before the ark of the Lord went on continually, and blew the trumpets; and the armed men went before them and the rear guard came after the ark of the Lord, while they continued to blow the trumpets.
14 Thus the second day they marched around the city once and returned to the camp; they did so for six days.
15 Then on the seventh day they rose early at the dawning of the day and marched around the city in the same manner seven times; only on that day they marched around the city seven times.
16 At the seventh time, when the priests blew the trumpets, Joshua said to the people, "Shout! For the Lord has given you the city.

20 So the people shouted, and priests blew the trumpets; and when the people heard the sound of the trumpet, the people shouted with a great shout and the wall fell down flat, so that the people went up into the city, every man straight ahead, and they took the city.
21 They utterly destroyed everything in the city, both man and woman, young and old, and ox and sheep and donkey, with the edge of the sword.

Samson and the Philistines

This story demonstrates that human weakness can coexist with faith and devotion to God. Weakened by the desire of Delilah, Samson gives up the source of his great strength. As a result, he is blinded and imprisoned. However, the story ends with a victory; Samson carries out a divine plan and manages to kill thousands of Philistines. Samson perished when executing this last act.

Bible Stories   *The Conquest of Jericho*

Judges 13

6 Then the woman came and told her husband, saying, "A man of God came to me and his appearance was like the appearance of the angel of God, very awesome. And I did not ask him where he came from, nor did he tell me his name.

7 "But he said to me, 'Behold, you shall conceive and give birth to a son, and now you shall not drink wine or strong drink nor eat any unclean thing, for the boy shall be a Nazirite to God from the womb to the day of his death.'

24 Then the woman gave birth to a son and named him Samson; and the child grew up and the Lord blessed him.

Judges 16

1 Now Samson went to Gaza and saw a harlot there, and went in to her.

2 When it was told to the Gazites, saying, "Samson has come here," they surrounded the place and lay in wait for him all night at the gate of the city. And they kept silent all night, saying, "Let us wait until the morning light, then we will kill him."

3 Now Samson lay until midnight, and at midnight he arose and took hold of the doors of the city gate and the two posts and pulled them up along with the bars; then he put them on his shoulders and carried them up to the top of the mountain which is opposite Hebron.

4 After this it came about that he loved a woman in the valley of Sorek, whose name was Delilah.

5 The lords of the Philistines came up to her and said to her, "Entice him, and see where his great strength lies and how we may overpower him that we may bind him to afflict him. Then we will each give you eleven hundred pieces of silver."

6 So Delilah said to Samson, "Please tell me where your great strength is and how you may be bound to afflict you."

7 Samson said to her, "If they bind me with seven fresh cords that have not been dried, then I will become weak and be like any other man."

8 Then the lords of the Philistines brought up to her seven fresh cords that had not been dried, and she bound him with them.

9 Now she had men lying in wait in an inner room. And she said to him, "The Philistines are upon you, Samson!" But he snapped the cords as a string of tow snaps when it touches fire. So his strength was not discovered.

10 Then Delilah said to Samson, "Behold, you have deceived me and told me lies; now please tell me how you may be bound."

11 He said to her, "If they bind me tightly with new ropes which have not been used, then I will become weak and be like any other man."

12 So Delilah took new ropes and bound him with them and said to him, "The Philistines are upon

you, Samson!" For the men were lying in wait in the inner room. But he snapped the ropes from his arms like a thread.
13 Then Delilah said to Samson, "Up to now you have deceived me and told me lies; tell me how you may be bound." And he said to her, "If you weave the seven locks of my hair with the web [and fasten it with a pin, then I will become weak and be like any other man."
14 So while he slept, Delilah took the seven locks of his hair and wove them into the web]. And she fastened it with the pin and said to him, "The Philistines are upon you, Samson!" But he awoke from his sleep and pulled out the pin of the loom and the web.
15 Then she said to him, "How can you say, 'I love you,' when your heart is not with me? You have deceived me these three times and have not told me where your great strength is."
16 It came about when she pressed him daily with her words and urged him, that his soul was annoyed to death.
17 So he told her all that was in his heart and said to her, "A razor has never come on my head, for I have been a Nazirite to God from my mother's womb. If I am shaved, then my strength will leave me and I will become weak and be like any other man."
18 When Delilah saw that he had told her all that was in his heart, she sent and called the lords of the Philistines, saying, "Come up once more, for he has told me all that is in his heart." Then the lords of the Philistines came up to her and brought the money in their hands.
19 She made him sleep on her knees, and called for a man and had him shave off the seven locks of his hair. Then she began to afflict him, and his strength left him.
20 She said, "The Philistines are upon you, Samson!" And he awoke from his sleep and said, "I will go out as at other times and shake myself free." But he did not know that the Lord had departed from him.
21 Then the Philistines seized him and gouged out his eyes; and they brought him down to Gaza and bound him with bronze chains, and he was a grinder in the prison.
22 However, the hair of his head began to grow again after it was shaved off.
23 Now the lords of the Philistines assembled to offer a great sacrifice to Dagon their god, and to rejoice, for they said, "Our god has given Samson our enemy into our hands."
24 When the people saw him, they praised their god, for they said, "Our god has given our enemy into our hands, Even the destroyer of our country, Who has slain many of us."
25 It so happened when they were in high spirits, that they said, "Call for Samson, that he may amuse us." So they called for Samson from the prison, and he entertained them.

Bible Stories   II - 23   *Samson and the Philistines*

And they made him stand between the pillars.

26 Then Samson said to the boy who was holding his hand, "Let me feel the pillars on which the house rests, that I may lean against them."

27 Now the house was full of men and women, and all the lords of the Philistines were there. And about 3,000 men and women were on the roof looking on while Samson was amusing them.

28 Then Samson called to the Lord and said, "O Lord God, please remember me and please strengthen me just this time, O God, that I may at once be avenged of the Philistines for my two eyes."

29 Samson grasped the two middle pillars on which the house rested, and braced himself against them, the one with his right hand and the other with his left.

30 And Samson said, "Let me die with the Philistines!" And he bent with all his might so that the house fell on the lords and all the people who were in it. So the dead whom he killed at his death were more than those whom he killed in his life.

31 Then his brothers and all his father's household came down, took him, brought him up and buried him between Zorah and Eshtaol in the tomb of Manoah his father. Thus he had judged Israel twenty years.

David and Goliath

During the time of David, the Philistines represented a serious threat to the Israelites. In this story the Philistines are personified by Goliath, a ten-foot tall giant while David is a simple and ordinary shepherd, an unsuitable contender to Goliath. The theme of this narrative is that God can choose ordinary people to do extraordinary work. David's great love for God transpires throughout the entire story. He is the only contender that asked for God's protection when facing Goliath. The story tells of God's deliverance to those who love and trust Him.

1 Samuel 17

12 Now David was the son of the Ephrathite of Bethlehem in Judah, whose name was Jesse, and he had eight sons. And Jesse was old in the days of Saul, advanced in years among men.

13 The three older sons of Jesse had gone after Saul to the battle. And the names of his three sons who went to the battle were Eliab the firstborn, and the second to him Abinadab, and the third Shammah.

14 David was the youngest. Now the three oldest followed Saul,

15 but David went back and forth from Saul to tend his father's flock at Bethlehem.

16 The Philistine came forward morning and evening for forty days and took his stand.

17 Then Jesse said to David his son, "Take now for your brothers an ephah of this roasted grain and these ten loaves and run to the camp to your brothers.

18 "Bring also these ten cuts of cheese to the commander of their thousand, and look into the welfare of your brothers, and bring back news of them.

19 "For Saul and they and all the men of Israel are in the valley of Elah, fighting with the Philistines."

20 So David arose early in the morning and left the flock with a keeper and took the supplies and went as Jesse had commanded him. And he came to the circle of the camp while the army was going out in battle array shouting the war cry.

21 Israel and the Philistines drew up in battle array, army against army.

22 Then David left his baggage in the care of the baggage keeper, and ran to the battle line and entered in order to greet his brothers.

23 As he was talking with them, behold, the champion, the Philistine from Gath named Goliath, was coming up from the army of the Philistines, and he spoke these same words; and David heard them.

24 When all the men of Israel saw the man, they fled from him and were greatly afraid.

25 The men of Israel said, "Have you seen this man who is coming up? Surely he is coming up to defy Israel. And it will be that the king will enrich the man who kills him with great riches and will give him his daughter and make his father's house free in Israel."

26 Then David spoke to the men who were standing by him, saying, "What will be done for the man who kills this Philistine and takes away the reproach from Israel? For who is this uncircumcised Philistine, that he should taunt the armies of the living God?"

27 The people answered him in accord with this word, saying, "Thus it will be done for the man who kills him."

28 Now Eliab his oldest brother heard when he spoke to the men; and Eliab's anger burned against David and he said, "Why have you come down? And with whom have you left those few sheep in the wilderness? I know your insolence and the wickedness of your heart; for you have come down in order to see the battle."

29 But David said, "What have I done now? Was it not just a question?"

30 Then he turned away from him to another and said the same thing; and the people answered the same thing as before.

31 When the words which David spoke were heard, they told them to Saul, and he sent for him.

32 David said to Saul, "Let no man's heart fail on account of him; your servant will go and fight with this Philistine."

33 Then Saul said to David, "You are not able to go against this Philistine to fight with him; for you are but a youth while he has been a warrior from his youth."

34 But David said to Saul, "Your servant was tending his father's sheep. When a lion or a bear came and took a lamb from the flock,

35 I went out after him and attacked him, and rescued it from his mouth; and when he rose up against me, I seized him by his beard and struck him and killed him.

36 "Your servant has killed both the lion and the bear; and this uncircumcised Philistine will be like one of them, since he has taunted the armies of the living God."

37 And David said, "The Lord who delivered me from the paw of the lion and from the paw of the bear, He will deliver me from the hand of this Philistine." And Saul said to David, "Go, and may the Lord be with you."

38 Then Saul clothed David with his garments and put a bronze helmet on his head, and he clothed him with armor.

39 David girded his sword over his armor and tried to walk, for he had not tested them. So David said to Saul, "I cannot go with these, for I have not tested them." And David took them off.

40 He took his stick in his hand and chose for himself five smooth stones from the brook, and put them in the shepherd's bag which he had, even in his pouch, and his sling was in his hand; and he approached the Philistine.

41 Then the Philistine came on and approached David, with the shield-bearer in front of him.

42 When the Philistine looked and saw David, he disdained him; for he was but a youth, and ruddy, with a handsome appearance.

43 The Philistine said to David, "Am I a dog, that you come to me with sticks?" And the Philistine cursed David by his gods.

44 The Philistine also said to David, "Come to me, and I will give your flesh to the birds of the sky and the beasts of the field."

45 Then David said to the Philistine, "You come to me with a sword, a spear, and a javelin, but I come to you in the name of the Lord of hosts, the God of the armies of Israel, whom you have taunted.

46 "This day the Lord will deliver you up into my hands, and I will strike you down and remove your head from you. And I will give the dead bodies of the army of the

Bible Stories *David and Goliath*

Philistines this day to the birds of the sky and the wild beasts of the earth, that all the earth may know that there is a God in Israel,
47 And that all this assembly may know that the Lord does not deliver by sword or by spear; for the battle is the Lord'S and He will give you into our hands."
48 Then it happened when the Philistine rose and came and drew near to meet David, that David ran quickly toward the battle line to meet the Philistine.
49 And David put his hand into his bag and took from it a stone and slung it, and struck the Philistine on his forehead. And the stone sank into his forehead, so that he fell on his face to the ground.
50 Thus David prevailed over the Philistine with a sling and a stone, and he struck the Philistine and killed him; but there was no sword in David's hand.
51 Then David ran and stood over the Philistine and took his sword and drew it out of its sheath and killed him, and cut off his head with it. When the Philistines saw that their champion was dead, they fled.

Bathsheba, David's Great Sin

God's great plans for David are overshadowed by his "great sin": he manages to have Bathsheba's husband killed in order to marry her. This is a story of power, contrition, and restoration. David committed this sin during the pinnacle of his power. The results were devastating: one of his children died; the people's respect for David was lowered; he entered in battles with neighboring countries; he was not allowed to build the Temple; and his beloved son Absalom revolted against him. However, David's love for God remained unchanged throughout his life. His love and contrition are characterized in a large number of psalms that have brought, and will continue to bring generations closer to God.

2 Samuel 11

1 Then it happened in the spring, at the time when kings go out to battle, that David sent Joab and his servants with him and all Israel, and they destroyed the sons of Ammon and besieged Rabbah. But David stayed at Jerusalem.
2 Now when evening came David arose from his bed and walked around on the roof of the king's house, and from the roof he saw a woman bathing; and the woman was very beautiful in appearance.
3 So David sent and inquired about the woman. And one said, "Is this not Bathsheba, the daughter of Eliam, the wife of Uriah the Hittite?"
4 David sent messengers and took her, and when she came to him, he lay with her; and when she had purified herself from her uncleanness, she returned to her house.
5 The woman conceived; and she sent and told David, and said, "I am pregnant."

6 Then David sent to Joab, saying, "Send me Uriah the Hittite." So Joab sent Uriah to David.

7 When Uriah came to him, David asked concerning the welfare of Joab and the people and the state of the war.

8 Then David said to Uriah, "Go down to your house, and wash your feet." And Uriah went out of the king's house, and a present from the king was sent out after him.

9 But Uriah slept at the door of the king's house with all the servants of his lord, and did not go down to his house.

10 Now when they told David, saying, "Uriah did not go down to his house," David said to Uriah, "Have you not come from a journey? Why did you not go down to your house?"

11 Uriah said to David, "The ark and Israel and Judah are staying in temporary shelters, and my lord Joab and the servants of my lord are camping in the open field. Shall I then go to my house to eat and to drink and to lie with my wife? By your life and the life of your soul, I will not do this thing."

12 Then David said to Uriah, "Stay here today also, and tomorrow I will let you go." So Uriah remained in Jerusalem that day and the next.

13 Now David called him, and he ate and drank before him, and he made him drunk; and in the evening he went out to lie on his bed with his lord's servants, but he did not go down to his house.

14 Now in the morning David wrote a letter to Joab and sent it by the hand of Uriah.

15 He had written in the letter, saying, "Place Uriah in the front line of the fiercest battle and withdraw from him, so that he may be struck down and die."

16 So it was as Joab kept watch on the city, that he put Uriah at the place where he knew there were valiant men.

17 The men of the city went out and fought against Joab, and some of the people among David's servants fell; and Uriah the Hittite also died.

18 Then Joab sent and reported to David all the events of the war.

19 He charged the messenger, saying, "When you have finished telling all the events of the war to the king,

20 and if it happens that the king's wrath rises and he says to you, 'Why did you go so near to the city to fight? Did you not know that they would shoot from the wall?

21 'Who struck down Abimelech the son of Jerubbesheth? Did not a woman throw an upper millstone on him from the wall so that he died at Thebez? Why did you go so near the wall?'-- then you shall say, 'Your servant Uriah the Hittite is dead also.' "

22 So the messenger departed and came and reported to David all that Joab had sent him to tell.

23 The messenger said to David, "The men prevailed against us and came out against us in the field,

but we pressed them as far as the entrance of the gate.

24 "Moreover, the archers shot at your servants from the wall; so some of the king's servants are dead, and your servant Uriah the Hittite is also dead."

25 Then David said to the messenger, "Thus you shall say to Joab, 'Do not let this thing displease you, for the sword devours one as well as another; make your battle against the city stronger and overthrow it'; and so encourage him."

26 Now when the wife of Uriah heard that Uriah her husband was dead, she mourned for her husband.

27 When the time of mourning was over, David sent and brought her to his house and she became his wife; then she bore him a son. But the thing that David had done was evil in the sight of the Lord.

2 Samuel 12

1 Then the Lord sent Nathan to David. And he came to him and said, "There were two men in one city, the one rich and the other poor.

2 "The rich man had a great many flocks and herds.

3 "But the poor man had nothing except one little ewe lamb Which he bought and nourished; And it grew up together with him and his children. It would eat of his bread and drink of his cup and lie in his bosom, And was like a daughter to him.

4 "Now a traveler came to the rich man, And he was unwilling to take from his own flock or his own herd, To prepare for the wayfarer who had come to him; Rather he took the poor man's ewe lamb and prepared it for the man who had come to him."

5 Then David's anger burned greatly against the man, and he said to Nathan, "As the Lord lives, surely the man who has done this deserves to die.

6 "He must make restitution for the lamb fourfold, because he did this thing and had no compassion."

7 Nathan then said to David, "You are the man! Thus says the Lord God of Israel, 'It is I who anointed you king over Israel and it is I who delivered you from the hand of Saul.

8 'I also gave you your master's house and your master's wives into your care, and I gave you the house of Israel and Judah; and if that had been too little, I would have added to you many more things like these!

9 'Why have you despised the word of the Lord by doing evil in His sight? You have struck down Uriah the Hittite with the sword, have taken his wife to be your wife, and have killed him with the sword of the sons of Ammon.

10 'Now therefore, the sword shall never depart from your house, because you have despised Me and have taken the wife of Uriah the Hittite to be your wife.'

11 "Thus says the Lord, 'Behold, I will raise up evil against you from your own household; I will even take your wives before your eyes and give them to your companion, and he will lie with your wives in broad daylight.

12 'Indeed you did it secretly, but I will do this thing before all Israel, and under the sun.' "

13 Then David said to Nathan, "I have sinned against the Lord." And Nathan said to David, "The Lord also has taken away your sin; you shall not die.

14 "However, because by this deed you have given occasion to the enemies of the Lord to blaspheme, the child also that is born to you shall surely die."

15 So Nathan went to his house. Then the Lord struck the child that Uriah's widow bore to David, so that he was very sick.

16 David therefore inquired of God for the child; and David fasted and went and lay all night on the ground.

17 The elders of his household stood beside him in order to raise him up from the ground, but he was unwilling and would not eat food with them.

Bathsheba, David's Great Sin

18 Then it happened on the seventh day that the child died. And the servants of David were afraid to tell him that the child was dead, for they said, "Behold, while the child was still alive, we spoke to him and he did not listen to our voice. How then can we tell him that the child is dead, since he might do himself harm!"

19 But when David saw that his servants were whispering together, David perceived that the child was dead; so David said to his servants, "Is the child dead?" And they said, "He is dead."

20 So David arose from the ground, washed, anointed himself, and changed his clothes; and he came into the house of the Lord and worshiped. Then he came to his own house, and when he requested, they set food before him and he ate.

21 Then his servants said to him, "What is this thing that you have done? While the child was alive, you fasted and wept; but when the child died, you arose and ate food."

22 He said, "While the child was still alive, I fasted and wept; for I said, 'Who knows, the Lord may be gracious to me, that the child may live.'

23 "But now he has died; why should I fast? Can I bring him back again? I will go to him, but he will not return to me."

24 Then David comforted his wife Bathsheba, and went in to her and lay with her; and she gave birth to a son, and he named him Solomon. Now the Lord loved him

25 And sent word through Nathan the prophet, and he named him Jedidiah for the Lord's sake.

Solomon's Wisdom

The biblical tradition associates wisdom with Solomon. At the beginning of his reign, a prayer for wisdom was his first request to God. This story illustrates how God responds to the prayers that are just. This narrative describes how Solomon yearned for discernment and how he was able to apply this gift to every-day life situations.

1 Kings 3

3 Now Solomon loved the Lord, walking in the statutes of his father David, except he sacrificed and burned incense on the high places.

4 The king went to Gibeon to sacrifice there, for that was the great high place; Solomon offered a thousand burnt offerings on that altar.

5 In Gibeon the Lord appeared to Solomon in a dream at night; and God said, "Ask what you wish me to give you."

6 Then Solomon said, "You have shown great lovingkindness to Your servant David my father, according as he walked before You in truth and righteousness and uprightness of heart toward You; and You have reserved for him this great lovingkindness, that You have given him a son to sit on his throne, as it is this day.

7 "Now, O Lord my God, You have made Your servant king in place of my father David, yet I am but a little child; I do not know how to go out or come in.

8 "Your servant is in the midst of Your people which You have chosen, a great people who are too many to be numbered or counted.

9 "So give Your servant an understanding heart to judge Your people to discern between good and evil. For who is able to judge this great people of Yours?"

10 It was pleasing in the sight of the Lord that Solomon had asked this thing.

11 God said to him, "Because you have asked this thing and have not asked for yourself long life, nor have asked riches for yourself, nor have you asked for the life of your enemies, but have asked for yourself discernment to understand justice,

12 Behold, I have done according to your words. Behold, I have given you a wise and discerning heart, so that there has been no one like you before you, nor shall one like you arise after you.

13 "I have also given you what you have not asked, both riches and honor, so that there

will not be any among the kings like you all your days. 14 "If you walk in My ways, keeping My statutes and commandments, as your father David walked, then I will prolong your days."
15 Then Solomon awoke, and behold, it was a dream. And he came to Jerusalem and stood before the ark of the covenant of the Lord, and offered burnt offerings and made peace offerings, and made a feast for all his servants.

16 Then two women who were harlots came to the king and stood before him.
17 The one woman said, "Oh, my lord, this woman and I live in the same house; and I gave birth to a child while she was in the house.
18 "It happened on the third day after I gave birth, that this woman also gave birth to a child, and we were together. There was no stranger with us in the house, only the two of us in the house.
19 "This woman's son died in the night, because she lay on it.
20 "So she arose in the middle of the night and took my son from beside me while your maidservant slept, and laid him in her bosom, and laid her dead son in my bosom.
21 "When I rose in the morning to nurse my son, behold, he was dead; but when I looked at him carefully in the morning, behold, he was not my son, whom I had borne."
22 Then the other woman said, "No! For the living one is my son, and the dead one is your son." But the first woman said, "No! For the dead one is your son, and the living one is my son." Thus they spoke before the king.
23 Then the king said, "The one says, 'This is my son who is living, and your son is the dead one'; and the other says, 'No! For your son is the dead one, and my son is the living one.' "
24 The king said, "Get me a sword." So they brought a sword before the king.
25 The king said, "Divide the living child in two, and give half to the one and half to the other."
26 Then the woman whose child was the living one spoke to the king, for she was deeply stirred over her son and said, "Oh, my lord, give her the living child, and by no means kill him." But the other said, "He shall be neither mine nor yours; divide him!"
27 Then the king said, "Give the first woman the living child, and by no means kill him. She is his mother."
28 When all Israel heard of the judgment which the king had handed down, they feared the king, for they saw that the wisdom of God was in him to administer justice.

Daniel in the Lions' Den

This narrative shows a soul in conflict. Daniel can neither disobey the Law of his God, nor escape the inexorable law of the royal decree of the king of the Medes and the Persians. Daniel prospered over other satraps which triggered their jealousy and envy. This situation culminates in the incarceration of Daniel in the lions' den. It is also a story of faith and deliverance: "God sent his angel and shut the lions' mouths". This story shows a man in the midst of a horrible situation who continues to hope and pray for God's help.

Daniel 6

1 It seemed good to Darius to appoint 120 satraps over the kingdom, that they would be in charge of the whole kingdom,

2 And over them three commissioners (of whom Daniel was one), that these satraps might be accountable to them, and that the king might not suffer loss.

3 Then this Daniel began distinguishing himself among the commissioners and satraps because he possessed an extraordinary spirit, and the king planned to appoint him over the entire kingdom.

4 Then the commissioners and satraps began trying to find a ground of accusation against Daniel in regard to government affairs; but they could find no ground of accusation or evidence of corruption, inasmuch as he was faithful, and no negligence or corruption was to be found in him.

5 Then these men said, "We will not find any ground of accusation against this Daniel unless we find it against him with regard to the law of his God."

6 Then these commissioners and satraps came by agreement to the king and spoke to him as follows: "King Darius, live forever!

7 "All the commissioners of the kingdom, the prefects and the satraps, the high officials and the governors have consulted together that the king should establish a statute and enforce an injunction that anyone who makes a petition to any god or man besides you, O king, for thirty days, shall be cast into the lions' den.

8 "Now, O king, establish the injunction and sign the document so that it may not be changed, according to the law of the Medes and Persians, which may not be revoked."

9 Therefore King Darius signed the document, that is, the injunction.

10 Now when Daniel knew that the document was signed, he entered his house (now in his roof chamber he had windows open toward Jerusalem); and he continued kneeling on his knees three times a day, praying and giving thanks before his God, as he had been doing previously.

11 Then these men came by agreement and found Daniel making petition and supplication before his God.

12 Then they approached and spoke before the king about the king's injunction, "Did you not sign an injunction that any man who makes a petition to any god or man besides you, O king, for thirty days, is to be cast into the lions' den?" The king replied, "The

statement is true, according to the law of the Medes and Persians, which may not be revoked."

13 Then they answered and spoke before the king, "Daniel, who is one of the exiles from Judah, pays no attention to you, O king, or to the injunction which you signed, but keeps making his petition three times a day."

14 Then, as soon as the king heard this statement, he was deeply distressed and set his mind on delivering Daniel; and even until sunset he kept exerting himself to rescue him.

15 Then these men came by agreement to the king and said to the king, "Recognize, O king, that it is a law of the Medes and Persians that no injunction or statute which the king establishes may be changed."

16 Then the king gave orders, and Daniel was brought in and cast into the lions' den. The king spoke and said to Daniel, "Your God whom you constantly serve will Himself deliver you."

17 A stone was brought and laid over the mouth of the den; and the king sealed it with his own signet ring and with the signet rings of his nobles, so that nothing would be changed in regard to Daniel.

18 Then the king went off to his palace and spent the night fasting, and no entertainment was brought before him; and his sleep fled from him.

19 Then the king arose at dawn, at the break of day, and went in haste to the lions' den.

20 When he had come near the den to Daniel, he cried out with a troubled voice. The king spoke and said to Daniel, "Daniel, servant of the living God, has your God, whom you constantly serve, been able to deliver you from the lions?"

21 Then Daniel spoke to the king, "O king, live forever!

22 "My God sent His angel and shut the lions' mouths and they have not harmed me, inasmuch as I was found innocent before Him; and also toward you, O king, I have committed no crime."

23 Then the king was very pleased and gave orders for Daniel to be taken up out of the den. So Daniel was taken up out of the den and no injury whatever was found on him, because he had trusted in his God.

24 The king then gave orders, and they brought those men who had maliciously accused Daniel, and they cast them, their children and their wives into the lions' den; and they had not reached the bottom of the den before the lions overpowered them and crushed all their bones.

25 Then Darius the king wrote to all the peoples, nations and men of every language who were living in all the land: "May your peace abound!

Daniel in the Lions' Den   *Bible Stories*

26 "I make a decree that in all the dominion of my kingdom men are to fear and tremble before the God of Daniel; For He is the living God and enduring forever, And His kingdom is one which will not be destroyed, And His dominion will be forever.
27 "He delivers and rescues and performs signs and wonders In heaven and on earth, Who has also delivered Daniel from the power of the lions."
28 So this Daniel enjoyed success in the reign of Darius and in the reign of Cyrus the Persian.

Jonah's Disobedience

This is a story of judgment and grace. Because Jonah's flight to Tarshish has an adverse effect on God's possibilities for Nineveh, God pursues the mediator, not to punish him but to turn him around. This narrative demonstrates the fatal consequences of ignoring God when he speaks to us. It shows that God can be severe but kind when we change our life in order to submit to His will. In this story God remains gracious toward those who deserve punishment.

Jonah 1

1 The word of the Lord came to Jonah the son of Amittai saying,
2 "Arise, go to Nineveh the great city and cry against it, for their wickedness has come up before Me."
3 But Jonah rose up to flee to Tarshish from the presence of the Lord. So he went down to Joppa, found a ship which was going to Tarshish, paid the fare and went down into it to go with them to Tarshish from the presence of the Lord.
4 The Lord hurled a great wind on the sea and there was a great storm on the sea so that the ship was about to break up.
5 Then the sailors became afraid and every man cried to his god, and they threw the cargo which was in the ship into the sea to lighten it for them. But Jonah had gone below into the hold of the ship, lain down and fallen sound asleep.
6 So the captain approached him and said, "How is it that you are sleeping? Get up, call on your god. Perhaps your god will be concerned about us so that we will not perish."
7 Each man said to his mate, "Come, let us cast lots so we may learn on whose account this calamity has struck us." So they cast lots and the lot fell on Jonah.
8 Then they said to him, "Tell us, now! On whose account has this calamity struck us? What is your occupation? And where do you come from? What is your country? From what people are you?"

9 He said to them, "I am a Hebrew, and I fear the Lord God of heaven who made the sea and the dry land."
10 Then the men became extremely frightened and they said to him, "How could you do this?" For the men knew that he was fleeing from the presence of the Lord, because he had told them.
11 So they said to him, "What should we do to you that the sea may become calm for us?"-- for the sea was becoming increasingly stormy.
12 He said to them, "Pick me up and throw me into the sea. Then the sea will become calm for you, for I know that on account of me this great storm has come upon you."
13 However, the men rowed desperately to return to land but they could not, for the sea was becoming even stormier against them.
14 Then they called on the Lord and said, "We earnestly pray, O Lord, do not let us perish on account of this man's life and do not put innocent blood on us; for You, O Lord, have done as You have pleased."
15 So they picked up Jonah, threw him into the sea, and the sea stopped its raging.
16 Then the men feared the Lord greatly, and they offered a sacrifice to the Lord and made vows.
17 And the Lord appointed a great fish to swallow Jonah, and Jonah was in the stomach of the fish three days and three nights.

Jonah 2

1 Then Jonah prayed to the Lord his God from the stomach of the fish,
2 And he said, "I called out of my distress to the Lord, And He answered me. I cried for help from the depth of Sheol; You heard my voice.
3 "For You had cast me into the deep, Into the heart of the seas, And the current engulfed me. All Your breakers and billows passed over me.
4 "So I said, 'I have been expelled from Your sight. Nevertheless I will look again toward Your holy temple.'
5 "Water encompassed me to the point of death. The great deep engulfed me, Weeds were wrapped around my head.
6 "I descended to the roots of the mountains. The earth with its bars was around me forever, But You have brought up my life from the pit, O Lord my God.
7 "While I was fainting away, I remembered the Lord, And my prayer came to You, Into Your holy temple.
8 "Those who regard vain idols Forsake their faithfulness,
9 But I will sacrifice to You With the voice of thanksgiving. That which I have vowed I will pay Salvation is from the Lord."
10 Then the Lord commanded the fish, and it vomited Jonah up onto the dry land.

Key for Bible Stories

BIBLE STORIES/ LAYERS	VERSES
The Creation	Genesis 1:1-31
The Creation of Adam and Eve	Genesis 2:7-9; 16-25
The Fall of Man	Genesis 3:1-24
Cain and Abel	Genesis 4:1-15
Noah and the Great Flood	Genesis 6:1-22 Genesis 7:1-5; 17-22; Genesis 8:1-22
The Doom of Sodom and Gomorrah	Genesis 19:1-26
The Offering of Isaac	Genesis 21:2-3 Genesis 22:1-18
The Birth of Moses	Exodus 1:15-22 Exodus 2:1-10
The Passover	Exodus 9:1-3 Exodus 11:1; 4-10 Exodus 12:21-33; 40-42
Exodus and the Crossing of the Red Sea	Exodus 14:5-31
The Ten Commandments	Exodus 20:1-19
The Golden Calf and Moses' Anger	Exodus 32:1-35 Exodus 34:1-9
The Conquest of Jericho	Joshua 6:1-16; 20-21
Samson and the Philistines	Judges 13:6-7; 24 Judges 16:1-31
David and Goliath	1 Samuel 17:12-51
Bathsheba, David's Great Sin	2 Samuel 11:1-27 2 Samuel 12:1-25
Solomon's Wisdom	1 Kings 3:3-28
Daniel in the Lion's Den	Daniel 6:1-28
Jonah's Disobedience	Jonah 1:1-17 Jonah 2:1-10

LAYERS

- Love
- Jesus' Deity
- The Holy Spirit
- Grace
- Sin, Forgiveness, and Redemption
- The Second Coming and Judgment
- Exhortations
- Petitions, Miracles, and Faith
- Worries
- Compassion
- Prayers

Third Collection

Paul and Peter

Matthew, Mark, Luke, and John

Love

Love will never cease. Our Father demonstrated His love for us when he sent His "only begotten Son" (John 3:16) to save this world. This layer shows the love that Christ always will have for us. It teaches us the love that we should have for God and our neighbors. In 1 Corinthians 13, Paul defines love for us. He tells us that love is patient, kind, and never faltering. It bears all things, brings hope to all things, and endures all things. Love is the greatest of the graces given by God.

Matthew 5

44 "But I say to you, love your enemies and pray for those who persecute you,

45 So that you may be sons of your Father who is in heaven; for He causes His sun to rise on the evil and the good, and sends rain on the righteous and the unrighteous.

46 "For if you love those who love you, what reward do you have? Do not even the tax collectors do the same?

47 "If you greet only your brothers, what more are you doing than others? Do not even the Gentiles do the same?

48 "Therefore you are to

Scriptures   *Love*

be perfect, as your heavenly Father is perfect."

Matthew 22

37 And He said to him, " 'You shall love the Lord your God with all your heart, and with all your soul, and with all your mind.'
38 "This is the great and foremost commandment.
39 "The second is like it, 'you shall love your neighbor as yourself.'
40 "On these two commandments depend the whole law and the prophets."

Luke 6

27 "But I say to you who hear, love your enemies, do good to those who hate you,
28 "Bless those who curse you, pray for those who mistreat you.
29 "Whoever hits you on the cheek, offer him the other also; and whoever takes away your coat, do not withhold your shirt from him either.
30 "Give to everyone who asks of you, and whoever takes away what is yours, do not demand it back.
31 "Treat others the same way you want them to treat you.
32 "If you love those who love you, what credit is that to you? For even sinners love those who love them.
33 "If you do good to those who do good to you, what credit is that to you? For even sinners do the same.
34 "If you lend to those from whom you expect to receive, what credit is that to you? Even sinners lend to sinners in order to receive back the same amount.
35 "But love your enemies, and do good, and lend, expecting nothing in return; and your reward will be great, and you will be sons of the Most High; for He Himself is kind to ungrateful and evil men.
36 "Be merciful, just as your Father is merciful."

John 3

16 "For God so loved the world, that He gave His only begotten Son, that whoever believes in Him shall not perish, but have eternal life."

John 13

1 Now before the Feast of the Passover, Jesus knowing that His hour had come that He would depart out of this world to the Father, having loved His own who were in the world, He loved them to the end.

13 "You call Me Teacher and Lord; and you are right, for so I am.
14 "If I then, the Lord and the Teacher, washed your feet, you also ought to wash one another's feet.

33 "Little children, I am with you a little while longer. You will seek Me; and as I said to the Jews, now I also say to you, 'Where I am going, you cannot come.'
34 "A new commandment I give to you, that you love one another, even as I have loved you, that you also love one another.
35 "By this all men will know that you are My disciples, if you have love for one another."

John 14

21 "He who has My commandments and keeps them is the one who loves Me; and he who loves Me will be loved by My Father, and I will love him and will disclose Myself to him."

23 Jesus answered and said to him, "If anyone loves Me, he will keep My word; and My Father will love him, and We will come to him and make Our abode with him.

John 15

9 "Just as the Father has loved Me, I have also loved you; abide in My love.
10 "If you keep My commandments, you will

Love   III - 4   *Scriptures*

abide in My love; just as I have kept My Father's commandments and abide in His love."

John 16

27 "For the Father Himself loves you, because you have loved Me and have believed that I came forth from the Father."

Romans 5

8 But God demonstrates His own love toward us, in that while we were yet sinners, Christ died for us.

Romans 12

9 Let love be without hypocrisy. Abhor what is evil; cling to what is good.
10 Be devoted to one another in brotherly love; give preference to one another in honor;
11 Not lagging behind in diligence, fervent in spirit, serving the Lord;
12 Rejoicing in hope, persevering in tribulation, devoted to prayer,
13 Contributing to the needs of the saints, practicing hospitality.
14 Bless those who persecute you; bless and do not curse.
15 Rejoice with those who rejoice, and weep with those who weep.
16 Be of the same mind toward one another; do not be haughty in mind, but associate with the lowly. Do not be wise in your own estimation.
17 Never pay back evil for evil to anyone. Respect what is right in the sight of all men.
18 If possible, so far as it depends on you, be at peace with all men.
19 Never take your own revenge, beloved, but leave room for the wrath of God, for it is written, "vengeance is mine, I will repay," says the Lord.
20 "But if your enemy is hungry, feed him, and if he is thirsty, give him a drink; for in so doing you will heap burning coals on his head."
21 Do not be overcome by evil, but overcome evil with good.

Romans 13

10 Love does no wrong to a neighbor; therefore love is the fulfillment of the law.

Romans 15

7 Therefore, accept one another, just as Christ also accepted us to the glory of God.

1 Corinthians 8

3 But if anyone loves God, he is known by Him.

1 Corinthians 13

4 Love is patient, love is kind and is not jealous; love does not brag and is not arrogant,
5 Does not act unbecomingly; it does not seek its own, is not provoked, does not take into account a wrong suffered,
6 Does not rejoice in unrighteousness, but rejoices with the truth;
7 Bears all things, believes all things, hopes all things, endures all things.
8 Love never fails; but if there are gifts of prophecy, they will be done away; if there are tongues, they will cease; if there is knowledge, it will be done away.

13 But now faith, hope, love, abide these three; but the greatest of these is love.

1 Corinthians 16

14 Let all that you do be done in love.

Ephesians 5

1 Therefore be imitators of God, as beloved children;
2 And walk in love, just as Christ also loved you and gave Himself up for us, an offering and a sacrifice to God as a fragrant aroma.

2 Thessalonians 3

5 May the Lord direct your hearts into the love of God and into the steadfastness of Christ.

1 Peter 4

8 Above all, keep fervent in your love for one another, because love covers a multitude of sins.
9 Be hospitable to one another without complaint.
10 As each one has received a special gift, employ it in serving one another as good stewards of the manifold grace of God.

1 John 3

1 See how great a love the Father has bestowed on us, that we would be called children of God; and such we are. For this reason the world does not know us, because it did not know Him.

11 For this is the message which you have heard from the beginning, that we should love one another;

14 We know that we have passed out of death into life, because we love the brethren. He who does not love abides in death.
15 Everyone who hates his brother is a murderer; and you know that no murderer has eternal life abiding in him.
16 We know love by this, that He laid down His life for us; and we ought to lay down our lives for the brethren.
17 But whoever has the world's goods, and sees his brother in need and closes his heart against him, how does the love of God abide in him?
18 Little children, let us not love with word or with tongue, but in deed and truth.

1 John 4

7 Beloved, let us love one another, for love is from God; and everyone who loves is born of God and knows God.
8 The one who does not love does not know God, for God is love.
9 By this the love of God was manifested in us, that God has sent His only begotten Son into the world so that we might live through Him.
10 In this is love, not that we loved God, but that He loved us and sent His Son to be the propitiation for our sins.
11 Beloved, if God so loved us, we also ought to love one another.
12 No one has seen God at any time; if we love one another, God abides in us, and His love is perfected in us.
13 By this we know that we abide in Him and He in us, because He has given us of His Spirit.
14 We have seen and testify that the Father has sent the Son to be the Savior of the world.
15 Whoever confesses that Jesus is the Son of God, God abides in him, and he in God.
16 We have come to know and have believed the love which God has for us. God is love, and the one who abides in love abides in God, and God abides in him.
17 By this, love is perfected with us, so that we may have confidence in the day of judgment; because as He is, so also are we in this world.
18 There is no fear in love; but perfect love casts out fear, because fear involves punishment, and the one who fears is not perfected in love.
19 We love, because He first loved us.
20 If someone says, "I love God," and hates his brother, he is a liar; for the one who does not love his brother whom he has seen, cannot love God whom he has not seen.
21 And this commandment we have from Him, that the one who loves God should love his brother also.

2 John 1

6 And this is love, that we walk according to His commandments. This is the commandment, just as you have heard from the beginning, that you should walk in it.

Jesus' Deity

This layer includes scriptures directed at demonstrating that Christ is God. Non-believers, throughout the ages, have tried to rob Him from His deity and present Him as a lesser god in a chain of demi-gods. The writers of the Gospel, made a great effort to affirm Jesus' Deity. Matthew, Mark, Luke, and John in their writings stress the fact that Jesus Christ is the Son of God and that together with the Father and the Holy Spirit conforms the Trinity, the core and essence of Christian belief.

Scriptures   *Jesus' Deity*

Matthew 28

18 And Jesus came up and spoke to them, saying, "All authority has been given to Me in heaven and on earth."

Mark 8

29 And He continued by questioning them, "But who do you say that I am?" Peter answered and said to Him, "You are the Christ."

Mark 14

61 But He kept silent and did not answer. Again the high priest was questioning Him, and saying to Him, "Are You the Christ, the Son of the Blessed One?"
62 And Jesus said, "I am; and you shall see the Son of Man sitting at the right hand of power, and coming with the clouds of heaven."

Luke 2

10 But the angel said to them, "Do not be afraid; for behold, I bring you good news of great joy which will be for all the people;
11 For today in the city of David there has been born for you a Savior, who is Christ the Lord.
12 "This will be a sign for you: you will find a baby wrapped in cloths and lying in a manger."
13 And suddenly there appeared with the angel a multitude of the heavenly host praising God and saying,
14 "Glory to God in the highest, And on earth peace among men with whom He is pleased."

Luke 8

24 They came to Jesus and woke Him up, saying, "Master, Master, we are perishing!" And He got up and rebuked the wind and the surging waves, and they stopped, and it became calm.
25 And He said to them, "Where is your faith?" They were fearful and amazed, saying to one another, "Who then is this, that He commands even the winds and the water, and they obey Him?"

Luke 22

19 And when He had taken some bread and given thanks, He broke it and gave it to them, saying, "This is My body which is given for you; do this in remembrance of Me."

John 1

1 In the beginning was the Word, and the Word was with God, and the Word was God.
2 He was in the beginning with God.
3 All things came into being through Him, and apart from Him nothing came into being that has come into being.
4 In Him was life, and the life was the Light of men.
5 The Light shines in the darkness, and the darkness did not comprehend it.

John 3

34 "For He whom God has sent speaks the words of God; for He gives the Spirit without measure.
35 "The Father loves the Son and has given all things into His hand.
36 "He who believes in the Son has eternal life; but he who does not obey the Son will not see life, but the wrath of God abides on him."

John 4

13 Jesus answered and said to her, "Everyone who drinks of this water will thirst again;
14 But whoever drinks of the water that I will give him shall never thirst; but the water that I will give him will become in him a well of water springing up to eternal life."

John 5

19 Therefore Jesus answered and was saying to them, "Truly, truly, I say to you, the Son can do nothing of Himself, unless it is something He sees the Father doing; for

Jesus' Deity   *Scriptures*

whatever the Father does, these things the Son also does in like manner.

20 "For the Father loves the Son, and shows Him all things that He Himself is doing; and the Father will show Him greater works than these, so that you will marvel.

21 "For just as the Father raises the dead and gives them life, even so the Son also gives life to whom He wishes.

22 "For not even the Father judges anyone, but He has given all judgment to the Son,

23 "So that all will honor the Son even as they honor the Father. He who does not honor the Son does not honor the Father who sent Him."

John 6

35 Jesus said to them, "I am the bread of life; he who comes to Me will not hunger, and he who believes in Me will never thirst.

36 "But I said to you that you have seen Me, and yet do not believe.

37 "All that the Father gives Me will come to Me, and the one who comes to Me I will certainly not cast out.

38 "For I have come down from heaven, not to do My own will, but the will of Him who sent Me.

39 "This is the will of Him who sent Me, that of all that He has given Me I lose nothing, but raise it up on the last day.

40 "For this is the will of My Father, that everyone who beholds the Son and believes in Him will have eternal life, and I Myself will raise him up on the last day."

44 "No one can come to Me unless the Father who sent Me draws him; and I will raise him up on the last day.

45 "It is written in the prophets, 'and they shall be taught of God.' Everyone who has heard and learned from the Father, comes to Me.

46 "Not that anyone has seen the Father, except the One who is from God; He has seen the Father.

47 "Truly, truly, I say to you, he who believes has eternal life.

48 "I am the bread of life.

49 "Your fathers ate the manna in the wilderness, and they died.

50 "This is the bread which comes down out of heaven, so that one may eat of it and not die.

51 "I am the living bread that came down out of heaven; if anyone eats of this bread, he will live forever; and the bread also which I will give for the life of the world is My flesh."

52 Then the Jews began to argue with one another, saying, "How can this man give us His flesh to eat?"

53 So Jesus said to them, "Truly, truly, I say to you, unless you eat the flesh of the Son of Man and drink His blood, you have no life in yourselves.

54 "He who eats My flesh and drinks My blood has eternal life, and I will raise him up on the last day.

55 "For My flesh is true food, and My blood is true drink.

56 "He who eats My flesh and drinks My blood abides in Me, and I in him.

57 "As the living Father sent Me, and I live because of the Father, so he who eats Me, he also will live because of Me.

58 "This is the bread which came down out of heaven; not as the fathers ate and died; he who eats this bread will live forever."

59 These things He said in the synagogue as He taught in Capernaum.

60 Therefore many of His disciples, when they heard this said, "This is a difficult statement; who can listen to it?"

61 But Jesus, conscious that His disciples grumbled at this, said to them, "Does this cause you to stumble?

62 "What then if you see the Son of Man ascending to where He was before?

63 "It is the Spirit who gives life; the flesh profits nothing; the words that I have spoken to you are spirit and are life.

64 "But there are some of you who do not believe." For Jesus knew from the beginning who they were who did not believe, and who it was that would betray Him.

65 And He was saying, "For this reason I have said to you, that no one can come to Me unless it has been granted him from the Father."
66 As a result of this many of His disciples withdrew and were not walking with Him anymore.
67 So Jesus said to the twelve, "You do not want to go away also, do you?"
68 Simon Peter answered Him, "Lord, to whom shall we go? You have words of eternal life.
69 "We have believed and have come to know that You are the Holy One of God."

John 7

38 "He who believes in Me, as the Scripture said, 'From his innermost being will flow rivers of living water.' "

John 8

12 Then Jesus again spoke to them, saying, "I am the Light of the world; he who follows Me will not walk in the darkness, but will have the Light of life."

24 "Therefore I said to you that you will die in your sins; for unless you believe that I am He, you will die in your sins."
25 So they were saying to Him, "Who are You?" Jesus said to them, "What have I been saying to you from the beginning?
26 "I have many things to speak and to judge concerning you, but He who sent Me is true; and the things which I heard from Him, these I speak to the world."
27 They did not realize that He had been speaking to them about the Father.
28 So Jesus said, "When you lift up the Son of Man, then you will know that I am He, and I do nothing on My own initiative, but I speak these things as the Father taught Me.
29 "And He who sent Me is with Me; He has not left Me alone, for I always do the things that are pleasing to Him."
30 As He spoke these things, many came to believe in Him.

42 Jesus said to them, "If God were your Father, you would love Me, for I proceeded forth and have come from God, for I have not even come on My own initiative, but He sent Me.
43 "Why do you not understand what I am saying? It is because you cannot hear My word."

47 "He who is of God hears the words of God; for this reason you do not hear them, because you are not of God."

51 "Truly, truly, I say to you, if anyone keeps My word he will never see death."

58 Jesus said to them, "Truly, truly, I say to you, before Abraham was born, I am."

John 10

7 So Jesus said to them again, "Truly, truly, I say to you, I am the door of the sheep.
8 "All who came before Me are thieves and robbers, but the sheep did not hear them.
9 "I am the door; if anyone enters through Me, he will be saved, and will go in and out and find pasture.
10 "The thief comes only to steal and kill and destroy; I came that they may have life, and have it abundantly.
11 "I am the good shepherd; the good shepherd lays down His life for the sheep.
12 "He who is a hired hand, and not a shepherd, who is not the owner of the sheep, sees the wolf coming, and leaves the sheep and flees, and the wolf snatches them and scatters them.
13 "He flees because he is a hired hand and is not concerned about the sheep.
14 "I am the good shepherd, and I know My own and My own know Me,
15 Even as the Father knows Me and I know the Father; and I lay down My life for the sheep.
16 "I have other sheep, which are not of this fold; I must bring them also, and they will hear My voice; and they will become one flock with one shepherd.
17 "For this reason the Father loves Me, because I lay down My life so that I may take it again.
18 "No one has taken it away from Me, but I lay it down on My own initiative. I have authority to lay it down, and I have authority to take it up again. This commandment I received from My Father."

27 "My sheep hear My voice, and I know them, and they follow Me;
28 "And I give eternal life to them, and they will never perish; and no one will snatch them out of My hand.
29 "My Father, who has given them to Me, is greater than all; and no one is able to snatch them out of the Father's hand."
30 "I and the Father are one."

37 "If I do not do the works of My Father, do not believe Me;"

John 11

25 Jesus said to her, "I am the resurrection and the life; he who believes in Me will live even if he dies,
26 And everyone who lives and believes in Me will never die. Do you believe this?"

Scriptures

Jesus' Deity

John 12

46 "I have come as Light into the world, so that everyone who believes in Me will not remain in darkness."

John 13

19 "From now on I am telling you before it comes to pass, so that when it does occur, you may believe that I am He."

John 14

1 "Do not let your heart be troubled; believe in God, believe also in Me.
2 "In My Father's house are many dwelling places; if it were not so, I would have told you; for I go to prepare a place for you.
3 "If I go and prepare a place for you, I will come again and receive you to Myself, that where I am, there you may be also."

6 Jesus said to him, "I am the way, and the truth, and the life; no one comes to the Father but through Me."

10 "Do you not believe that I am in the Father, and the Father is in Me? The words that I say to you I do not speak on My own initiative, but the Father abiding in Me does His works."

28 "You heard that I said to you, 'I go away, and I will come to you.' If you loved Me, you would have rejoiced because I go to the Father, for the Father is greater than I."

John 16

28 "I came forth from the Father and have come into the world; I am leaving the world again and going to the Father."

33 "These things I have spoken to you, so that in Me you may have peace. In the world you have tribulation, but take courage; I have overcome the world."

John 17

1 Jesus spoke these things; and lifting up His eyes to heaven, He said, "Father, the hour has come; glorify Your Son, that the Son may glorify You,
2 Even as You gave Him authority over all flesh, that to all whom You have given Him, He may give eternal life.
3 "This is eternal life, that they may know You, the only true God, and Jesus Christ whom You have sent.
4 "I glorified You on the earth, having accomplished the work which You have given Me to do.
5 "Now, Father, glorify Me together with Yourself, with the glory which I had with You before the world was."

9 "I ask on their behalf; I do not ask on behalf of the world, but of those whom You have given Me; for they are Yours;
10 "And all things that are Mine are Yours, and Yours are Mine; and I have been glorified in them.
11 "I am no longer in the world; and yet they themselves are in the world, and I come to You. Holy Father, keep them in Your name, the name which You have given Me, that they may be one even as We are."

23 "I in them and You in Me, that they may be perfected in unity, so that the world may know that You sent Me, and loved them, even as You have loved Me.
24 "Father, I desire that they also, whom You have given Me, be with Me where I am, so that they may see My glory which You have given Me, for You loved Me before the foundation of the world.
25 "O righteous Father, although the world has not known You, yet I have known You; and these have known that You sent Me;
26 And I have made Your name known to them, and will make it known, so that the love with which You loved Me may be in them, and I in them."

Jesus' Deity *Scriptures*

John 18

37 Therefore Pilate said to Him, "So You are a king?" Jesus answered, "You say correctly that I am a king. For this I have been born, and for this I have come into the world, to testify to the truth. Everyone who is of the truth hears My voice."

Acts 2

32 "This Jesus God raised up again, to which we are all witnesses.
33 "Therefore having been exalted to the right hand of God, and having received from the Father the promise of the Holy Spirit, He has poured forth this which you both see and hear."

1 Corinthians 8

5 For even if there are so-called gods whether in heaven or on earth, as indeed there are many gods and many lords,
6 Yet for us there is but one God, the Father, from whom are all things and we exist for Him; and one Lord, Jesus Christ, by whom are all things, and we exist through Him.

Philippians 2

5 Have this attitude in yourselves which was also in Christ Jesus,
6 Who, although He existed in the form of God, did not regard equality with God a thing to be grasped,
7 But emptied Himself, taking the form of a bond-servant, and being made in the likeness of men.
8 Being found in appearance as a man, He humbled Himself by becoming obedient to the point of death, even death on a cross.
9 For this reason also, God highly exalted Him, and bestowed on Him the name which is above every name,
10 So that at the name of Jesus every knee will bow, of those who are in heaven and on earth and under the earth,
11 And that every tongue will confess that Jesus Christ is Lord, to the glory of God the Father.

Colossians 1

12 Giving thanks to the Father, who has qualified us to share in the inheritance of the saints in Light.
13 For He rescued us from the domain of darkness, and transferred us to the kingdom of His beloved Son,
14 In whom we have redemption, the forgiveness of sins.
15 He is the image of the invisible God, the firstborn of all creation.
16 For by Him all things were created, both in the heavens and on earth, visible and invisible, whether thrones or dominions or rulers or authorities-- all things have been created through Him and for Him.
17 He is before all things, and in Him all things hold together.
18 He is also head of the body, the church; and He is the beginning, the firstborn from the dead, so that He Himself will come to have first place in everything.
19 For it was the Father's good pleasure for all the fullness to dwell in Him,
20 And through Him to reconcile all things to Himself, having made peace through the blood of His cross; through Him, I say, whether things on earth or things in heaven.

1 Timothy 2

5 For there is one God, and one mediator also between God and men, the man Christ Jesus,
6 Who gave Himself as a ransom for all, the testimony given at the proper time.

Hebrews 1

1 God, after He spoke long ago to the fathers in the prophets in many portions and in many ways,
2 In these last days has spoken to us in His Son, whom He appointed heir of all things, through whom also He made the world.
3 And He is the radiance of His glory and the exact representation of His nature, and upholds all things by the word of His

power. When He had made purification of sins, He sat down at the right hand of the Majesty on high, 4 having become as much better than the angels, as He has inherited a more excellent name than they.

5 For to which of the angels did He ever say, "You are my Son, today I have begotten you"? And again, "I will be a Father to Him and He shall be a Son to me"?

6 And when He again brings the firstborn into the world, He says, "And let all the angels of god worship Him."

7 And of the angels He says, "Who makes his angels winds, and his ministers a flame of fire."

8 But of the Son He says, "Your throne, O God, is forever and ever, and the righteous scepter is the scepter of his Kingdom.

9 "You have loved righteousness and hated lawlessness; therefore God, your God, has anointed you with the oil of gladness above your companions."

10 And, "you, Lord, in the beginning laid the foundation of the earth, and the heavens are the works of your hands;

11 They will perish, but you remain; and they all will become old like a garment,

12 And like a mantle you will roll them up; like a garment they will also be changed. But you are the same, and your years will not come to an end."

13 But to which of the angels has He ever said, "Sit at my right hand, until I make your enemies a footstool for your feet"?

14 Are they not all ministering spirits, sent out to render service for the sake of those who will inherit salvation?

2 Peter 1

16 For we did not follow cleverly devised tales when we made known to you the power and coming of our Lord Jesus Christ, but we were eyewitnesses of His majesty.

17 For when He received honor and glory from God the Father, such an utterance as this was made to Him by the Majestic Glory, "This is My beloved Son with whom I am well-pleased"--

18 And we ourselves heard this utterance made from heaven when we were with Him on the holy mountain.

1 John 2

22 Who is the liar but the one who denies that Jesus is the Christ? This is the antichrist, the one who denies the Father and the Son.

23 Whoever denies the Son does not have the Father; the one who confesses the Son has the Father also.

Jesus' Deity   *Scriptures*

1 John 5

1 Whoever believes that Jesus is the Christ is born of God, and whoever loves the Father loves the child born of Him.

5 Who is the one who overcomes the world, but he who believes that Jesus is the Son of God?
6 This is the One who came by water and blood, Jesus Christ; not with the water only, but with the water and with the blood. It is the Spirit who testifies, because the Spirit is the truth.

The Holy Spirit

The Holy Spirit is the eternal Spirit of God, God Himself, one of the three beautiful facets of the Lord. In the Old Testament, David as well as many characters throughout the Bible are many times touched by the Holy Spirit. When Jesus went back to heaven, however, he left the Holy Spirit in a different way. The Holy Spirit will convict the world in relation to sin, righteousness, and of judgment. The Holy Spirit is a powerful personality that can talk and be heard by us. He has feelings and emotions since He can be grieved. Jesus Christ told us that the only unforgiveable sin was to blaspheme against the Holy Spirit. (Matthew 12:31) In John 14 through 17, Jesus provides us with wonderful teachings about the Holy Spirit, the Comforter. The essential conditions for receiving the gift of the Holy Spirit is to be a true believer and be obedient to Christ's teachings.

Matthew 12

31 "Therefore I say to you, any sin and blasphemy shall be forgiven people, but blasphemy against the Spirit shall not be forgiven.
32 "Whoever speaks a word against the Son of Man, it shall be forgiven him; but whoever speaks against the Holy Spirit, it shall not be forgiven him, either in this age or in the age to come.

Luke 3

21 Now when all the people were baptized, Jesus was also baptized, and while He was praying, heaven was opened,
22 And the Holy Spirit descended upon Him in bodily form like a dove, and a voice came out of heaven, "You are My beloved Son, in You I am well-pleased."

John 1

32 John [The Baptist] testified saying, "I have seen the Spirit descending as a dove out of heaven, and He remained upon Him."

John 14

16 "I will ask the Father, and He will give you another Helper, that He may be with you forever;

17 "That is the Spirit of truth, whom the world cannot receive, because it does not see Him or know Him, but you know Him because He abides with you and will be in you."

26 "But the Helper, the Holy Spirit, whom the Father will send in My name, He will teach you all things, and bring to your remembrance all that I said to you."

John 15

26 "When the Helper comes, whom I will send to you from the Father, that is the Spirit of truth who proceeds from the Father, He will testify about Me,

27 "And you will testify also, because you have been with Me from the beginning."

John 16

7 "But I tell you the truth, it is to your advantage that I go away; for if I do not go away, the Helper will not come to you; but if I go, I will send Him to you.

8 "And He, when He comes, will convict the world concerning sin and righteousness and judgment;

9 "Concerning sin, because they do not believe in Me;"

Acts 2

1 When the day of Pentecost had come, they were all together in one place.

2 And suddenly there came from heaven a noise like a violent rushing wind, and it filled the whole house where they were sitting.

3 And there appeared to them tongues as of fire distributing themselves, and they rested on each one of them.

4 And they were all filled with the Holy Spirit and began to speak with other tongues, as the Spirit was giving them utterance.

5 Now there were Jews living in Jerusalem, devout men from every nation under heaven.

6 And when this sound occurred, the crowd came together, and were bewildered because each one of them was hearing them speak in his own language.

7 They were amazed and astonished, saying, "Why, are not all these who are speaking Galileans?

8 "And how is it that we each hear them in our own language to which we were born?

9 "Parthians and Medes and Elamites, and residents of Mesopotamia, Judea and Cappadocia, Pontus and Asia,

10 "Phrygia and Pamphylia, Egypt and the districts of Libya around Cyrene, and visitors from Rome, both Jews and proselytes,

11 "Cretans and Arabs-- we hear them in our own tongues speaking of the mighty deeds of God."

12 And they all continued in amazement and great perplexity, saying to one another, "What does this mean?"

13 "But others were mocking and saying, "They are full of sweet wine."

14 But Peter, taking his stand with the eleven, raised his voice and declared to them: "Men of Judea and all you who live in Jerusalem, let this be known to you and give heed to my words.

15 "For these men are not drunk, as you suppose, for it is only the third hour of the day;

16 "But this is what was spoken of through the prophet Joel:

17 'And it shall be in the last days,' God says, 'That I will pour forth of My Spirit on all mankind; and your sons and your daughters shall prophesy, and your young

men shall see visions, and your old men shall dream dreams;

18 'Even on my bondslaves, both men and women, I will in those days pour forth of My Spirit and they shall prophesy.

19 'And I will grant wonders in the sky above and signs on the earth below, blood, and fire, and vapor of smoke.

20 'The sun will be turned into darkness and the moon into blood, before the great and glorious day of the Lord shall come.

21 'And it shall be that everyone who calls on the name of the Lord will be saved."

Acts 4

31 And when they had prayed, the place where they had gathered together was shaken, and they were all filled with the Holy Spirit and began to speak the word of God with boldness.

Acts 8

14 Now when the apostles in Jerusalem heard that Samaria had received the word of God, they sent them Peter and John,

15 Who came down and prayed for them that they might receive the Holy Spirit.

16 For He had not yet fallen upon any of them; they had simply been baptized in the name of the Lord Jesus.

17 Then they began laying their hands on them, and they were receiving the Holy Spirit.

Acts 19

6 And when Paul had laid his hands upon them, the Holy Spirit came on them, and they began speaking with tongues and prophesying.

Romans 8

14 For all who are being led by the Spirit of God, these are sons of God.

15 For you have not received a spirit of slavery leading to fear again, but you have received a spirit of adoption as sons by which we cry out, "Abba! Father!"

16 The Spirit Himself testifies with our spirit that we are children of God,

26 In the same way the Spirit also helps our weakness; for we do not know how to pray as we should, but the Spirit Himself intercedes for us with groanings too deep for words;

27 And He who searches the hearts knows what the mind of the Spirit is, because He intercedes for the saints according to the will of God.

1 Corinthians 2

10 For to us God revealed them through the Spirit; for the Spirit searches all things, even the depths of God.

11 For who among men knows the thoughts of a man except the spirit of the man which is in him? Even so the thoughts of God no one knows except the Spirit of God.

12 Now we have received, not the spirit of the world, but the Spirit who is from God, so that we may know the things freely given to us by God,

13 Which things we also speak, not in words taught by human wisdom, but in those taught by the Spirit, combining spiritual thoughts with spiritual words.

14 But a natural man does not accept the things of the Spirit of God, for they are foolishness to him; and he cannot understand them, because they are spiritually appraised.

15 But he who is spiritual appraises all things, yet he himself is appraised by no one.

16 For who has known the mind of the Lord, that he will instruct him? But we have the mind of Christ.

1 Corinthians 12

3 Therefore I make known to you that no one speaking by the Spirit of God says, "Jesus is accursed"; and no one can say, "Jesus is Lord," except by the Holy Spirit.

4 Now there are varieties of gifts, but the same Spirit.

5 And there are varieties of ministries, and the same Lord.
6 There are varieties of effects, but the same God who works all things in all persons.
7 But to each one is given the manifestation of the Spirit for the common good.
8 For to one is given the word of wisdom through the Spirit, and to another the word of knowledge according to the same Spirit;
9 To another faith by the same Spirit, and to another gifts of healing by the one Spirit,
10 And to another the effecting of miracles, and to another prophecy, and to another the distinguishing of spirits, to another various kinds of tongues, and to another the interpretation of tongues.
11 But one and the same Spirit works all these things, distributing to each one individually just as He wills.
12 For even as the body is one and yet has many members, and all the members of the body, though they are many, are one body, so also is Christ.
13 For by one Spirit we were all baptized into one body, whether Jews or Greeks, whether slaves or free, and we were all made to drink of one Spirit.

Grace

Forgiveness by grace is a divine act of God by which He pardons all sins of those who believe in Christ and accepts them as righteous in the eye of the Law. Through grace, the sinner is forever freed from the guilt and penalty of sins. The purpose of grace is not to disregard the Law but to create inner soul conditions that allows us to receive Jesus' teachings and be saved through His infinite love. Paul is one of the voices of the New Testament that explains to us the meaning of grace. Romans 8:1 tells us that "there is now no condemnation for those who are in Christ Jesus. For the Law of the Spirit of life in Christ Jesus has set you free from the Law of sin and of death."

John 1

17 For the Law was given through Moses; grace and truth were realized through Jesus Christ.

John 3

17 "For God did not send the Son into the world to judge the world, but that the world might be saved through Him.
18 "He who believes in Him is not judged; he who does not believe has been judged already, because he has not believed in the name of the only begotten Son of God."

John 5

24 "Truly, truly, I say to you, he who hears My word, and believes Him who sent Me, has eternal life, and does not come into judgment, but has passed out of death into life."

Romans 3

20 Because by the works of the Law no flesh will be justified in His sight; for through the Law comes the knowledge of sin.
21 But now apart from the Law the righteousness of God has been manifested, being witnessed by the Law and the Prophets,
22 Even the righteousness of God through faith in Jesus Christ for all those who believe; for there is no distinction;
23 For all have sinned and fall short of the glory of God,
24 Being justified as a gift by His grace through the redemption which is in Christ Jesus;
25 Whom God displayed publicly as a propitiation in His blood through faith. This was to demonstrate His righteousness, because in the forbearance of God He passed over the sins previously committed;

Romans 4

7 "Blessed are those whose lawless deeds have been forgiven, and whose sins have been covered.
8 "Blessed is the man whose sin the Lord will not take into account."

14 For if those who are of the Law are heirs, faith is made void and the promise is nullified;
15 For the Law brings about wrath, but where there is no law, there also is no violation.
16 For this reason it is by faith, in order that it may be in accordance with grace, so that the promise will be guaranteed to all the descendants, not only to those who are of the Law, but also to those who are of the faith of Abraham, who is the father of us all,
17 (as it is written, "A father of many nations have i made you") in the presence of Him whom he believed, even God, who gives life to the dead and calls into being that which does not exist.

Romans 5

1 Therefore, having been justified by faith, we have peace with God through our Lord Jesus Christ,
2 Through whom also we have obtained our introduction by faith into this grace in which we stand; and we exult in hope of the glory of God.

8 But God demonstrates His own love toward us, in that while we were yet sinners, Christ died for us.

9 Much more then, having now been justified by His blood, we shall be saved from the wrath of God through Him.
10 For if while we were enemies we were reconciled to God through the death of His Son, much more, having been reconciled, we shall be saved by His life.
11 And not only this, but we also exult in God through our Lord Jesus Christ, through whom we have now received the reconciliation.
12 Therefore, just as through one man sin entered into the world, and death through sin, and so death spread to all men, because all sinned—
13 For until the Law sin was in the world, but sin is not imputed when there is no law.
14 Nevertheless death reigned from Adam until Moses, even over those who had not sinned in the likeness of the offense of Adam, who is a type of Him who was to come.
15 But the free gift is not like the transgression. For if by the transgression of the one the many died, much more did the grace of God and the gift by the grace of the one Man, Jesus Christ, abound to the many.
16 The gift is not like that which came through the one who sinned; for on the one hand the judgment arose from one transgression resulting in condemnation, but on the other hand the free gift arose from many transgressions resulting in justification.
17 For if by the transgression of the one, death reigned through the one, much more those who receive the abundance of grace and of the gift of righteousness will reign in life through the One, Jesus Christ.
18 So then as through one transgression there resulted condemnation to all men, even so through one act of righteousness there resulted justification of life to all men.
19 For as through the one man's disobedience the many were made sinners, even so through the obedience of the One the many will be made righteous.
20 The Law came in so that the transgression would increase; but where sin increased, grace abounded all the more,
21 So that, as sin reigned in death, even so grace would reign through righteousness to eternal life through Jesus Christ our Lord.

Romans 6

1 What shall we say then? Are we to continue in sin so that grace may increase?
2 May it never be! How shall we who died to sin still live in it?
3 Or do you not know that all of us who have been baptized into Christ Jesus have been baptized into His death?
4 Therefore we have been buried with Him through baptism into death, so that as Christ was raised from the dead through the glory of the Father, so we too might walk in newness of life.
14 For sin shall not be master over you, for you are not under Law but under grace.
15 What then? Shall we sin because we are not under Law but under grace? May it never be!
16 Do you not know that when you present yourselves to someone as slaves for obedience, you are slaves of the one whom you obey, either of sin resulting in death, or of obedience resulting in righteousness?
17 But thanks be to God that though you were slaves of sin, you became obedient from the heart to that form of teaching to which you were committed,
18 And having been freed from sin, you became slaves of righteousness.

Romans 7

5 For while we were in the flesh, the sinful passions, which were aroused by the Law, were at work in the members of our body to bear fruit for death.
6 But now we have been released from the Law, having died to that by which we were bound, so that we serve in newness of the Spirit and not in oldness of the letter.
7 What shall we say then? Is the Law sin? May

it never be! On the contrary, I would not have come to know sin except through the Law; for I would not have known about coveting if the Law had not said, "you shall not covet."

14 For we know that the Law is spiritual, but I am of flesh, sold into bondage to sin.
15 For what I am doing, I do not understand; for I am not practicing what I would like to do, but I am doing the very thing I hate.
16 But if I do the very thing I do not want to do, I agree with the Law, confessing that the Law is good.
17 So now, no longer am I the one doing it, but sin which dwells in me.
18 For I know that nothing good dwells in me, that is, in my flesh; for the willing is present in me, but the doing of the good is not.
19 For the good that I want, I do not do, but I practice the very evil that I do not want.
20 But if I am doing the very thing I do not want, I am no longer the one doing it, but sin which dwells in me.
21 I find then the principle that evil is present in me, the one who wants to do good.
22 For I joyfully concur with the Law of God in the inner man,
23 But I see a different Law in the members of my body, waging war against the Law of my mind and making me a prisoner of the Law of sin which is in my members.
24 Wretched man that I am! Who will set me free from the body of this death?
25 Thanks be to God through Jesus Christ our Lord! So then, on the one hand I myself with my mind am serving the Law of God, but on the other, with my flesh the Law of sin.

Romans 8

1 Therefore there is now no condemnation for those who are in Christ Jesus.
2 For the Law of the Spirit of life in Christ Jesus has set you free from the Law of sin and of death.
3 For what the Law could not do, weak as it was through the flesh, God did: sending His own Son in the likeness of sinful flesh and as an offering for sin, He condemned sin in the flesh,
4 So that the requirement of the Law might be fulfilled in us, who do not walk according to the flesh but according to the Spirit.

Romans 9

30 What shall we say then? That Gentiles, who did not pursue righteousness, attained righteousness, even the righteousness which is by faith;
31 But Israel, pursuing a Law of righteousness, did not arrive at that Law.
32 Why? Because they did not pursue it by faith, but as though it were by works. They stumbled over the stumbling stone,

Romans 10

11 For the Scripture says, "Whoever believes in him will not be disappointed."
12 For there is no distinction between Jew and Greek; for the same Lord is Lord of all, abounding in riches for all who call on Him;
13 For "Whoever will call on the name of the Lord will be saved."

Romans 11

1 I Say then, God has not rejected His people, has He? May it never be! For I too am an Israelite, a descendant of Abraham, of the tribe of Benjamin.
2 God has not rejected His people whom He foreknew. Or do you not know what the Scripture says in the passage about Elijah, how he pleads with God against Israel?
3 "Lord, they have killed your prophets, they have torn down your altars, and I alone am left, and they are seeking my life."
4 But what is the divine response to him? "I have kept for myself seven thousand men who have not bowed the knee to Baal."
5 In the same way then, there has also come to be at the present time a remnant according to God's gracious choice.
6 But if it is by grace, it is no longer on the basis of works, otherwise grace is no longer grace.

7 What then? What Israel is seeking, it has not obtained, but those who were chosen obtained it, and the rest were hardened;
8 Just as it is written, "God gave them a spirit of stupor, eyes to see not and ears to hear not, down to this very day."

2 Corinthians 3

16 But whenever a person turns to the Lord, the veil is taken away.
17 Now the Lord is the Spirit, and where the Spirit of the Lord is, there is liberty.
18 But we all, with unveiled face, beholding as in a mirror the glory of the Lord, are being transformed into the same image from glory to glory, just as from the Lord, the Spirit.

2 Corinthians 5

17 Therefore if anyone is in Christ, he is a new creature; the old things passed away; behold, new things have come.
18 Now all these things are from God, who reconciled us to Himself through Christ and gave us the ministry of reconciliation,
19 Namely, that God was in Christ reconciling the world to Himself, not counting their trespasses against them, and He has committed to us the word of reconciliation.
20 Therefore, we are ambassadors for Christ, as though God were making an appeal through us; we beg you on behalf of Christ, be reconciled to God.
21 He made Him who knew no sin to be sin on our behalf, so that we might become the righteousness of God in Him.

Galatians 2

16 Nevertheless knowing that a man is not justified by the works of the Law but through faith in Christ Jesus, even we have believed in Christ Jesus, so that we may be justified by faith in Christ and not by the works of the Law; since by the works of the Law no flesh will be justified.
17 "But if, while seeking to be justified in Christ, we ourselves have also been found sinners, is Christ then a minister of sin? May it never be!
18 "For if I rebuild what I have once destroyed, I prove myself to be a transgressor.
19 "For through the Law I died to the Law, so that I might live to God.
20 "I have been crucified with Christ; and it is no longer I who live, but Christ lives in me; and the life which I now live in the flesh I live by faith in the Son of God, who loved me and gave Himself up for me.

21 "I do not nullify the grace of God, for if righteousness comes through the Law, then Christ died needlessly."

Galatians 3

21 Is the Law then contrary to the promises of God? May it never be! For if a law had been given which was able to impart life, then righteousness would indeed have been based on law.
22 But the Scripture has shut up everyone under sin, so that the promise by faith in Jesus Christ might be given to those who believe.
23 But before faith came, we were kept in custody under the law, being shut up to the faith which was later to be revealed.
24 Therefore the Law has become our tutor to lead us to Christ, so that we may be justified by faith.
25 But now that faith has come, we are no longer under a tutor.
26 For you are all sons of God through faith in Christ Jesus.
27 For all of you who were baptized into Christ have clothed yourselves with Christ.
28 There is neither Jew nor Greek, there is neither slave nor free man, there is neither male nor female; for you are all one in Christ Jesus.

Galatians 5

13 For you were called to freedom, brethren; only do not turn your freedom into an opportunity for the flesh, but through love serve one another.
14 For the whole Law is fulfilled in one word, in the statement, "You shall love your neighbor as yourself."
15 But if you bite and devour one another, take care that you are not consumed by one another.
16 But I say, walk by the Spirit, and you will not carry out the desire of the flesh.
17 For the flesh sets its desire against the Spirit, and the Spirit against the flesh; for these are in opposition to one another, so that you may not do the things that you please.
18 But if you are led by the Spirit, you are not under the Law.
19 Now the deeds of the flesh are evident, which are: immorality, impurity, sensuality,
20 Idolatry, sorcery, enmities, strife, jealousy, outbursts of anger, disputes, dissensions, factions,
21 Envying, drunkenness, carousing, and things like these, of which I forewarn you, just as I have forewarned you, that those who practice such things will not inherit the kingdom of God.
22 But the fruit of the Spirit is love, joy, peace, patience, kindness, goodness, faithfulness,
23 Gentleness, self-control; against such things there is no law.

Scriptures   *Grace*

24 Now those who belong to Christ Jesus have crucified the flesh with its passions and desires.
25 If we live by the Spirit, let us also walk by the Spirit.
26 Let us not become boastful, challenging one another, envying one another.

Ephesians 2

1 And you were dead in your trespasses and sins,
2 In which you formerly walked according to the course of this world, according to the prince of the power of the air, of the spirit that is now working in the sons of disobedience.
3 Among them we too all formerly lived in the lusts of our flesh, indulging the desires of the flesh and of the mind, and were by nature children of wrath, even as the rest.
4 But God, being rich in mercy, because of His great love with which He loved us,
5 Even when we were dead in our transgressions, made us alive together with Christ (by grace you have been saved),
6 And raised us up with Him, and seated us with Him in the heavenly places in Christ Jesus,
7 So that in the ages to come He might show the surpassing riches of His grace in kindness toward us in Christ Jesus.
8 For by grace you have been saved through faith; and that not of yourselves, it is the gift of God;
9 Not as a result of works, so that no one may boast.
10 For we are His workmanship, created in Christ Jesus for good works, which God prepared beforehand so that we would walk in them.

13 But now in Christ Jesus you who formerly were far off have been brought near by the blood of Christ.
14 For He Himself is our peace, who made both groups into one and broke down the barrier of the dividing wall,

Ephesians 6

24 Grace be with all those who love our Lord Jesus Christ with incorruptible love.

2 Timothy 1

8 Therefore do not be ashamed of the testimony of our Lord or of me His prisoner, but join with me in suffering for the gospel according to the power of God,
9 Who has saved us and called us with a holy calling, not according to our works, but according to His own purpose and grace which was granted us in Christ Jesus from all eternity,

Hebrews 9

14 How much more will the blood of Christ, who through the eternal Spirit offered Himself without blemish to God, cleanse your conscience from dead works to serve the living God?
15 For this reason He is the mediator of a new covenant, so that, since a death has taken place for the redemption of the transgressions that were committed under the first covenant, those who have been called may receive the promise of the eternal inheritance.
16 For where a covenant is, there must of necessity be the death of the one who made it.
17 For a covenant is valid only when men are dead, for it is never in force while the one who made it lives.

22 And according to the Law, one may almost say, all things are cleansed with blood, and without shedding of blood there is no forgiveness.
23 Therefore it was necessary for the copies of the things in the heavens to be cleansed with these, but the heavenly things themselves with better sacrifices than these.
24 For Christ did not enter a holy place made with hands, a mere copy of the true one,

but into heaven itself, now to appear in the presence of God for us;
25 Nor was it that He would offer Himself often, as the high priest enters the holy place year by year with blood that is not his own.
26 Otherwise, He would have needed to suffer often since the foundation of the world; but now once at the consummation of the ages He has been manifested to put away sin by the sacrifice of Himself.

Hebrews 10

26 For if we go on sinning willfully after receiving the knowledge of the truth, there no longer remains a sacrifice for sins,
27 But a terrifying expectation of judgment and the fury of a fire which will consume the adversaries.
28 Anyone who has set aside the Law of Moses dies without mercy on the testimony of two or three witnesses.
29 How much severer punishment do you think he will deserve who has trampled under foot the Son of God, and has regarded as unclean the blood of the covenant by which he was sanctified, and has insulted the Spirit of grace?

1 Peter 2

23 And while being reviled, He did not revile in return; while suffering, He uttered no threats, but kept entrusting Himself to Him who judges righteously;
24 And He Himself bore our sins in His body on the cross, so that we might die to sin and live to righteousness; for by His wounds you were healed.
25 For you were continually straying like sheep, but now you have returned to the Shepherd and Guardian of your souls.

1 Peter 3

18 For Christ also died for sins once for all, the just for the unjust, so that He might bring us to God, having been put to death in the flesh, but made alive in the spirit;

Sin, Forgiveness, and Redemption

What is sin? Sinners are "everyone who practices sin lawlessness". (1 John 3:4) James 3:16 tells us that "to one who knows the right thing to do and does not do it, to him it is sin." Sin has always been a mystery. Could God have made man in a way that he does not sin? God gave man the freedom to think and choose. By giving man free will, man has the choice to disobey God and, thus, sin. According to the Bible there are several types of sins: Original sin, a sin that was imputed to all generations from the times of Adam and Eve. This inherited moral corruption is what caused man's proneness to sin such as those explained by Paul in Romans 13:5-14. The sins described by Paul includes adultery, murder, stealing, drunkenness, sexual promiscuity, and jealousy. Another type of sin is the unpardonable sin. This includes any blasphemy pronounced against the Holy Spirit (Matthew 12:31). In John 9:3, Jesus correlates sins with physical illness. He tells His disciples that a man, blind that He cured, neither was caused by his own sin nor sin inherited by his parents. His blindness had the purpose that the works of God might be displayed in him.

Forgiveness cannot be explained without understanding the grace of God. In pardoning sin, God absolves the sinner from the condemnation of the law and on the account of the work of Christ. By forgiving our sins --through grace-- God removes guilt and offers salvation. By forgiving our sins God demonstrates his love towards us. In Romans 5, Paul tells us that "while we were yet sinners, Christ died for us. Much more then, having now been justified by His blood, we shall be saved from the wrath of God through Him."

Redemption is an individual act of freewill which comes from the inner desire to change present circumstances after God has forgiven our sins. It can be defined as a tribute or moral payment to God. Ephesians 1:7 tell us: "In Him we have redemption through His blood, the forgiveness of our trespasses to the riches of His grace."

Matthew 6

14 "For if you forgive others for their transgressions, your heavenly Father will also forgive you."

Matthew 16

26 "For what will it profit a man if he gains the whole world and forfeits his sour? Or what will a man give in excahnge for his soul?"

Matthew 18

21 Then Peter came and said to Him, "Lord, how often shall my brother sin against me and I forgive him? Up to seven times?"
22 Jesus said to him, "I do not say to you, up to seven times, but up to seventy times seven."

Mark 9

43 "If your hand causes you to stumble, cut it off; it is better for you to enter life crippled, than, having your two hands, to go into hell, into the unquenchable fire,
44 [Where their worm does not die, and the fire is not quenched.]
45 "If your foot causes you to stumble, cut it off; it is better for you to enter life lame, than, having your two feet, to be cast into hell,
46 [Where their worm does not die, and the fire is not quenched.]
47 "If your eye causes you to stumble, throw it out; it is better for you to enter the kingdom of god with one eye, than, having two eyes, to be cast into hell,
48 "Where their worm does not die, and the fire is not quenched.
49 "For everyone will be salted with fire."

Mark 11

25 "Whenever you stand praying, forgive, if you have anything against anyone, so that your Father who is in heaven will also forgive you your transgressions.
26 ["But if you do not forgive, neither will your Father who is in heaven forgive your transgressions."]

Luke 5

32 "I have not come to call the righteous but sinners to repentance."

Luke 6

36 "Be merciful, just as your Father is merciful.
37 "Do not judge, and you will not be judged; and do not condemn, and you will not be condemned; pardon, and you will be pardoned."

Sin, Forgiveness, and Redemption — *Scriptures*

Luke 15

7 "I tell you that in the same way, there will be more joy in heaven over one sinner who repents than over ninety-nine righteous persons who need no repentance.
8 "Or what woman, if she has ten silver coins and loses one coin, does not light a lamp and sweep the house and search carefully until she finds it?

Luke 17

3 "Be on your guard! If your brother sins, rebuke him; and if he repents, forgive him.
4 "And if he sins against you seven times a day, and returns to you seven times, saying, 'I repent,' forgive him."

Luke 18

24 And Jesus looked at him and said, "How hard it is for those who are wealthy to enter the kingdom of God!
25 "For it is easier for a camel to go through the eye of a needle than for a rich man to enter the kingdom of God."

John 3

5 Jesus answered, "Truly, truly, I say to you, unless one is born of water and the Spirit he cannot enter into the kingdom of God.
6 "That which is born of the flesh is flesh, and that which is born of the Spirit is spirit.
7 "Do not be amazed that I said to you, 'You must be born again.'
8 "The wind blows where it wishes and you hear the sound of it, but do not know where it comes from and where it is going; so is everyone who is born of the Spirit."

John 8

31 So Jesus was saying to those Jews who had believed Him, "If you continue in My word, then you are truly disciples of Mine;"

34 Jesus answered them, "Truly, truly, I say to you, everyone who commits sin is the slave of sin."

John 9

1 As He passed by, He saw a man blind from birth.
2 And His disciples asked Him, "Rabbi, who sinned, this man or his parents, that he would be born blind?"
3 Jesus answered, "It was neither that this man sinned, nor his parents; but it was so that the works of God might be displayed in him."

John 15

22 "If I had not come and spoken to them, they would not have sin, but now they have no excuse for their sin."

Acts 2

38 Peter said to them, "Repent, and each of you be baptized in the name of Jesus Christ for the forgiveness of your sins; and you will receive the gift of the Holy Spirit.

39 "For the promise is for you and your children and for all who are far off, as many as the Lord our God will call to Himself."

Romans 2

1 Therefore you have no excuse, everyone of you who passes judgment, for in that which you judge another, you condemn yourself; for you who judge practice the same things.

2 And we know that the judgment of God rightly falls upon those who practice such things.

3 But do you suppose this, O man, when you pass judgment on those who practice such things and do the same yourself, that you will escape the judgment of God?

4 Or do you think lightly of the riches of His kindness and tolerance and patience, not knowing that the kindness of God leads you to repentance?

5 But because of your stubbornness and unrepentant heart you are storing up wrath for yourself in the day of wrath and revelation of the righteous judgment of God,

Romans 13

5 Therefore it is necessary to be in subjection, not only because of wrath, but also for conscience' sake.

6 For because of this you also pay taxes, for rulers are servants of God, devoting themselves to this very thing.

7 Render to all what is due them: tax to whom tax is due; custom to whom custom; fear to whom fear; honor to whom honor.

8 Owe nothing to anyone except to love one another; for he who loves his neighbor has fulfilled the law.

9 For this, "You shall not commit adultery, you shall not murder, you shall not steal, you shall not covet," and if there is any other commandment, it is summed up in this saying, "You shall love your neighbor as yourself."

10 Love does no wrong to a neighbor; therefore love is the fulfillment of the law.

11 Do this, knowing the time, that it is already the hour for you to awaken from sleep; for now salvation is nearer to us than when we believed.

12 The night is almost gone, and the day is near. Therefore let us lay aside the deeds of darkness and put on the armor of light.

13 Let us behave properly as in the day, not in carousing and drunkenness, not in sexual promiscuity and sensuality, not in strife and jealousy.

14 But put on the Lord Jesus Christ, and make no provision for the flesh in regard to its lusts.

1 Corinthians 6

9 Or do you not know that the unrighteous will not inherit the kingdom of God? Do not be deceived; neither fornicators, nor idolaters, nor adulterers, nor effeminate, nor homosexuals,

10 Nor thieves, nor the covetous, nor drunkards, nor revilers, nor swindlers, will inherit the kingdom of God.

11 Such were some of you; but you were washed, but you were sanctified, but you were justified in the name of the Lord Jesus Christ and in the Spirit of our God.

15 Do you not know that your bodies are members of Christ? Shall I then take away the members of Christ and make them members of a prostitute? May it never be!

16 Or do you not know that the one who joins himself to a prostitute is one body with

her? For He says, "The two shall become one flesh."

17 But the one who joins himself to the Lord is one spirit with Him.

18 Flee immorality. Every other sin that a man commits is outside the body, but the immoral man sins against his own body.

19 Or do you not know that your body is a temple of the Holy Spirit who is in you, whom you have from God, and that you are not your own?

20 For you have been bought with a price: therefore glorify God in your body.

1 Corinthians 8

12 And so, by sinning against the brethren and wounding their conscience when it is weak, you sin against Christ.

1 Corinthians 10

13 No temptation has overtaken you but such as is common to man; and God is faithful, who will not allow you to be tempted beyond what you are able, but with the temptation will provide the way of escape also, so that you will be able to endure it.

Ephisians 4

22 That, in reference to your former manner of life, you lay aside the old self, which is being corrupted in accordance with the lusts of deceit,

23 And that you be renewed in the spirit of your mind,

24 And put on the new self, which in the likeness of God has been created in righteousness and holiness of the truth.

26 Be angry, and yet do not sin; do not let the sun go down on your anger,

Colossians 3

2 Set your mind on the things above, not on the things that are on earth.

3 For you have died and your life is hidden with Christ in God.

4 When Christ, who is our life, is revealed, then you also will be revealed with Him in glory.

5 Therefore consider the members of your earthly body as dead to immorality, impurity, passion, evil desire, and greed, which amounts to idolatry.

6 For it is because of these things that the wrath of God will come upon the sons of disobedience,

7 And in them you also once walked, when you were living in them.

8 But now you also, put them all aside: anger, wrath, malice, slander, and abusive speech from your mouth.

9 Do not lie to one another, since you laid aside the old self with its evil practices,

10 And have put on the new self who is being renewed to a true knowledge according to the image of the One who created him—

1 Timothy 6

12 Fight the good fight of faith; take hold of the eternal life to which you were called, and you made the good confession in the presence of many witnesses.

2 Timothy 4

7 I have fought the good fight, I have finished the course, I have kept the faith;

8 In the future there is laid up for me the crown of righteousness, which the Lord, the righteous Judge, will award to me on that day; and not only to me, but also to all who have loved His appearing.

Hebrews 4

12 For the word of God is living and active and sharper than any two-edged sword, and piercing as far as the division of soul and spirit, of both joints and marrow, and able to judge the thoughts and intentions of the heart.

13 And there is no creature hidden from His sight, but all things are open and laid bare to the eyes of Him with whom we have to do.

14 Therefore, since we have a great high priest who has passed through the heavens, Jesus the Son of God, let us hold fast our confession.
15 For we do not have a high priest who cannot sympathize with our weaknesses, but One who has been tempted in all things as we are, yet without sin.
16 Therefore let us draw near with confidence to the throne of grace, so that we may receive mercy and find grace to help in time of need.

Hebrews 12

7 It is for discipline that you endure; God deals with you as with sons; for what son is there whom his father does not discipline?
8 But if you are without discipline, of which all have become partakers, then you are illegitimate children and not sons.
9 Furthermore, we had earthly fathers to discipline us, and we respected them; shall we not much rather be subject to the Father of spirits, and live?
10 For they disciplined us for a short time as seemed best to them, but He disciplines us for our good, so that we may share His holiness.
11 All discipline for the moment seems not to be joyful, but sorrowful; yet to those who have been trained by it, afterwards it yields the peaceful fruit of righteousness.

James 1

13 Let no one say when he is tempted, "I am being tempted by God"; for God cannot be tempted by evil, and He Himself does not tempt anyone.
14 But each one is tempted when he is carried away and enticed by his own lust.
15 Then when lust has conceived, it gives birth to sin; and when sin is accomplished, it brings forth death.

James 3

16 For where jealousy and selfish ambition exist, there is disorder and every evil thing.

James 4

17 Therefore, to one who knows the right thing to do and does not do it, to him it is sin.

James 5

19 My brethren, if any among you strays from the truth and one turns him back,
20 Let him know that he who turns a sinner from the error of his way will save his soul from death and will cover a multitude of sins.

1 Peter 1

23 For you have been born again not of seed which is perishable but imperishable, that is, through the living and enduring word of God.

1 Peter 3

8 To sum up, all of you be harmonious, sympathetic, brotherly, kindhearted, and humble in spirit;
9 Not returning evil for evil or insult for insult, but giving a blessing instead; for you were called for the very purpose that you might inherit a blessing.
10 For, "The one who desires life, to love and see good days, must keep his tongue from evil and his lips from speaking deceit.
11 "He must turn away from evil and do good; he must seek peace and pursue it.
12 "For the eyes of the Lord are toward the righteous, and his ears attend to their prayer, but the face of the Lord is against those who do evil."

2 Peter 2

9 Then the Lord knows how to rescue the godly from temptation, and to keep the unrighteous under punishment for the day of judgment,

20 For if, after they have escaped the defilements of the world by the knowledge of the Lord and Savior Jesus Christ, they are again entangled in them and are overcome, the last state has become worse for them than the first.
21 For it would be better for them not to have known the way of righteousness, than having known it, to turn away from the holy commandment handed on to them.

1 John 1

5 This is the message we have heard from Him and announce to you, that God is Light, and in Him there is no darkness at all.
6 If we say that we have fellowship with Him and yet walk in the darkness, we lie and do not practice the truth;
7 But if we walk in the Light as He Himself is in the Light, we have fellowship with one another, and the blood of Jesus His Son cleanses us from all sin.
8 If we say that we have no sin, we are deceiving ourselves and the truth is not in us.
9 If we confess our sins, He is faithful and righteous to forgive us our sins and to cleanse us from all unrighteousness.
10 If we say that we have not sinned, we make Him a liar and His word is not in us.

1 John 2

7 Beloved, I am not writing a new commandment to you, but an old commandment which you have had from the beginning; the old commandment is the word which you have heard.

8 On the other hand, I am writing a new commandment to you, which is true in Him and in you, because the darkness is passing away and the true Light is already shining.
9 The one who says he is in the Light and yet hates his brother is in the darkness until now.
10 The one who loves his brother abides in the Light and there is no cause for stumbling in him.
11 But the one who hates his brother is in the darkness and walks in the darkness, and does not know where he is going because the darkness has blinded his eyes.
12 I am writing to you, little children, because your sins have been forgiven you for His name's sake.

15 Do not love the world nor the things in the world. If anyone loves the world, the love of the Father is not in him.
16 For all that is in the world, the lust of the flesh and the lust of the eyes and the boastful pride of life, is not from the Father, but is from the world.
17 The world is passing away, and also its lusts; but the one who does the will of God lives forever.

1 John 3

4 Everyone who practices sin also practices lawlessness; and sin is lawlessness.
5 You know that He appeared in order to take away sins; and in Him there is no sin.
6 No one who abides in Him sins; no one who sins has seen Him or knows Him.
7 Little children, make sure no one deceives you; the one who practices righteousness is righteous, just as He is righteous;
8 the one who practices sin is of the devil; for the devil has sinned from the beginning. The Son of God appeared for this purpose, to destroy the works of the devil.
9 No one who is born of God practices sin, because His seed abides in him; and he cannot sin, because he is born of God.

1 John 5

16 If anyone sees his brother committing a sin not leading to death, he shall ask and God will for him give life to those who commit sin not leading to death. There is a sin leading to death; I do not say that he should make request for this.
17 All unrighteousness is sin, and there is a sin not leading to death.
18 We know that no one who is born of God sins; but He who was born of God keeps him, and the evil one does not touch him.
19 We know that we are of God, and that the whole world lies in the power of the evil one.
20 And we know that the Son of God has come, and has given us understanding so that we may know Him who is true; and we are in Him who is true, in His Son Jesus Christ. This is the true God and eternal life.

The Second Coming and Judgment

The Second Coming of Christ and Judgment are two interrelated themes. When Christ came the first time, the glory of his deity was veiled in a human body. When Christ comes again, the veil will be removed and we will see His great glory and judgment. In the New Testament, all Bible writers make reference to the Second Coming and Judgment. For instance, in the Synoptic Gospels, Matthew, Mark and Luke (Matthew 24:21-44; Mark 13: 24-37; and Luke 17:22-37) describe the Second Coming in a similar manner. Revelation 1: 7 uses the most vivid words to describe this event: "Behold, he is coming with the clouds, and every eye will see Him, even those who pierced Him; and all the tribes of the earth will mourn over Him. So it is to be. Amen." The fundamental difference between the First and Second Coming of Jesus is that during His first mission on earth He did not judge but showed the path for salvation and eternal life. The main purpose of the Second Coming is to judge people that did not accept Him. They will be condemned and will not be raised to eternal life. In John 12:48,

Jesus tells us that "He who rejects Me, and does not receive My sayings, has one who judges him; the word I spoke is what will judge him at the last day".

Matthew 12

36 "But I tell you that every careless word that people speak, they shall give an accounting for it in the day of judgment.
37 "For by your words you will be justified, and by your words you will be condemned."

Matthew 16

27 "For the Son of Man is going to come in the glory of His Father with His angels, and will then repay every man according to his deeds."

Matthew 24

21 "For then there will be a great tribulation, such as has not occurred since the beginning of the world until now, nor ever will.
22 "Unless those days had been cut short, no life would have been saved; but for the sake of the elect those days will be cut short.
23 "Then if anyone says to you, 'Behold, here is the Christ,' or 'There He is,' do not believe him.
24 "For false Christs and false prophets will arise and will show great signs and wonders, so as to mislead, if possible, even the elect.
25 "Behold, I have told you in advance.
26 "So if they say to you, 'Behold, He is in the wilderness,' do not go out, or, 'Behold, He is in the inner rooms,' do not believe them.
27 "For just as the lightning comes from the east and flashes even to the west, so will the coming of the Son of Man be.
28 "Wherever the corpse is, there the vultures will gather.
29 "But immediately after the tribulation of those days the sun will be darkened, and the moon will not give its light, and the stars will fall from the sky, and the powers of the heavens will be shaken.
30 "And then the sign of the Son of Man will appear in the sky, and then all the tribes of the earth will mourn, and they will see the Son of Man coming on the clouds of the sky with power and great glory.
31 "And He will send forth His angels with a great trumpet and they will gather together His elect from the four winds, from one end of the sky to the other.
32 "Now learn the parable from the fig tree: when its branch has already become tender and puts forth its leaves, you know that summer is near;
33 "So, you too, when you see all these things, recognize that He is near, right at the door.
34 "Truly I say to you, this generation will not pass away until all these things take place.
35 "Heaven and earth will pass away, but My words will not pass away.
36 "But of that day and hour no one knows, not even the angels of heaven, nor the Son, but the Father alone.
37 "For the coming of the Son of Man will be just like the days of Noah.
38 "For as in those days before the flood they were eating and drinking, marrying and giving in marriage, until the day that Noah entered the ark,
39 And they did not understand until the flood came and took them all away; so will the coming of the Son of Man be.
40 "Then there will be two men in the field; one will be taken and one will be left.
41 "Two women will be grinding at the mill; one will be taken and one will be left.
42 "Therefore be on the alert, for you do not know which day your Lord is coming.
43 "But be sure of this, that if the head of the house had known at what time of the night the thief was coming, he would have been on the alert and would not have allowed his house to be broken into.
44 "For this reason you also must be ready; for the Son of Man is coming at an hour when you do not think He will."

Mark 13

24 "But in those days, after that tribulation, the sun will be darkened and the moon will not give its light,
25 "And the stars will be falling from heaven, and the powers that are in the heavens will be shaken.

Scriptures — *The Second Coming and Judgment*

26 "Then they will see the son of man coming in clouds with great power and glory.
27 "And then He will send forth the angels, and will gather together His elect from the four winds, from the farthest end of the earth to the farthest end of heaven.
28 "Now learn the parable from the fig tree: when its branch has already become tender and puts forth its leaves, you know that summer is near.
29 "Even so, you too, when you see these things happening, recognize that He is near, right at the door.
30 "Truly I say to you, this generation will not pass away until all these things take place.
31 "Heaven and earth will pass away, but My words will not pass away.
32 "But of that day or hour no one knows, not even the angels in heaven, nor the Son, but the Father alone.
33 "Take heed, keep on the alert; for you do not know when the appointed time will come.
34 "It is like a man away on a journey, who upon leaving his house and putting his slaves in charge, assigning to each one his task, also commanded the doorkeeper to stay on the alert.
35 "Therefore, be on the alert-- for you do not know when the master of the house is coming, whether in the evening, at midnight, or when the rooster crows, or in the morning--
36 "In case he should come suddenly and find you asleep.
37 "What I say to you I say to all, 'Be on the alert!' "

Luke 12

40 "You too, be ready; for the Son of Man is coming at an hour that you do not expect."

Luke 17

22 And He said to the disciples, "The days will come when you will long to see one of the days of the Son of Man, and you will not see it.
23 "They will say to you, 'Look there! Look here!' Do not go away, and do not run after them.
24 "For just like the lightning, when it flashes out of one part of the sky, shines to the other part of the sky, so will the Son of Man be in His day.
25 "But first He must suffer many things and be rejected by this generation.
26 "And just as it happened in the days of Noah, so it will be also in the days of the Son of Man:
27 They were eating, they were drinking, they were marrying, they were being given in marriage, until the day that Noah entered the ark, and the flood came and destroyed them all.
28 "It was the same as happened in the days of Lot: they were eating, they were drinking, they were buying, they were selling, they were planting, they were building;
29 But on the day that Lot went out from Sodom it rained fire and brimstone from heaven and destroyed them all.

The Second Coming and Judgment   *Scriptures*

30 "It will be just the same on the day that the Son of Man is revealed.
31 "On that day, the one who is on the housetop and whose goods are in the house must not go down to take them out; and likewise the one who is in the field must not turn back.
32 "Remember Lot's wife.
33 "Whoever seeks to keep his life will lose it, and whoever loses his life will preserve it.
34 "I tell you, on that night there will be two in one bed; one will be taken and the other will be left.
35 "There will be two women grinding at the same place; one will be taken and the other will be left.
36 ["Two men will be in the field; one will be taken and the other will be left."]
37 And answering they said to Him, "Where, Lord?" And He said to them, "Where the body is, there also the vultures will be gathered."

John 12

48 "He who rejects Me and does not receive My sayings, has one who judges him; the word I spoke is what will judge him at the last day."

1 Corinthians 15

51 Behold, I tell you a mystery; we will not all sleep, but we will all be changed,
52 In a moment, in the twinkling of an eye, at the last trumpet; for the trumpet will sound, and the dead will be raised imperishable, and we will be changed.
53 For this perishable must put on the imperishable, and this mortal must put on immortality.
54 But when this perishable will have put on the imperishable, and this mortal will have put on immortality, then will come about the saying that is written, "Death is swallowed up in victory."

2 Corinthians 5

10 For we must all appear before the judgment seat of Christ, so that each one may be recompensed for his deeds in the body, according to what he has done, whether good or bad.

Philippians 3

20 For our citizenship is in heaven, from which also we eagerly wait for a Savior, the Lord Jesus Christ;
21 Who will transform the body of our humble state into conformity with the body of His glory, by the exertion of the power that He has even to subject all things to Himself.

1 Thessalonians 1

10 And to wait for His Son from heaven, whom He raised from the dead, that is Jesus, who rescues us from the wrath to come.

1 Thessalonians 4

13 But we do not want you to be uninformed, brethren, about those who are asleep, so that you will not grieve as do the rest who have no hope.
14 For if we believe that Jesus died and rose again, even so God will bring with Him those who have fallen asleep in Jesus.
15 For this we say to you by the word of the Lord, that we who are alive and remain until the coming of the Lord, will not precede those who have fallen asleep.
16 For the Lord Himself will descend from heaven with a shout, with the voice of the archangel and with the trumpet of God, and the dead in Christ will rise first.
17 Then we who are alive and remain will be caught up together with them in the clouds to meet the Lord in the air, and so we shall always be with the Lord.

Hebrews 9

27 And inasmuch as it is appointed for men to die once and after this comes judgment,
28 So Christ also, having been offered once to bear the sins of many, will appear a second time for salvation without reference to sin, to those who eagerly await Him.

1 Peter 5

4 And when the Chief Shepherd appears, you will receive the unfading crown of glory.

2 Peter 3

10 But the day of the Lord will come like a thief, in which the heavens will pass away with a roar and the elements will be destroyed with intense heat, and the earth and its works will be burned up.
11 Since all these things are to be destroyed in this way, what sort of people ought you to be in holy conduct and godliness,
12 Looking for and hastening the coming of the day of God, because of which the heavens will be destroyed by burning, and the elements will melt with intense heat!
13 But according to His promise we are looking for new heavens and a new earth, in which righteousness dwells.

Revelation 1

7 Behold, he is coming with the clouds, and every eye will see Him, even those who pierced Him; and all the tribes of the earth will mourn over Him. So it is to be. Amen.

Revelation 6

12 I looked when He broke the sixth seal, and there was a great earthquake; and the sun became black as sackcloth made of hair, and the whole moon became like blood;
13 And the stars of the sky fell to the earth, as a fig tree casts its unripe figs when shaken by a great wind.
14 The sky was split apart like a scroll when it is rolled up, and every mountain and island were moved out of their places.
15 Then the kings of the earth and the great men and the commanders and the rich and the strong and every slave and free man hid themselves in the caves and among the rocks of the mountains;
16 And they said to the mountains and to the rocks, "Fall on us and hide us from the presence of Him who sits on the throne, and from the wrath of the Lamb;
17 For the great day of their wrath has come, and who is able to stand?"

Revelation 20

11 Then I saw a great white throne and Him who sat upon it, from whose presence earth and heaven fled away, and no place was found for them.
12 And I saw the dead, the great and the small, standing before the throne, and books were opened; and another book was opened, which is the book of life; and the dead were judged from the things which were written in the books, according to their deeds.

13 And the sea gave up the dead which were in it, and death and Hades gave up the dead which were in them; and they were judged, every one of them according to their deeds.
14 Then death and Hades were thrown into the lake of fire. This is the second death, the lake of fire.
15 And if anyone's name was not found written in the book of life, he was thrown into the lake of fire.

Revelation 21

1 Then I saw a new heaven and a new earth; for the first heaven and the first earth passed away, and there is no longer any sea.
2 And I saw the holy city, new Jerusalem, coming down out of heaven from God, made ready as a bride adorned for her husband.
3 And I heard a loud voice from the throne, saying, "Behold, the tabernacle of God is among men, and He will dwell among them, and they shall be His people, and God Himself will be among them,
4 And He will wipe away every tear from their eyes; and there will no longer be any death; there will no longer be any mourning, or crying, or pain; the first things have passed away."
5 And He who sits on the throne said, "Behold, I am making all things new." And He said, "Write, for these words are faithful and true."
6 Then He said to me, "It is done. I am the Alpha and the Omega, the beginning and the end. I will give to the one who thirsts from the spring of the water of life without cost.
7 "He who overcomes will inherit these things, and I will be his God and he will be My son.
8 "But for the cowardly and unbelieving and abominable and murderers and immoral persons and sorcerers and idolaters and all liars, their part will be in the lake that burns with fire and brimstone, which is the second death."
22 I saw no temple in it, for the Lord God the Almighty and the Lamb are its temple.
23 And the city has no need of the sun or of the moon to shine on it, for the glory of God has illumined it, and its lamp is the Lamb.
24 The nations will walk by its light, and the kings of the earth will bring their glory into it.
25 In the daytime (for there will be no night there) its gates will never be closed;
26 And they will bring the glory and the honor of the nations into it;
27 And nothing unclean, and no one who practices abomination and lying, shall ever come into it, but only those whose names are written in the Lamb's book of life.

Exhortations

This layer groups different messages from Christ and the Apostles. These scriptures are intended to improve our Christian life and our relationship with God and reach salvation. In some of the scriptures one can almost hear the voice of the Lord telling us how to follow His teaching and His Father's Will.

Matthew 5

3 "Blessed are the poor in spirit, for theirs is the kingdom of heaven.
4 "Blessed are those who mourn, for they shall be comforted.
5 "Blessed are the gentle, for they shall inherit the earth.
6 "Blessed are those who hunger and thirst for righteousness, for they shall be satisfied.
7 "Blessed are the merciful, for they shall receive mercy.
8 "Blessed are the pure in heart, for they shall see God.
9 "Blessed are the peacemakers, for they shall be called sons of God.

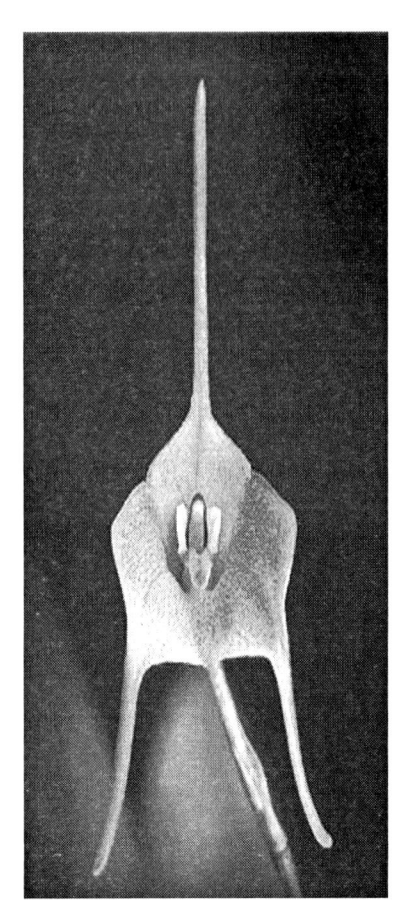

10 "Blessed are those who have been persecuted for the sake of righteousness, for theirs is the kingdom of heaven.
11 "Blessed are you when people insult you and persecute you, and falsely say all kinds of evil against you because of Me."

Matthew 6

19 "Do not store up for yourselves treasures on earth, where moth and rust destroy, and where thieves break in and steal.
20 "But store up for yourselves treasures in heaven, where neither moth nor rust destroys, and where thieves do not break in or steal;
21 For where your treasure is, there your heart will be also."

Matthew 7

21 "Not everyone who says to Me, 'Lord, Lord,' will enter the kingdom of heaven, but he who does the will of My Father who is in heaven will enter."

Matthew 10

37 "He who loves father or mother more than Me is not worthy of Me; and he who loves son or daughter more than Me is not worthy of Me."

Matthew 15

11 "It is not what enters into the mouth that defiles the man, but what proceeds out of the mouth, this defiles the man."

Matthew 18

4 "Whoever then humbles himself as this child, he is the greatest in the kingdom of heaven.

10 "See that you do not despise one of these little ones, for I say to you that their angels in heaven continually see the face of My Father who is in heaven.

12 "What do you think? If any man has a hundred sheep, and one of them has gone astray, does he not leave the ninety-nine on the mountains and go and search for the one that is straying?
13 "If it turns out that he finds it, truly I say to you, he rejoices over it more than over the ninety-nine which have not gone astray.
14 "So it is not the will of your Father who is in heaven that one of these little ones perish."

Mark 2

27 Jesus said to them, "The Sabbath was made for man, and not man for the Sabbath.
28 "So the Son of Man is Lord even of the Sabbath."

Exhortations   *Scriptures*

Mark 8

38 "For whoever is ashamed of Me and My words in this adulterous and sinful generation, the Son of Man will also be ashamed of him when He comes in the glory of His Father with the holy angels."

Luke 6

38 "Give, and it will be given to you. They will pour into your lap a good measure-- pressed down, shaken together, and running over. For by your standard of measure it will be measured to you in return."

44 "For each tree is known by its own fruit. For men do not gather figs from thorns, nor do they pick grapes from a briar bush."

Luke 11

33 "No one, after lighting a lamp, puts it away in a cellar nor under a basket, but on the lampstand, so that those who enter may see the light.

34 "The eye is the lamp of your body; when your eye is clear, your whole body also is full of light; but when it is bad, your body also is full of darkness.

35 "Then watch out that the light in you is not darkness.

36 "If therefore your whole body is full of light, with no dark part in it, it will be wholly illumined, as when the lamp illumines you with its rays."

Luke 12

8 "And I say to you, everyone who confesses Me before men, the Son of Man will confess him also before the angels of God;

9 "But he who denies Me before men will be denied before the angels of God."

51 "Do you suppose that I came to grant peace on earth? I tell you, no, but rather division;

52 "For from now on five members in one household will be divided, three against two and two against three.

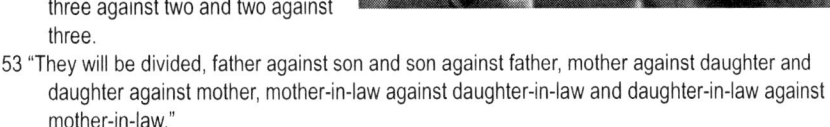

53 "They will be divided, father against son and son against father, mother against daughter and daughter against mother, mother-in-law against daughter-in-law and daughter-in-law against mother-in-law."

Luke 14

27 "Whoever does not carry his own cross and come after Me cannot be My disciple."

Scriptures   III - 39   *Exhortations*

Luke 18

29 And He said to them, "Truly I say to you, there is no one who has left house or wife or brothers or parents or children, for the sake of the kingdom of God,
30 "Who will not receive many times as much at this time and in the age to come, eternal life."

John 8

47 "He who is of God hears the words of God; for this reason you do not hear them, because you are not of God."

John 12

25 "He who loves his life loses it, and he who hates his life in this world will keep it to life eternal.
26 "If anyone serves Me, he must follow Me; and where I am, there My servant will be also; if anyone serves Me, the Father will honor him."

John 15

19 "If you were of the world, the world would love its own; but because you are not of the world, but I chose you out of the world, because of this the world hates you."

John 20

28 Thomas answered and said to Him, "My Lord and my God!"
29 Jesus said to him, "Because you have seen Me, have you believed? Blessed are they who did not see, and yet believed."

Acts 16

31 They said, "Believe in the Lord Jesus, and you will be saved, you and your household."

Romans 12

2 And do not be conformed to this world, but be transformed by the renewing of your mind, so that you may prove what the will of God is, that which is good and acceptable and perfect.
4 For just as we have many members in one body and all the members do not have the same function,
5 So we, who are many, are one body in Christ, and individually members one of another.
6 Since we have gifts that differ according to the grace given to us, each of us is to exercise them accordingly: if prophecy, according to the proportion of his faith;
7 If service, in his serving; or he who teaches, in his teaching;
8 Or he who exhorts, in his exhortation; he who gives, with liberality; he who leads, with diligence; he who shows mercy, with cheerfulness.

Romans 13

12 The night is almost gone, and the day is near. Therefore let us lay aside the deeds of darkness and put on the armor of light.

Romans 14

8 For if we live, we live for the Lord, or if we die, we die for the Lord; therefore whether we live or die, we are the Lord's.
9 For to this end Christ died and lived again, that He might be Lord both of the dead and of the living.

1 Corinthians 3

7 So then neither the one who plants nor the one who waters is anything, but God who causes the growth.

16 Do you not know that you are a temple of God and that the Spirit of God dwells in you?
17 If any man destroys the temple of God, God will destroy him, for the temple of God is holy, and that is what you are.

2 Corinthians 7

10 For the sorrow that is according to the will of God produces a repentance without regret, leading to salvation, but the sorrow of the world produces death.

2 Corinthians 12

9 And He has said to me, "My grace is sufficient for you, for power is perfected in weakness." Most gladly, therefore, I will rather boast about my weaknesses, so that the power of Christ may dwell in me.
10 Therefore I am well content with weaknesses, with insults, with distresses, with persecutions, with difficulties, for Christ's sake; for when I am weak, then I am strong.

Ephesians 6

13 Therefore, take up the full armor of God, so that you will be able to resist in the evil day, and having done everything, to stand firm.
14 Stand firm therefore, having girded your loins with truth, and having put on the breastplate of righteousness,
15 And having shod your feet with the preparation of the gospel of peace;
16 In addition to all, taking up the shield of faith with which you will be able to extinguish all the flaming arrows of the evil one.
17 And take the helmet of salvation, and the sword of the Spirit, which is the word of God.

Philippians 2

3 Do nothing from selfishness or empty conceit, but with humility of mind regard one another as more important than yourselves;
4 Do not merely look out for your own personal interests, but also for the interests of others.

1 Timothy 6

7 For we have brought nothing into the world, so we cannot take anything out of it either.
8 If we have food and covering, with these we shall be content.

2 Timothy 2

19 Nevertheless, the firm foundation of God stands, having this seal, "The Lord knows those who are His," and, "Everyone who names the name of the Lord is to abstain from wickedness."

Hebrews 11

1 Now faith is the assurance of things hoped for, the conviction of things not seen.

Hebrews 12

14 Pursue peace with all men, and the sanctification without which no one will see the Lord.
15 See to it that no one comes short of the grace of God; that no root of bitterness springing up causes trouble, and by it many be defiled;

Hebrews 13

2 Do not neglect to show hospitality to strangers, for by this some have entertained angels without knowing it.
3 Remember the prisoners, as though in prison with them, and those who are ill-treated, since you yourselves also are in the body.
4 Marriage is to be held in honor among all, and the marriage bed is to be undefiled; for fornicators and adulterers God will judge.
5 Make sure that your character is free from the love of money, being content with what you have; for He Himself has said, "I will never desert you, nor will I ever forsake you,"
6 So that we confidently say, "The Lord is my helper, I will not be afraid. What will man do to me?"

James 1

12 Blessed is a man who perseveres under trial; for once he has been approved, he will receive the crown of life which the Lord has promised to those who love Him.

James 3

5 So also the tongue is a small part of the body, and yet it boasts of great things. See how great a forest is set aflame by such a small fire!
6 And the tongue is a fire, the very world of iniquity; the tongue is set among our members as that which defiles the entire body, and sets on fire the course of our life, and is set on fire by hell.

7 For every species of beasts and birds, of reptiles and creatures of the sea, is tamed and has been tamed by the human race.
8 But no one can tame the tongue; it is a restless evil and full of deadly poison.
9 With it we bless our Lord and Father, and with it we curse men, who have been made in the likeness of God;
10 From the same mouth come both blessing and cursing. My brethren, these things ought not to be this way.
11 Does a fountain send out from the same opening both fresh and bitter water?
12 Can a fig tree, my brethren, produce olives, or a vine produce figs? Nor can salt water produce fresh.

James 5

12 But above all, my brethren, do not swear, either by heaven or by earth or with any other oath; but your yes is to be yes, and your no, no, so that you may not fall under judgment.

1 Peter 3

14 But even if you should suffer for the sake of righteousness, you are blessed. And do not fear their intimidation, and do not be troubled,
15 But sanctify Christ as Lord in your hearts, always being ready to make a defense to everyone who asks you to give an account for the hope that is in you, yet with gentleness and reverence;

1 Peter 4

12 Beloved, do not be surprised at the fiery ordeal among you, which comes upon you for your testing, as though some strange thing were happening to you;
13 But to the degree that you share the sufferings of Christ, keep on rejoicing, so that also at the revelation of His glory you may rejoice with exultation.
14 If you are reviled for the name of Christ, you are blessed, because the Spirit of glory and of God rests on you.

2 Peter 3

9 The Lord is not slow about His promise, as some count slowness, but is patient toward you, not wishing for any to perish but for all to come to repentance.

1 John 2

25 This is the promise which He Himself made to us: eternal life.

1 John 4

1 Beloved, do not believe every spirit, but test the spirits to see whether they are from God, because many false prophets have gone out into the world.
2 By this you know the Spirit of God: every spirit that confesses that Jesus Christ has come in the flesh is from God;
3 And every spirit that does not confess Jesus is not from God; this is the spirit of the antichrist, of which you have heard that it is coming, and now it is already in the world.

2 John 1

10 If anyone comes to you and does not bring this teaching, do not receive him into your house, and do not give him a greeting;
11 For the one who gives him a greeting participates in his evil deeds.

Jude 1

20 But you, beloved, building yourselves up on your most holy faith, praying in the Holy Spirit,
21 Keep yourselves in the love of God, waiting anxiously for the mercy of our Lord Jesus Christ to eternal life.
22 And have mercy on some, who are doubting;
23 Save others, snatching them out of the fire; and on some have mercy with fear, hating even the garment polluted by the flesh.
24 Now to Him who is able to keep you from stumbling, and to make you stand in the presence of His glory blameless with great joy,
25 To the only God our Savior, through Jesus Christ our Lord, be glory, majesty, dominion and authority, before all time and now and forever. Amen.

Petitions, Miracles, and Faith

    Multiple scriptures support that, as Christians, we should pray to our Father in Heaven through Our Lord Jesus and our requests will be granted. They also show that our Father wants to fulfill our desires. However, these statements are many times qualified. It tells that we need to ask with the right motives (James 4:3), that we need to believe and have faith in God. (Matthew 21:21-22) It also tells us that if two people or more are in agreement with our petitions, the Lord will grant our requests. (Matthew 18:19) As Christians we need to trust the Lord and understand that, under the right circumstances, He is willing to fulfill our needs and grant us our heart's desires.

    Miracles are events through which God may answer our petitions. The occurrence of a miracle involves the intervention of a power that is not limited by the laws of nature. An integral part of the Bible are the miracles performed by Jesus. The Bible writers appeal to miracles as a way to provide conclusive proof of Christ's divine nature. The Gospels attribute 35 miracles to Jesus all performed during His 3 years of Ministry. These miracles can be classified in four categories: bodily cures, miracles over forces of nature, cures of demoniacs, and raised from the dead.

    An indispensable condition for God to answer our petitions is faith. Matthew 21:22 tells us that "all things you ask in prayer, believing you will receive." The word faith implies trust. Faith is the result of teaching and our openness to understand the testimony of God. Faith in Jesus secures our relationship with Him, His attention to our needs, and our salvation.

Matthew 7

7 "Ask, and it will be given to you; seek, and you will find; knock, and it will be opened to you.
8 "For everyone who asks receives, and he who seeks finds, and to him who knocks it will be opened.
9 "Or what man is there among you who, when his son asks for a loaf, will give him a stone?
10 "Or if he asks for a fish, he will not give him a snake, will he?
11 "If you then, being evil, know how to give good gifts to your children, how much more will your Father who is in heaven give what is good to those who ask Him!"

Matthew 8

8 But the centurion said, "Lord, I am not worthy for You to come under my roof, but just say the word, and my servant will be healed.
9 "For I also am a man under authority, with soldiers under me; and I say to this one, 'Go!' and he goes, and to another, 'Come!' and he comes, and to my slave, 'Do this!' and he does it."
10 Now when Jesus heard this, He marveled and said to those who were following, "Truly I say to you, I have not found such great faith with anyone in Israel."

13 And Jesus said to the centurion, "Go; it shall be done for you as you have believed." And the servant was healed that very moment.

Matthew 17

20 And He said to them, "Because of the littleness of your faith; for truly I say to you, if you have faith the size of a mustard seed, you will say to this mountain, 'Move from here to there,' and it will move; and nothing will be impossible to you."

Matthew 18

19 "Again I say to you, that if two of you agree on earth about anything that they may ask, it shall be done for them by My Father who is in heaven.
20 "For where two or three have gathered together in My name, I am there in their midst."

Matthew 19

26 And looking at them Jesus said to them, "With people this is impossible, but with God all things are possible."

Matthew 21

21 And Jesus answered and said to them, "Truly I say to you, if you have faith and do not doubt, you will not only do what was done to the fig tree, but even if you say to this mountain, 'Be taken up and cast into the sea,' it will happen.
22 "And all things you ask in prayer, believing, you will receive."

Matthew 26

39 And He went a little beyond them, and fell on His face and prayed, saying, "My Father, if it is possible, let this cup pass from Me; yet not as I will, but as You will."
40 And He came to the disciples and found them sleeping, and said to Peter, "So, you men could not keep watch with Me for one hour?
41 "Keep watching and praying that you may not enter into temptation; the spirit is willing, but the flesh is weak."

Mark 5

27 After hearing about Jesus, she came up in the crowd behind Him and touched His cloak.
28 For she thought, "If I just touch His garments, I will get well."
29 Immediately the flow of her blood was dried up; and she felt in her body that she was healed of her affliction.
30 Immediately Jesus, perceiving in Himself that the power proceeding from Him had gone forth, turned around in the crowd and said, "Who touched My garments?"
31 And His disciples said to Him, "You see the crowd pressing in on You, and You say, 'Who touched Me?' "
32 And He looked around to see the woman who had done this.
33 But the woman fearing and trembling, aware of what had happened to her, came and fell down before Him and told Him the whole truth.
34 And He said to her, "Daughter, your faith has made you well; go in peace and be healed of your affliction."

Mark 7

31 Again He went out from the region of Tyre, and came through Sidon to the Sea of Galilee, within the region of Decapolis.
32 They brought to Him one who was deaf and spoke with difficulty, and they implored Him to lay His hand on him.
33 Jesus took him aside from the crowd, by himself, and put His fingers into his ears, and after spitting, He touched his tongue with the saliva;
34 And looking up to heaven with a deep sigh, He said to him, "Ephphatha!" that is, "Be opened!"
35 And his ears were opened, and the impediment of his tongue was removed, and he began speaking plainly.

Mark 11

23 "Truly I say to you, whoever says to this mountain, 'Be taken up and cast into the sea,' and does not doubt in his heart, but believes that what he says is going to happen, it will be granted him.
24 "Therefore I say to you, all things for which you pray and ask, believe that you have received them, and they will be granted you."

Luke 4

40 While the sun was setting, all those who had any who were sick with various diseases brought them to Him; and laying His hands on each one of them, He was healing them.

Luke 5

12 While He was in one of the cities, behold, there was a man covered with leprosy; and when he saw Jesus, he fell on his face and implored Him, saying, "Lord, if You are willing, You can make me clean."
13 And He stretched out His hand and touched him, saying, "I am willing; be cleansed." And immediately the leprosy left him.

Luke 6

19 And all the people were trying to touch Him, for power was coming from Him and healing them all.

Luke 7

11 Soon afterwards He went to a city called Nain; and His disciples were going along with Him, accompanied by a large crowd.
12 Now as He approached the gate of the city, a dead man was being carried out, the only son of his mother, and she was a widow; and a sizeable crowd from the city was with her.
13 When the Lord saw her, He felt compassion for her, and said to her, "Do not weep."
14 And He came up and touched the coffin; and the bearers came to a halt. And He said, "Young man, I say to you, arise!"
15 The dead man sat up and began to speak. And Jesus gave him back to his mother.

Luke 8

41 And there came a man named Jairus, and he was an official of the synagogue; and he fell at Jesus' feet, and began to implore Him to come to his house;
42 For he had an only daughter, about twelve years old, and she was dying. But as He went, the crowds were pressing against Him.

49 While He was still speaking, someone came from the house of the synagogue official, saying, "Your daughter has died; do not trouble the Teacher anymore."
50 But when Jesus heard this, He answered him, "Do not be afraid any longer; only believe, and she will be made well."
51 When He came to the house, He did not allow anyone to enter with Him, except Peter and John and James, and the girl's father and mother.
52 Now they were all weeping and lamenting for her; but He said, "Stop weeping, for she has not died, but is asleep."

Petitions, Miracles, and Faith   *Scriptures*

53 And they began laughing at Him, knowing that she had died.
54 He, however, took her by the hand and called, saying, "Child, arise!"
55 And her spirit returned, and she got up immediately; and He gave orders for something to be given her to eat.

Luke 11

8 "I tell you, even though he will not get up and give him anything because he is his friend, yet because of his persistence he will get up and give him as much as he needs.
9 "So I say to you, ask, and it will be given to you; seek, and you will find; knock, and it will be opened to you.
10 "For everyone who asks, receives; and he who seeks, finds; and to him who knocks, it will be opened.
11 "Now suppose one of you fathers is asked by his son for a fish; he will not give him a snake instead of a fish, will he?
12 "Or if he is asked for an egg, he will not give him a scorpion, will he?
13 "If you then, being evil, know how to give good gifts to your children, how much more will your heavenly Father give the Holy Spirit to those who ask Him?"

Luke 13

11 And there was a woman who for eighteen years had had a sickness caused by a spirit; and she was bent double, and could not straighten up at all.
12 When Jesus saw her, He called her over and said to her, "Woman, you are freed from your sickness."
13 And He laid His hands on her; and immediately she was made erect again and began glorifying God.

Luke 17

6 And the Lord said, "If you had faith like a mustard seed, you would say to this mulberry tree, 'Be uprooted and be planted in the sea'; and it would obey you."

John 11

1 Now a certain man was sick, Lazarus of Bethany, the village of Mary and her sister Martha.
2 It was the Mary who anointed the Lord with ointment, and wiped His feet with her hair, whose brother Lazarus was sick.
3 So the sisters sent word to Him, saying, "Lord, behold, he whom You love is sick."

32 Therefore, when Mary came where Jesus was, she saw Him, and fell at His feet, saying to Him, "Lord, if You had been here, my brother would not have died."
33 When Jesus therefore saw her weeping, and the Jews who came with her also weeping, He was deeply moved in spirit and was troubled,
34 And said, "Where have you laid him?" They said to Him, "Lord, come and see."
35 Jesus wept.
36 So the Jews were saying, "See how He loved him!"
37 But some of them said, "Could not this man, who opened the eyes of the blind man, have kept this man also from dying?"
38 So Jesus, again being deeply moved within, came to the tomb. Now it was a cave, and a stone was lying against it.
39 Jesus said, "Remove the stone." Martha, the sister of the deceased, said to Him, "Lord, by this time there will be a stench, for he has been dead four days."
40 Jesus said to her, "Did I not say to you that if you believe, you will see the glory of God?"
41 So they removed the stone. Then Jesus raised His eyes, and said, "Father, I thank You that You have heard Me.
42 "I knew that You always hear Me; but because of the people standing around I said it, so that they may believe that You sent Me."
43 When He had said these things, He cried out with a loud voice, "Lazarus, come forth."
44 The man who had died came forth, bound hand and foot with wrappings, and his face was wrapped around with a cloth. Jesus said to them, "Unbind him, and let him go."

John 14
13 "Whatever you ask in My name, that will I do, so that the Father may be glorified in the Son.
14 "If you ask Me anything in My name, I will do it."

John 15
7 "If you abide in Me, and My words abide in you, ask whatever you wish, and it will be done for you.
8 "My Father is glorified by this, that you bear much fruit, and so prove to be My disciples."
16 "You did not choose Me but I chose you, and appointed you that you would go and bear fruit, and that your fruit would remain, so that whatever you ask of the Father in My name He may give to you.

John 16
23 "In that day you will not question Me about anything. Truly, truly, I say to you, if you ask the Father for anything in My name, He will give it to you."
24 "Until now you have asked for nothing in My name; ask and you will receive, so that your joy may be made full."

Romans 8
31 What then shall we say to these things? if God is for us, who is against us?
32 He who did not spare his own son, but delivered him over for us all, how will he not also with him freely give us all things?

Hebrews 11
6 And without faith it is impossible to please Him, for he who comes to God must believe that He is and that He is a rewarder of those who seek Him.
7 By faith Noah, being warned by God about things not yet seen, in reverence prepared an ark for the salvation of his household, by which he condemned the world, and became an heir of the righteousness which is according to faith.
8 By faith Abraham, when he was called, obeyed by going out to a place which he was to receive for an inheritance; and he went out, not knowing where he was going.
9 By faith he lived as an alien in the land of

promise, as in a foreign land, dwelling in tents with Isaac and Jacob, fellow heirs of the same promise;
10 For he was looking for the city which has foundations, whose architect and builder is God.
11 By faith even Sarah herself received ability to conceive, even beyond the proper time of life, since she considered Him faithful who had promised.

James 1

2 Consider it all joy, my brethren, when you encounter various trials,
3 Knowing that the testing of your faith produces endurance.
4 And let endurance have its perfect result, so that you may be perfect and complete, lacking in nothing.

6 But he must ask in faith without any doubting, for the one who doubts is like the surf of the sea, driven and tossed by the wind.
7 For that man ought not to expect that he will receive anything from the Lord,

James 4

3 You ask and do not receive, because you ask with wrong motives, so that you may spend it on your pleasures.

James 5

13 Is anyone among you suffering? Then he must pray. Is anyone cheerful? He is to sing praises.
14 Is anyone among you sick? Then he must call for the elders of the church and they are to pray over him, anointing him with oil in the name of the Lord;
15 And the prayer offered in faith will restore the one who is sick, and the Lord will raise him up, and if he has committed sins, they will be forgiven him.
16 Therefore, confess your sins to one another, and pray for one another so that you may be healed. The effective prayer of a righteous man can accomplish much.

1 John 5

14 This is the confidence which we have before Him, that, if we ask anything according to His will, He hears us.
15 And if we know that He hears us in whatever we ask, we know that we have the requests which we have asked from Him.

Worries

God clearly commands us not to worry and place trust in His divine care. The fact that we need not worry is exemplified by Luke 12:29-30: "And do not seek what you will eat and what you will drink, and do not keep worrying. For all these things the nations of the world eagerly seek: but your Father knows that you need these things." As Christians we need to understand that to worry about the future is useless. Worry affects a man or woman's judgment and lessens his or her power of decision. The alternative to worry is prayer and the trust that our Lord will fulfill our needs.

Matthew 6

25 "For this reason I say to you, do not be worried about your life, as to what you will eat or what you will drink; nor for your body, as to what you will put on. Is not life more than food, and the body more than clothing?
26 "Look at the birds of the air, that they do not sow, nor reap nor gather into barns, and yet your heavenly Father feeds them. Are you not worth much more than they?
27 "And who of you by being worried can add a single hour to his life?
28 "And why are you worried about clothing? Observe how the lilies of the field grow; they do not toil nor do they spin,
29 "Yet I say to you that not even Solomon in all his glory clothed himself like one of these.
30 "But if God so clothes the grass of the field, which is alive today and tomorrow is thrown into the furnace, will He not much more clothe you? You of little faith!

31 "Do not worry then, saying, 'What will we eat?' or 'What will we drink?' or 'What will we wear for clothing?'
32 "For the Gentiles eagerly seek all these things; for your heavenly Father knows that you need all these things.
33 "But seek first His kingdom and His righteousness, and all these things will be added to you.
34 "So do not worry about tomorrow; for tomorrow will care for itself. Each day has enough trouble of its own."

Matthew 10

28 "Do not fear those who kill the body but are unable to kill the soul; but rather fear Him who is able to destroy both soul and body in hell.
29 "Are not two sparrows sold for a cent? And yet not one of them will fall to the ground apart from your Father.
30 "But the very hairs of your head are all numbered.
31 "So do not fear; you are more valuable than many sparrows."

Matthew 11

28 "Come to Me, all who are weary and heavy-laden, and I will give you rest.
29 "Take My yoke upon you and learn from Me, for I am gentle and humble in heart, and you will find rest for your souls.
30 "For My yoke is easy and My burden is light."

Luke 12

29 "And do not seek what you will eat and what you will drink, and do not keep worrying.
30 "For all these things the nations of the world eagerly seek; but your Father knows that you need these things.
31 "But seek His kingdom, and these things will be added to you."

Philippians 4

6 Be anxious for nothing, but in everything by prayer and supplication with thanksgiving let your requests be made known to God.
7 And the peace of God, which surpasses all comprehension, will guard your hearts and your minds in Christ Jesus.

11 Not that I speak from want, for I have learned to be content in whatever circumstances I am.

12 I know how to get along with humble means, and I also know how to live in prosperity; in any and every circumstance I have learned the secret of being filled and going hungry, both of having abundance and suffering need.
13 I can do all things through Him who strengthens me.

1 Peter 5

6 Therefore humble yourselves under the mighty hand of God, that He may exalt you at the proper time,
7 Casting all your anxiety on Him, because He cares for you.
10 After you have suffered for a little while, the God of all grace, who called you to His eternal glory in Christ, will Himself perfect, confirm, strengthen and establish you.
11 To Him be dominion forever and ever. Amen.

Compassion

This layer tries to show an important part of Jesus' heart. It shows Jesus' humanity and compassion for us.

Matthew 9

36 Seeing the people, He felt compassion for them, because they were distressed and dispirited like sheep without a shepherd.

Matthew 20

32 And Jesus stopped and called them, and said, "What do you want Me to do for you?"
33 They said to Him, "Lord, we want our eyes to be opened."
34 Moved with compassion, Jesus touched their eyes; and immediately they regained their sight and followed Him.

Mark 1

40 And a leper came to Jesus, beseeching Him and falling on his knees before Him, and saying, "If You are willing, You can make me clean."
41 Moved with compassion, Jesus stretched out His hand and touched him, and said to him, "I am willing; be cleansed."
42 Immediately the leprosy left him and he was cleansed.

Mark 6

34 When Jesus went ashore, He saw a large crowd, and He felt compassion for them because they were like sheep without a shepherd; and He began to teach them many things.

Luke 7

13 When the Lord saw her, He felt compassion for her, and said to her, "Do not weep."
14 And He came up and touched the coffin; and the bearers came to a halt. And He said, "Young man, I say to you, arise!"
15 The dead man sat up and began to speak. And Jesus gave him back to his mother.
16 Fear gripped them all, and they began glorifying God, saying, "A great prophet has arisen among us!" and, "God has visited His people!"

John 11

32 Therefore, when Mary came where Jesus was, she saw Him, and fell at His feet, saying to Him, "Lord, if You had been here, my brother would not have died."
33 When Jesus therefore saw her weeping, and the Jews who came with her also weeping, He was deeply moved in spirit and was troubled,
34 And said, "Where have you laid him?" They said to Him, "Lord, come and see."
35 Jesus wept.
36 So the Jews were saying, "See how He loved him!"

Prayers

This layer brings together a series of scriptures that involves praying. These are beautiful words from Matthew, Paul, Peter, and John that can help to illuminate our Christian life.

Matthew 6

9 "Pray, then, in this way: 'Our Father who is in heaven, Hallowed be Your name.
10 'Your kingdom come. Your will be done, On earth as it is in heaven.
11 'Give us this day our daily bread.
12 'And forgive us our debts, as we also have forgiven our debtors.
13 'And do not lead us into temptation, but deliver us from evil. [For Yours is the kingdom and the power and the glory forever. Amen.]'

1 Corinthians 1

3 Grace to you and peace from God our Father and the Lord Jesus Christ.
4 I thank my God always concerning you for the grace of God which was given you in Christ Jesus,
5 That in everything you were enriched in Him, in all speech and all knowledge,
6 Even as the testimony concerning Christ was confirmed in you,
7 So that you are not lacking in any gift, awaiting eagerly the revelation of our Lord Jesus Christ,
8 Who will also confirm you to the end, blameless in the day of our Lord Jesus Christ.
9 God is faithful, through whom you were called into fellowship with His Son, Jesus Christ ou our Lord.

2 Corinthians 1

2 Grace to you and peace from God our Father and the Lord Jesus Christ.
3 Blessed be the God and Father of our Lord Jesus Christ, the Father of mercies and God of all comfort,

4 Who comforts us in all our affliction so that we will be able to comfort those who are in any affliction with the comfort with which we ourselves are comforted by God.
5 For just as the sufferings of Christ are ours in abundance, so also our comfort is abundant through Christ.
6 But if we are afflicted, it is for your comfort and salvation; or if we are comforted, it is for your comfort, which is effective in the patient enduring of the same sufferings which we also suffer;
7 And our hope for you is firmly grounded, knowing that as you are sharers of our sufferings, so also you are sharers of our comfort.

2 Corinthians 2

14 But thanks be to God, who always leads us in triumph in Christ, and manifests through us the sweet aroma of the knowledge of Him in every place.

Galatians 1

3 Grace to you and peace from God our Father and the Lord Jesus Christ,
4 Who gave Himself for our sins so that He might rescue us from this present evil age, according to the will of our God and Father,
5 To whom be the glory forevermore. Amen.

Ephesians 1

2 Grace to you and peace from God our Father and the Lord Jesus Christ.
3 Blessed be the God and Father of our Lord Jesus Christ, who has blessed us with every spiritual blessing in the heavenly places in Christ,
4 Just as He chose us in Him before the foundation of the world, that we would be holy and blameless before Him. In love
5 He predestined us to adoption as sons through Jesus Christ to Himself, according to the kind intention of His will,
6 To the praise of the glory of His grace, which He freely bestowed on us in the Beloved.
7 In Him we have redemption through His blood, the forgiveness of our trespasses, according to the riches of His grace
8 Which He lavished on us. In all wisdom and insight
9 He made known to us the mystery of His will, according to His kind intention which He purposed in Him
10 With a view to an administration suitable to the fullness of the times, that is, the summing up of all things in Christ, things in the heavens and things on the earth. In Him
11 Also we have obtained an inheritance, having been predestined according to His purpose who works all things after the counsel of His will,
12 To the end that we who were the first to hope in Christ would be to the praise of His glory.
13 In Him, you also, after listening to the message of truth, the gospel of your salvation-- having also believed, you were sealed in Him with the Holy Spirit of promise,
14 Who is given as a pledge of our inheritance, with a view to the redemption of God's own possession, to the praise of His glory.

Ephesians 3

14 For this reason I bow my knees before the Father,
15 From whom every family in heaven and on earth derives its name,
16 That He would grant you, according to the riches of His glory, to be strengthened with power through His Spirit in the inner man,
17 So that Christ may dwell in your hearts through faith; and that you, being rooted and grounded in love,
18 May be able to comprehend with all the saints what is the breadth and length and height and depth,
19 And to know the love of Christ which surpasses knowledge, that you may be filled up to all the fullness of God.
20 Now to Him who is able to do far more abundantly beyond all that we ask or think, according to the power that works within us,

Scriptures   III - 53   *Prayers*

21 To Him be the glory in the church and in Christ Jesus to all generations forever and ever. Amen.

1 Thessalonians 1

2 We give thanks to God always for all of you, making mention of you in our prayers;
3 Constantly bearing in mind your work of faith and labor of love and steadfastness of hope in our Lord Jesus Christ in the presence of our God and Father,
4 Knowing, brethren beloved by God, His choice of you;
5 For our gospel did not come to you in word only, but also in power and in the Holy Spirit and with full conviction; just as you know what kind of men we proved to be among you for your sake.

2 Timothy 4

18 The Lord will rescue me from every evil deed, and will bring me safely to His heavenly kingdom; to Him be the glory forever and ever. Amen.

Hebrews 13

20 Now the God of peace, who brought up from the dead the great Shepherd of the sheep through the blood of the eternal covenant, even Jesus our Lord,
21 Equip you in every good thing to do His will, working in us that which is pleasing in His sight, through Jesus Christ, to whom be the glory forever and ever. Amen.

1 Peter 1

3 Blessed be the God and Father of our Lord Jesus Christ, who according to His great mercy has caused us to be born again to a living hope through the resurrection of Jesus Christ from the dead,
4 To obtain an inheritance which is imperishable and undefiled and will not fade away, reserved in heaven for you,
5 Who are protected by the power of God through faith for a salvation ready to be revealed in the last time.

2 John 1

3 Grace, mercy and peace will be with us, from God the Father and from Jesus Christ, the Son of the Father, in truth and love.

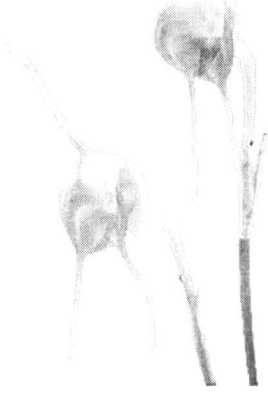

Key for Scriptures

LAYERS	SCRIPTURES & VERSES
LOVE	Matthew 5:44-48 Matthew 22: 37-40 Luke 6:27-36 John 3:16 John 13:1; 13-14; 33-35 John 14: 21; 23 John 15: 9-10 John 16; 27 Romans 5:8 Romans 12:9-21 Romans 13:10 Romans 15:7 1Corinthians 8:3 1Corinthians 13: 4-8; 13 1Corinthians 16:14 Ephesians 5:1-2 2 Thessalonians 3:5 1 Peter 4:8-10 1 John 3:1; 11; 14-18 1 John 4:7-21 2 John 1:6
JESUS' DEITY	Matthew 28:18 Mark 8:29 Mark 14:61-62 Luke 2: 10-14 Luke 8:24-25 Luke 22:19 John 1: 1-5 John 3: 34-36
JESUS' DEITY	John 4: 13-14 John 5: 19-23 John 6: 35-40; 44-69 John 7:38 John 8:12; 24-30; 42-43; 47; 51; 58 John 10: 7-18; 27-30; 37 John 11: 25-26 John 12: 46 John 13:19 John 14:1-3; 6; 10; 28 John 16:28; 33 John 17:1-5; 9-11; 23-26 John 18:37 Acts 2:32-33 1 Corinthians 8:5-6 Philippians 2:5-11 Colossians 1:12-20 1 Timothy 2:5-6 Hebrews 1: 1-14 2 Peter 1:16-18 1 John 2: 22-23 1 John 5:1; 5-6
THE HOLY SPIRIT	Matthew 12:31-32 Luke 3:21-22 John 1:32 John 14:16-17; 26 John 15: 26-27 John 16: 7-9 Acts 2:1-21 Acts 4:31 Acts 8:14-17 Acts 19:6 Romans 8:14-16; 26-27 1 Corinthians 2:10-16 1 Corinthians 12:3-13
GRACE	John 1:17 John 3:17-18 John 5:24 Romans 3:20-25 Romans 4:7-8; 14-17 Romans 5:1-2; 8-21 Romans 6:1-4; 14-18 Romans 7:5-7; 14-25 Romans 8:1-4 Romans 9:30-32 Romans 10:11-13 Romans 11:1-8 2 Corinthians 3:16-18 2 Corinthians 5:17-21 Galatians 2:16-21 Galatians 3:21-28 Galatians 5:13-26 Ephesians 2:1-10; 13-14 Ephesians 6:24 2 Timothy 1:8-9 Hebrews 9:14-17; 22-26 Hebrews 10:26-29 1 Peter 2:23-25 1 Peter 3:18

LAYERS	SCRIPTURES & VERSES
SIN, FORGIVENESS, AND REDEMPTION	Matthew 6:14 Matthew 16:26 Matthew 18:21-22 Mark 9: 43-49 Mark 11:25-26 Luke 5:32 Luke 6:36-37 Luke 15:7-8 Luke 17:3-4 Luke 18:24-25 John 3:5-8 John 8:31; 34 John 9:1-3 John 15:22 Acts 2:38-39 Romans 2:1-5 Romans 13:5-14 1 Corinthians 6:9-11; 15-20 1 Corinthians 8:12 1 Corinthians 10:13 Ephesians 4:22-24; 26 Colossians 3:2-10 1 Timothy 6:12 2 Timothy 4:7-8 Hebrews 4:12-16 Hebrews 12:7-11 James 1:13-15 James 3:16 James 4:17 James 5:19-20 1 Peter 1:23 1 Peter 3:8-12 2 Peter 2:9; 20-21 1 John 1:5-10 1 John 2:7-12; 15-17 1 John 3:4-9 1 John 5:16-20
THE SECOND COMING AND JUDGMENT	Matthew 12:36-37 Matthew 16:27 Matthew 24:21-44 Mark 13:24-37 Luke 12:40 Luke 17:22-37 John 12:48 1 Corinthians 15:51-54 2 Corinthians 5:10 Philippians 3:20-21 1 Thessalonians 1:10 1 Thessalonians 4:13-17 Hebrews 9: 27-28 1 Peter 5:4 2 Peter 3:10-13 Revelation 1:7 Revelation 6:12-17 Revelation 20:11-15 Revelation 21:1-8; 22-27

EXHORTATIONS	Matthew 5:3-11 Matthew 6:19-21 Matthew 7:21 Matthew 10:37 Matthew 15:11 Matthew 18:4; 10; 12-14 Mark 2:27-28 Mark 8: 38 Luke 6:38; 44 Luke 11:33-36 Luke 12:8-9; 51-53 Luke 14:27 Luke 18:29-30 John 8:47 John 12:25-26 John 15:19 John 20:28-29 Acts 16:31 Romans 12:2; 4-8 Romans 13:12 Romans 14:8-9 1 Corinthians 3:7; 16-17 2 Corinthians 7:10 2 Corinthians 12:9-10 Ephesians 6:13-17 Philippians 2:3-4 1 Timothy 6:7-8 2 Timothy 2:19 Hebrews 11:1 Hebrews 12:14-15 Hebrews 13:2-6 James 1:12 James 3:5-12 James 5:12 1 Peter 3:14-15 1 Peter 4:12-14 2 Peter 3:9 1 John 2:25 1 John 4:1-3 2 John 1:10-11 Jude 1:20-25
PETITIONS, MIRACLES, AND FAITH	Matthew 7:7-11 Matthew 8:8-10; 13 Matthew 17:20 Matthew 18:19-20 Matthew 19:26 Matthew 21:21-22 Matthew 26:39-41 Mark 5:27-34 Mark 7:31-35 Mark 11:23-24 Luke 4:40 Luke 5:12-13 Luke 6:19 Luke 7:11-15 Luke 8:41-42; 49-55 Luke 11:8-13 Luke 13:11-13 Luke 17:6 John 11:1-3; 32-44 John 14:13-14

LAYERS	SCRIPTURES & VERSES
PETITIONS, MIRACLES, AND FAITH	John 15:7-8; 16 John 16:23-24 Romans 8:31-32 Hebrews 11:6-11 James 1:2-4; 6-7 James 4:3 James 5:13-16 1 John 5:14-15
WORRIES	Matthew 6:25-34 Matthew 10:28-31 Matthew 11:28-30 Luke 12:29-31 Philippians 4:6-7; 11-13 1 Peter 5:6-7; 10-11
COMPASSION	Matthew 9:36 Matthew 20:32-34 Mark 1:40-42 Mark 6:34 Luke 7:13-16 John 11:32-36
PRAYERS	Matthew 6:9-13 1 Corinthians 1:3-9 2 Corinthians 1:2-7 2 Corinthians: 2:14 Galatians 1:3-5 Ephesians 1:2-14 Ephesians 3:14-21 1 Thessalonians 1:2-5 2 Timothy 4:18 Hebrews 13:20-21 1 Peter 1:3-5 2 John 1:3

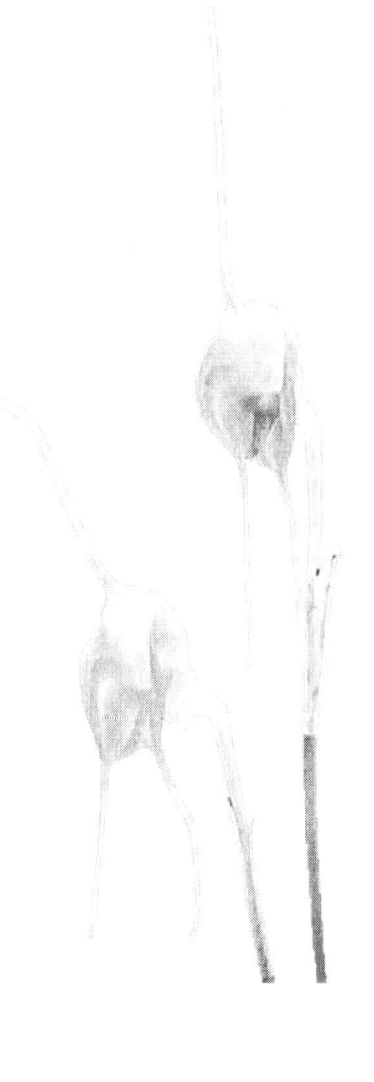

LAYERS from:

- Matthew
- Mark
- Luke
- John

"Therefore I speak to them in parables; because while seeing they do not see, and while hearing they do not hear, nor do they understand."

Matthew 13:13

Fourth Collection

Matthew, Mark, Luke, and John

MATTHEW

Matthew 7

The House on the Rock and on the Sand
Also in Luke 6: 46-49

The basic theme of this parable is that Jesus declares that obedience to His word is the only sure foundation for life. In this parable, Jesus makes a very strong plea for men to listen to His word and "act on them".

24 "Therefore everyone who hears these words of Mine and acts on them, may be compared to a wise man who built his house on the rock.
25 "And the rain fell, and the floods came, and the winds blew and slammed against that house; and yet it did not fall, for it had been founded on the rock.
26 "Everyone who hears these words of Mine and does not act on them, will be like a foolish

man who built his house on the sand.
27 "The rain fell, and the floods came, and the winds blew and slammed against that house; and it fell-- and great was its fall."
28 When Jesus had finished these words, the crowds were amazed at His teaching;
29 For He was teaching them as one having authority, and not as their scribes.

Matthew 13

The Sower
Also in Mark 4:3-20 and Luke 8:4-15

(This parable is explained in Matthew 13:18-24. Text is included below.)

1 That day Jesus went out of the house and was sitting by the sea.
2 And large crowds gathered to Him, so He got into a boat and sat down, and the whole crowd was standing on the beach.
3 And He spoke many things to them in parables, saying, "Behold, the sower went out to sow;
4 And as he sowed, some seeds fell beside the road, and the birds came and ate them up.
5 "Others fell on the rocky places, where they did not have much soil; and immediately they sprang up, because they had no depth of soil.
6 "But when the sun had risen, they were scorched; and because they had no root, they withered away.
7 "Others fell among the thorns, and the thorns came up and choked them out.
8 "And others fell on the good soil and yielded a crop, some a hundredfold, some sixty, and some thirty."

Jesus explains the parable of the Sower:

"Hear then the parable of the sower. "When anyone hears the word of the kingdom and does not understand it, the evil one comes and snatches away what has been sown in his heart. This is the one on whom seed was sown beside the road. "The one on whom seed was sown on the rocky places, this is the man who hears the word and immediately receives it with joy; yet he has no firm root in himself, but is only temporary, and when affliction or persecution arises because of the word, immediately he falls away. "And the one on whom seed was sown among the thorns, this is the man who hears the word, and the worry of the world and the deceitfulness of wealth choke the word, and it becomes unfruitful. "And the one on whom seed was sown on the good soil, this is the man who hears the word and understands it; who indeed bears fruit and brings forth, some a hundredfold, some sixty, and some thirty."

Matthew 13

The Tares

In Palestine, tares were considered the curse of the farmers. In their early stages of growing, farmers cannot distinguish the difference between tares and wheat. However, as they grow, the difference is quite apparent; but, by that time, their roots are so intertwined that the tares, the bad seed, cannot be separated from the wheat, the good seed. With this parable, Jesus reminds us that there always will be a hostile power in the world, seeking to destroy the good seed. He tells us that, for the believer, sometimes it is hard to distinguish who has the good words of God and who doesn't. In Matthew 7:15, Jesus warns us against hostile powers "who come to you in sheep clothing, but inwardly are ravenous wolves". Also in this parable, Jesus reminds us that the time of judgment will come.

24 Jesus presented another parable to them, saying, "The kingdom of heaven may be compared to a man who sowed good seed in his field.
25 "But while his men were sleeping, his enemy came and sowed tares among the wheat, and went away.
26 "But when the wheat sprouted and bore grain, then the tares became evident also.
27 "The slaves of the landowner came and said to him, 'Sir, did you not sow good seed in your field? How then does it have tares?'
28 "And he said to them, 'An enemy has done this!' The slaves said to him, 'Do you want us, then, to go and gather them up?'
29 "But he said, 'No; for while you are gathering

up the tares, you may uproot the wheat with them.

30 'Allow both to grow together until the harvest; and in the time of the harvest I will say to the reapers, "First gather up the tares and bind them in bundles to burn them up; but gather the wheat into my barn."

Matthew 13

The Leaven

Also in Luke 13:21

In Palestine, bread was baked at home. Leaven is a little piece of dough kept over from a previous baking. The introduction of the leaven in the baking causes a transformation in the dough. Unleavened bread is hard, dry, and unappealing. Bread baked with leaven is soft, porous, and tasty. Jesus teaches us that before His coming the Good News regarding the kingdom had not been revealed to men and with His coming there is opportunity to transform our lives.

33 He spoke another parable to them, "The kingdom of heaven is like leaven, which a woman took and hid in three pecks of flour until it was all leavened."
34 All these things Jesus spoke to the crowds in parables, and He did not speak to them without a parable.
35 This was to fulfill what was spoken through the prophet: "I will open my mouth in parables; I will utter things hidden since the foundation of the world."

Matthew 13

The Hidden Treasure

In Palestine, ordinary people used the ground as the safest place to keep their most cherished belongings. Jesus teaches us that man will experience a great joy when he finds the kingdom and that he will give up everything to make the treasure safe and his own. Jesus reminds us that it is worth any sacrifice to enter the kingdom of God.

44 "The kingdom of heaven is like a treasure hidden in the field, which a man found and hid again; and from joy over it he goes and sells all that he has and buys that field."

Matthew 13

The Pearl of Great Price

In the ancient world, men greatly valued good quality pearls. Jesus compares the beauty of the kingdom with a valuable pearl. This parable suggests that finding and accepting the kingdom will bring true happiness and joy, and that after receiving it, men will do anything to retain it.

45 "Again, the kingdom of heaven is like a merchant seeking fine pearls,
46 "And upon finding one pearl of great value, he went and sold all that he had and bought it."

Matthew 13

The Drag Net

The drag net was a method of fishing in Palestine. The net was a great square with cords at each corner, and weighted so that, at rest, it floated in the water. When the boat moved, the net took the shape of a great cone to which all types of fish were drawn. At shore, the catch was separated: useless material was tossed away while the good catch was saved in containers. This parable tells us about he time of judgment and vividly describes the torment of those that are separated from the kingdom.

47 "Again, the kingdom of heaven is like a dragnet cast into the sea, and gathering fish of every kind;
48 "And when it was filled, they drew it up on the beach; and they sat down and gathered the good fish into containers, but the bad they threw away.
49 "So it will be at the end of the age; the angels will come forth and take out the wicked from among the righteous,
50 "And will throw them into the furnace of fire; in that place there will be weeping and gnashing of teeth.
51 "Have you understood all these things?" They said to Him, "Yes."

Matthew 13

The Old Gifts Used in a New Way

This parable refers to the Scribes that have received the teaching of Jesus. The Scribes belonged to the sect of the Pharisees, who supplemented the ancient written Law with the account of their traditions. Sometimes the effects were devastating: scriptures became obscure and their work rendered no positive effects. The Scribes were public teachers and frequently came into confrontation with Jesus. However, some of the Scribes showed themselves friendly to the gospel and its preachers. (Acts 5:34-39 and Acts 23:9) With the coming of Jesus, the old system of belief was renewed. Jesus praises the Scribes that have accepted Him and sees added value in maintaining both, the old and new traditions.

52 And Jesus said to them, "Therefore every scribe who has become a disciple of the kingdom of heaven is like a head of a household, who brings out of his treasure things new and old."
53 When Jesus had finished these parables, He departed from there.

Matthew 18

The Unmerciful Servant

The main concept of this parable is repeated, many times, throughout the New Testament. It is part of the so called "golden rule", "do unto others as you would have them do unto you". The wicked slave after being forgiven by his master, is incapable of forgiving his own debtors. This action receives great condemnation on the part of his master. The behavior of the slave opposes the biblical principle stated in Matthew 7:12 and Luke 6:32: "Therefore, however you want people to treat you, so treat them, for this is the Law of the Prophets".

23 "For this reason the kingdom of heaven may be compared to a king who wished to settle accounts with his slaves.
24 "When he had begun to settle them, one who owed him ten thousand talents was brought to him.
25 "But since he did not have the means to repay, his lord commanded him to be sold, along with his wife and children and all that he had, and repayment to be made.
26 "So the slave fell to the ground and prostrated himself before him, saying, 'Have patience with me and I will repay you everything.'
27 "And the lord of that slave felt compassion and released him and forgave him the debt.
28 "But that slave went out and found one of his fellow slaves who owed him a hundred denarii; and he seized him and began to choke him, saying, 'Pay back what you owe.'
29 "So his fellow slave fell to the ground and began to plead with him, saying, 'Have patience with me and I will repay you.'
30 "But he was unwilling and went and threw him in prison until he should pay back what was owed.

31 "So when his fellow slaves saw what had happened, they were deeply grieved and came and reported to their lord all that had happened.
32 "Then summoning him, his lord said to him, 'You wicked slave, I forgave you all that debt because you pleaded with me.
33 'Should you not also have had mercy on your fellow slave, in the same way that I had mercy on you?'
34 "And his lord, moved with anger, handed him over to the torturers until he should repay all that was owed him.
35 "My heavenly Father will also do the same to you, if each of you does not forgive his brother from your heart."

Matthew 20

The Laborers in the Vineyard

This parable contains truth which goes to the very heart of the Christian faith. All men are precious to God and the particular time when they come to Christ is irrelevant. What matters is that they found their way. In this parable the master pays the workers for coming to work and not for the time or extent of their labor. The concept that God has the divine right to choose and bless His elect, permeates throughout this parable.

1 "For the kingdom of heaven is like a landowner who went out early in the morning to hire laborers for his vineyard.
2 "When he had agreed with the laborers for a denarius for the day, he sent them into his vineyard.
3 "And he went out about the third hour and saw others standing idle in the market place;
4 And to those he said, 'You also go into the vineyard, and whatever is right I will give you.' And so they went.
5 "Again he went out about the sixth and the ninth hour, and did the same thing.
6 "And about the eleventh hour he went out and found others standing around; and he said to them, 'Why have you been standing here idle all day long?'
7 "They said to him, 'Because no one hired us.' He said to them, 'You go into the vineyard too.'
8 "When evening came, the owner of the vineyard said to his foreman, 'Call the laborers and pay them their wages, beginning with the last group to the first.'
9 "When those hired about the eleventh hour came, each one received a denarius.
10 "When those hired first came, they thought that they would receive more; but each of them also received a denarius.
11 "When they received it, they grumbled at the landowner,
12 Saying, 'These last men have worked only one hour, and you have made them equal to us who have borne the burden and the scorching heat of the day.'

13 "But he answered and said to one of them, 'Friend, I am doing you no wrong; did you not agree with me for a denarius?
14 'Take what is yours and go, but I wish to give to this last man the same as to you.
15 'Is it not lawful for me to do what I wish with what is my own? Or is your eye envious because I am generous?'
16 "So the last shall be first, and the first last."

Matthew 21

The Two Sons

This parable deals with two very imperfect people; however, the son that in the end obeys was better than the other. This parable has a message to believers: Christianity should be based on performance and not on false promises.

28 "But what do you think? A man had two sons, and he came to the first and said, 'Son, go work today in the vineyard.'
29 "And he answered, 'I will not'; but afterward he regretted it and went.
30 "The man came to the second and said the same thing; and he answered, 'I will, sir'; but he did not go.
31 "Which of the two did the will of his father?" They said, "The first." Jesus said to them, "Truly I say to you that the tax collectors and prostitutes will get into the kingdom of God before you."

Matthew 21

The Vineyard
Also in Mark 12:1-11 and Luke 20:9-18

The Jewish nation as the vineyard of God was a familiar prophetic picture. This parable comprises four basic concepts: It speaks of free will: the landowner left the vine-growers to do the task as they liked. It speaks of patience: the landowner sent different messengers to reason with the vine-growers. It speaks of judgment: in the end the landowner took the vineyard from the cultivators and gave it to others. It speaks of accountability: men will finally face a day when they will answer for their actions. This parable ends with a quote from Psalm 118:22: "The stone which the builders rejected, this became the chief corner stone". This suggests that Christ was aware that many had rejected Him but He was also certain that at the end, He will come with glory and reign among the nations. This parable also bears a promise of deliverance to the Gentiles regarding the kingdom of God.

33 "Listen to another parable. There was a landowner who planted a vineyard and put a wall around it and dug a wine press in it, and build a tower, and rented it out to vine-growers and went on a journey.
34 "When the harvest time approached, he sent his slaves to the vine-growers to receive his produce.
35 "The vine-growers took his slaves and beat one, and killed another, and stoned a third.
36 "Again he sent another group of slaves larger than the first; and they did the same thing to them.
37 "But afterward he sent his son to them, saying, 'They will respect my son.'
38 "But when the vine-growers saw the son, they said among themselves, 'This is the heir; come, let us kill him and seize his inheritance.'
39 "They took him, and threw him out of the vineyard and killed him.
40 "Therefore when the owner of the vineyard comes, what will he do to those vine-growers?"
41 They said to Him, "He will bring those wretches to a wretched end, and will rent out the vineyard to other vine-growers who will pay him the proceeds at the proper seasons."
42 Jesus said to them, "Did you never read in the Scriptures, 'The stone which the builders rejected, this became the chief corner stone; this came about from the Lord, and it is marvelous in our eyes'??
43 "Therefore I say to you, the kingdom of God will be taken away from you and given to a people, producing the fruit of it.
44 "And he who falls on this stone will be broken to pieces; but on whomever it falls, it will scatter him like dust."
45 When the chief priests and the Pharisees

heard His parables, they understood that He was speaking about them.

46 When they sought to seize Him, they feared the people, because they considered Him to be a prophet.

Matthew 22

The Marriage of the King's Son

In this parable, Jesus alludes to the fact that Jews, as the chosen people, had been constantly invited to the "feast." However, when Christ offered to be part of the New Covenant, they openly rejected the invitation. An invitation was then offered to the Gentiles who never dreamed of participating in the kingdom. This parable reminds us that the invitation of God is a joyful one. It shows us that God is concerned with what we miss by not being part of His kingdom and not on how we will be punished if we miss this opportunity. This parable shows us that we need to wear new garments when we accept the Lord, that is, that we cannot continue our present life when we come to Christ.

1 Jesus spoke to them again in parables, saying,
2 "The kingdom of heaven may be compared to a king who gave a wedding feast for his son.
3 "And he sent out his slaves to call those who had been invited to the wedding feast, and they were unwilling to come.
4 "Again he sent out other slaves saying, 'Tell those who have been invited, "Behold, I have prepared my dinner; my oxen and my fattened livestock are all butchered and everything is ready; come to the wedding feast."'
5 "But they paid no attention and went their way, one to his own farm, another to his business,
6 And the rest seized his slaves and mistreated them and killed them.
7 "But the king was enraged, and he sent his armies and destroyed those murderers and set their city on fire.
8 "Then he said to his slaves, 'The wedding is ready, but those who were invited were not worthy.
9 'Go therefore to the main highways, and as many as you find there, invite to the wedding feast.'
10 "Those slaves went out into the streets and gathered together all they found, both evil and good; and the wedding hall was filled with dinner guests.
11 "But when the king came in to look over the dinner guests, he saw a man there who was not dressed in wedding clothes,
12 And he said to him, 'Friend, how did you come in here without wedding clothes?' And the man was speechless.
13 "Then the king said to the servants, 'Bind him hand and foot, and throw him into the outer darkness; in that place there will be weeping and gnashing of teeth.'
14 "For many are called, but few are chosen."

Matthew 25

The Ten Virgins

In Palestine, a wedding was a great occasion and celebration that involved the whole village. The bridal party, usually comprised of ten virgins, was to be on alert since the exact day of the wedding was imprecise and dependent on the time of the arrival of the bridegroom. The bridegroom could come unexpectedly and in the middle of the night. With the parable Jesus reminded the Jews that they were the chosen people and for centuries had been preparing to receive the Messiah. However, when Christ came, they were totally unprepared and were shut out. This parable also urges those who have not accepted Christ to do so before it is too late. It tells all believers that it is easy to defer our responsibilities with God until there is no time left for amendments. It assures us that it will be an hour of final judgment.

1 "Then the kingdom of heaven will be comparable to ten virgins, who took their lamps and went out to meet the bridegroom.
2 "Five of them were foolish, and five were prudent.
3 "For when the foolish took their lamps, they took no oil with them,
4 But the prudent took oil in flasks along with their lamps.

5 "Now while the bridegroom was delaying, they all got drowsy and began to sleep.
6 "But at midnight there was a shout, 'Behold, the bridegroom! Come out to meet him.'
7 "Then all those virgins rose and trimmed their lamps.
8 "The foolish said to the prudent, 'Give us some of your oil, for our lamps are going out.'
9 "But the prudent answered, 'No, there will not be enough for us and you too; go instead to the dealers and buy some for yourselves.'
10 "And while they were going away to make the purchase, the bridegroom came, and those who were ready went in with him to the wedding feast; and the door was shut.
11 "Later the other virgins also came, saying, 'Lord, lord, open up for us.'
12 "But he answered, 'Truly I say to you, I do not know you.'
13 "Be on the alert then, for you do not know the day nor the hour."

Matthew 25

The Talents

The talent was not a coin; it was a "weight". Its value depended on whether the coinage involved was copper, gold or silver. This parable was originally directed to the Scribes and Pharisees and their rigid views regarding salvation, works, and the Law. However, this parable has a very clear application to modern Christianity and our relationship with God. It tells us that God gives man different gifts and that it is of extreme importance how we use these gifts to honor Him. The parable also tells us that whatever talent we have, small or great, we must make the best use of it to serve God and that, as a result of this action, God will bless us.

14 "For it is just like a man about to go on a journey, who called his own slaves and entrusted his possessions to them.
15 "To one he gave five talents, to another, two, and to another, one, each according to his own ability; and he went on his journey.
16 "Immediately the one who had received the five talents went and traded with them, and gained five more talents.
17 "In the same manner the one who had received the two talents gained two more.
18 "But he who received the one talent went away, and dug a hole in the ground and hid his master's money.
19 "Now after a long time the master of those slaves came and settled accounts with them.
20 "The one who had received the five talents came up and brought five more talents, saying, 'Master, you entrusted five talents to me. See, I have gained five more talents.'
21 "His master said to him, 'Well done, good and faithful slave. You were faithful with a few things, I will put you in charge of many things; enter into the joy of your master.'

22 "Also the one who had received the two talents came up and said, 'Master, you entrusted two talents to me. See, I have gained two more talents.'
23 "His master said to him, 'Well done, good and faithful slave. You were faithful with a few things, I will put you in charge of many things; enter into the joy of your master.'
24 "And the one also who had received the one talent came up and said, 'Master, I knew you to be a hard man, reaping where you did not sow and gathering where you scattered no seed.
25 'And I was afraid, and went away and hid your talent in the ground. See, you have what is yours.'
26 "But his master answered and said to him, 'You wicked, lazy slave, you knew that I reap where I did not sow and gather where I scattered no seed.
27 'Then you ought to have put my money in the bank, and on my arrival I would have received my money back with interest.
28 'Therefore take away the talent from him, and give it to the one who has the ten talents.'
29 "For to everyone who has, more shall be given, and he will have an abundance; but from the one who does not have, even what he does have shall be taken away.
30 "Throw out the worthless slave into the outer darkness; in that place there will be weeping and gnashing of teeth."

Matthew 25

The Sheep and Goats

This parable starts with an opening that alludes to the Second Coming of Christ. The rest of the parable centers on one theme: God will judge us in accordance with our commitment to help others in need. It teaches us to help our fellow brothers and sisters in simple matters and when they are overtaken by great difficulties. It tells us that our help should be unselfish and centered in the good teaching of Jesus and that to fail this mandate will lead to eternal condemnation.

31 "But when the Son of Man comes in His glory, and all the angels with Him, then He will sit on His glorious throne.
32 "All the nations will be gathered before Him; and He will separate them from one another, as the shepherd separates the sheep from the goats;
33 "And He will put the sheep on His right, and the goats on the left.
34 "Then the King will say to those on His right, 'Come, you who are blessed of My Father, inherit the kingdom prepared for you from the foundation of the world.
35 'For I was hungry, and you gave Me something to eat; I was thirsty, and

Parables   *Matthew*

you gave Me something to drink; I was a stranger, and you invited Me in;
36 Naked, and you clothed Me; I was sick, and you visited Me; I was in prison, and you came to Me.'
37 "Then the righteous will answer Him, 'Lord, when did we see You hungry, and feed You, or thirsty, and give You something to drink?
38 'And when did we see You a stranger, and invite You in, or naked, and clothe You?
39 'When did we see You sick, or in prison, and come to You?'
40 "The King will answer and say to them, 'Truly I say to you, to the extent that you did it to one of these brothers of Mine, even the least of them, you did it to Me.'
41 "Then He will also say to those on His left, 'Depart from Me, accursed ones, into the eternal fire which has been prepared for the devil and his angels;
42 For I was hungry, and you gave Me nothing to eat; I was thirsty, and you gave Me nothing to drink;
43 I was a stranger, and you did not invite Me in; naked, and you did not clothe Me; sick, and in prison, and you did not visit Me.'
44 "Then they themselves also will answer, 'Lord, when did we see You hungry, or thirsty, or a stranger, or naked, or sick, or in prison, and did not take care of You?'
45 "Then He will answer them, 'Truly I say to you, to the extent that you did not do it to one of the least of these, you did not do it to Me.'
46 "These will go away into eternal punishment, but the righteous into eternal life."

MARK

Mark 4

The Seed Growing Secretly

This parable refers to the limited understanding human beings have on how the kingdom of God works and highlights the fact that no man has ever possessed the secrets of the kingdom. It tells that with the advent of Jesus, we may be able to recognize the glory of God. In this parable, as in many others, our Lord Jesus uses an illustration from nature to describe the coming and expansion of the kingdom. It encourages us to accept by faith those things related to the kingdom that are beyond our human understanding.

26 And He was saying, "The kingdom of God is like a man who casts seed upon the soil;
27 And he goes to bed at night and gets up by day, and the seed sprouts and grows-- how, he himself does not know.
28 "The soil produces crops by itself; first the blade, then the head, then the mature grain in the head.
29 "But when the crop permits, he immediately puts in the sickle, because the harvest has come."

Mark 4

The Mustard Seed
Also in Matthew 13:31-32 and Luke 13:18-20

For the Jews, the mustard seed stood for the smallest possible thing. In the Old Testament one of the ways to describe a great empire was through the symbol of a tree where tributary nations found shelter and protection. This parable departs from these two ancient themes. It is another of Jesus' parables associating the kingdom with nature. This parable suggests that the kingdom will grow and will come to us in its final glory and form when Christ returns. It shows that the kingdom is always watchful and provides protection for those who follow Jesus. It tells us that we should not be dismayed by small beginnings and should keep our focus and faith in God. This parable foretells that the future Church of Christ will be like a tree where all nations meet.

30 And He said, "How shall we picture the kingdom of God, or by what parable shall we present it?
31 "It is like a mustard seed, which, when sown upon the soil, though it is smaller than all the seeds that are upon the soil,
32 Yet when it is sown, it grows up and becomes larger than all the garden plants and forms large branches; so that the birds of the air can nest under its shade."
33 With many such parables He was speaking the word to them, so far as they were able to hear it;
34 And He did not speak to them without a parable; but He was explaining everything privately to His own disciples.

Mark 13

The Fig Tree
Also in Matthew 24:32-35, and Luke 21:29-33

This parable makes direct reference to the Second Coming. It indicates that as a man can tell by the signs of nature when the summer is coming, in the same way, he can tell by the signs of the world when the Second Coming is near. This parable, similar to the ones included in Matthew and Luke, seems to imply that the Second Coming will occur within the lifetime of the generation that walked with Jesus. In this parable, Jesus used the word generation referring to a body of living beings in the line of direct descent from an ancestor and that He used the term untied to any specific time frame.

28 "Now learn the parable from the fig tree; when its branch has already become tender and puts forth its leaves, you know that summer is near.
29 "Even so, you too, when you see these things happening, recognize that He is near, right at the door.
30 "Truly I say to you, this generation will not pass away until all these things take place.
31 "Heaven and earth will pass away, but My words will not pass away.

Mark 13

Watchfulness

This parable commands us to be alert since Jesus will come again. It tells us that the Spirit of God assigns us tasks to perform and that it is our responsibility to carry them out according to our abilities. It says that we should not be unprepared at the time of the final judgment.

33 "Take heed, keep on the alert; for you do not know when the appointed time will come.
34 "It is like a man away on a journey, who upon leaving his house and putting his slaves in charge, assigning to each one his task, also commanded the doorkeeper to stay on the alert.
35 "Therefore, be on the alert-- for you do not know when the master of the house is coming, whether in the evening, at midnight, or when the rooster crows, or in the morning--
36 In case he should come suddenly and find you asleep.
37 "What I say to you I say to all, 'Be on the alert!'

LUKE

Luke 5

The New Cloth and an Old Garment
Also in Matthew 9: 16 and Mark 2: 21
The New Wine in Old Bottles
Also in Matthew 9:17 and Mark 2:22

These are two parables in one. Through these parables, Jesus warns us against our limitation to accommodate the new and our ability to cling to the old. A new garment placed in an old will tear the old. Bottles in Palestine were made of skin. When new wine was put into an old bottle, the skin, which was dry and hard, would burst. These parables denounced the religious establishment in the time of Christ. The attachment for old traditions made them miss the coming of Jesus.

36 And He was also telling them a parable: "No one tears a piece of cloth from a new garment and puts it on an old garment; otherwise he will both tear the new, and the piece from the new will not match the old.
37 "And no one puts new wine into old wineskins; otherwise the new wine will burst the skins and it will be spilled out, and the skins will be ruined.
38 "But new wine must be put into fresh wineskins.
39 "And no one, after drinking old wine wishes for new; for he says, 'The old is good enough.'"

Luke 7

The Two Debtors

This parable speaks of the abundant grace of God and his willingness to forgive helpless sinners. Jesus reiterates this concept in Luke 5:32. He tells us that he has not come "to call the righteous but sinners to repentance."

41 "A moneylender had two debtors: one owed five hundred denarii, and the other fifty.
42 "When they were unable to repay, he graciously forgave them both. So which of them will love him more?"
43 Simon answered and said, "I suppose the one whom he forgave more." And He said to him, "You have judged correctly."

Luke 8

The Candle Under a Bushel
Also in Matthew 5:14-16; Mark 4:21-23

In this parable Jesus is equated to "light." This is done many times throughout the New Testament. In John 8:12, Jesus said: "I am the Light of the world; he who follows Me will not walk in darkness but will have the Light of life." In John 3:20, Jesus warned us that "everyone who does evil hates the Light, and does not come to the Light for fear that his deeds will be exposed." In this parable, Jesus tells the religious institutions to avoid secrets, and instead, be transparent. It invites us to use our discernment when listening to the world.

16 "Now no one after lighting a lamp covers it over with a container, or puts it under a bed; but he puts it on a lampstand, so that those who come in may see the light.
17 "For nothing is hidden that will not become evident, nor anything secret that will not be known and come to light.
18 "So take care how you listen; for whoever has, to him more shall be given; and whoever does not have, even what he thinks he has shall be taken away from him."

Luke 10

The Good Samaritan

This is one of the best known parables in the New Testament. Its main focus is part of the great commandment that Jesus gave us: "You shall love your neighbor as yourself". (Matthew 22:39) There are four main characters in this parable: the traveller, the priest, the Levite, and the Samaritan. Help to the injured traveller must had been expected from the priest and the Levite. However, only the Samaritan offered assistance and turned this offer into action. The fact that the Jews did not deal with Samaritans and that help came from somebody outside the Jewish faith, is what makes this story striking. Repeatedly, Jesus told us to love our neighbors. In Luke 6: 32 Jesus said; "If you love those who love you, what credit is that to you? For even sinners love those who love them." The Samaritan of our story, not only loved his neighbor but helped a person that might have wronged him in the past. This parable comprise all the main principles of Christianity: love, grace, and forgiveness.

30 Jesus replied and said, "A man was going down from Jerusalem to Jericho, and fell among robbers, and they stripped him and beat him, and went away leaving him half dead.

31 "And by chance a priest was going down on that road, and when he saw him, he passed by on the other side.

32 "Likewise a Levite also, when he came to the place and saw him, passed by on the other side.

33 "But a Samaritan, who was on a journey, came upon him; and when he saw him, he felt compassion,

34 And came to him and bandaged up his wounds, pouring oil and wine on them; and he put him on his own beast, and brought him to an inn and took care of him.

35 "On the next day he took out two denarii and gave them to the innkeeper and said, 'Take care of him; and whatever more you spend, when I return I will repay you.'

36 "Which of these three do you think proved to be a neighbor to the man who fell into the robbers' hands?"

37 And he said, "The one who showed mercy toward him." Then Jesus said to him, "Go and do the same."

Luke 11

The Importunate Friend at Midnight

The center theme of this parable is prayer. Matthew 7:7 tells us: "Ask, and it will be given to you; seek, and you will find; knock, and it will be opened to you". The fascinating part of this parable is that the favor was granted mainly as a result of the "persistence" of the petitioner.

5 Then He said to them, "Suppose one of you has a friend, and goes to him at midnight and says to him, 'Friend, lend me three loaves;
6 For a friend of mine has come to me from a journey, and I have nothing to set before him';
7 And from inside he answers and says, 'Do not bother me; the door has already been shut and my children and I are in bed; I cannot get up and give you anything.'
8 "I tell you, even though he will not get up and give him anything because he is his friend, yet because of his persistence he will get up and give him as much as he needs.

Luke 12

The Rich Fool

Jesus spoke this parable to those who have an abundant supply of possessions. There are several features that distinguish the main character of the parable. He never saw beyond himself; he never saw beyond the present day; he forgot that God was the one in control of his life; and he had little regard for his soul after death. In Matthew 6:19-21, the Lord tells us "Do not store up for yourselves treasures on earth, where moth and rust destroy, and where thieves break in and steal. But store up for yourselves treasures in heaven, where neither moth nor rust destroys and where thieves do not break in or steal; for where your treasure is, there your heart will be also."

16 And He told them a parable, saying, "The land of a rich man was very productive.
17 "And he began reasoning to himself, saying, 'What shall I do, since I have no place to store my crops?'
18 "Then he said, 'This is what I will do: I will tear down my barns and build larger ones, and there I will store all my grain and my goods.
19 'And I will say to my soul, "Soul, you have many goods laid up for many years to come; take your ease, eat, drink and be merry."'
20 "But God said to him, 'You fool! This very night your soul is required of you; and now who will own what you have prepared?'
21 "So is the man who stores up treasure for himself, and is not rich toward God."

Luke 12

The Servants Watching

This parable has three separate but intertwined meanings: it speaks of the Second Coming of Jesus; it speaks of our need to be ready; and it tells us about the transformation we experience when we receive Christ. Jesus, in this parable as well as in many other parts of the New Testament, emphasizes, over and over, the need to be prepared for His return.

35 "Be dressed in readiness, and keep your lamps lit.
36 "Be like men who are waiting for their master when he returns from the wedding feast, so that they may immediately open the door to him when he comes and knocks.
37 "Blessed are those slaves whom the master will find on the alert when he comes; truly I say to you, that he will gird himself to serve, and have them recline at the table, and will come up and wait on them.
38 "Whether he comes in the second watch, or even in the third, and finds them so, blessed are those slaves.
39 "But be sure of this, that if the head of the house had known at what hour the thief was coming, he would not have allowed his house to be broken into.
40 "You too, be ready; for the Son of Man is coming at an hour that you do not expect."

Luke 12

The Steward

This parable has similar meaning as the parable in Luke 12:30-40. It speaks of the Second Coming of Jesus and of our need to be ready. However, different from the other parables, this one focuses on sin, punishment, and final judgment. The last verse states that those "who did not know" will receive less slashes than those who knew that the master was coming and did not get ready. This central theme is found several times in the New Testament. In John 15:22, the Lord said: "If I had not come and spoken to them, they would not have sin, but now they have no excuse for their sin." In this parable, Jesus regarded the coming of His kingdom as a time of judgment.

42 And the Lord said, "Who then is the faithful and sensible steward, whom his master will put in charge of his servants, to give them their rations at the proper time?
43 "Blessed is that slave whom his master finds so doing when he comes.
44 "Truly I say to you that he will put him in charge of all his possessions.
45 "But if that slave says in his heart, 'My master will be a long time in coming,' and begins to beat the slaves, both men and women, and to eat and drink and get drunk;
46 The master of that slave will come on a day when he does not expect him and at an hour he does not know, and will cut him in pieces, and assign him a place with the unbelievers.
47 "And that slave who knew his master's will and did not get ready or act in accord with his will, will receive many lashes,
48 "But the one who did not know it, and committed deeds worthy of a flogging, will receive but few. From everyone who has been given much, much will be required; and to whom they entrusted much, of him they will ask all the more.

Luke 13

The Fig Tree in the Vineyard

This parable combines grace, mercy, and warnings. The parable teaches that if we do not produce fruits, our lives are senseless. It also teaches us that the Lord is patient, full of grace, and that He will give us time to turn around our lives and come to Him. In this parable, Jesus perceives himself as judge and will demand that we will be cut off if we persist in carrying out a life outside His grace. This parable has a parallel story in the New Testament. "When Jesus was traveling with His disciples he saw a fig tree by the road. "He came to it and found nothing on it except leaves only; and He said to it, "No longer shall there ever be any fruit from you." And at once the fig tree withered." (Matthew 21:19)

6 And He began telling this parable: "A man had a fig tree which had been planted in his vineyard; and he came looking for fruit on it and did not find any.
7 "And he said to the vineyard-keeper, 'Behold, for three years I have come looking for fruit on this fig tree without finding any. Cut it down! Why does it even use up the ground?'
8 "And he answered and said to him, 'Let it alone, sir, for this year too, until I dig around it and put in fertilizer;
9 And if it bears fruit next year, fine; but if not, cut it down.'

Luke 14

The Great Supper

In Palestine, when a man made a feast, the day was announced beforehand and invitations circulated days before; however, the exact time was not announced. The day of the feast, the servants were sent out to notify the guest of the exact time of the celebration. This might have been what Jesus had in mind when He told this parable. This parable is directed at the Jewish people who refused God's invitation to participate in the new covenant. It was also directed at the Gentiles by expressing that with the advent of Christ we are partakers of the good news and are part of the feast.

16 But He said to him, "A man was giving a big dinner, and he invited many;
17 And at the dinner hour he sent his slave to say to those who had been invited, 'Come; for everything is ready now.'
18 "But they all alike began to make excuses. The first one said to him, 'I have bought a piece of land and I need to go out and look at it; please consider me excused.'
19 "Another one said, 'I have bought five yoke of oxen, and I am going to try them out; please consider me excused.'
20 "Another one said, 'I have married a wife, and for that reason I cannot come.'
21 "And the slave came back and reported this to his master. Then the head of the household became angry and said to his slave, 'Go out at once into the streets and lanes of the city and bring in here the poor and crippled and blind and lame.'
22 "And the slave said, 'Master, what you commanded has been done, and still there is room.'
23 "And the master said to the slave, 'Go out into the highways and along the hedges, and compel them to come in, so that my house may be filled.
24 'For I tell you, none of those men who were invited shall taste of my dinner.'

Luke 14

Building a Tower and a King Going to War

With this parable, Jesus is telling us of the possible cost of following Him. He tells us that either when building a tower or planning a battle, it is required to consider costs. In Matthew 10:34-36, Jesus warned us about the potential price we may pay if we decide to follow him: "I did not come to bring peace, but a sword. "For I came to set a man against his father, and a daughter against her mother, and a daughter-in-law against her mother-in-law; And a man's enemies will be the members of his household."

28 "For which one of you, when he wants to build a tower, does not first sit down and calculate the cost to see if he has enough to complete it?
29 "Otherwise, when he has laid a foundation and is not able to finish, all who observe it begin to ridicule him,
30 Saying, 'This man began to build and was not able to finish.'
31 "Or what king, when he sets out to meet another king in battle, will not first sit down and consider whether he is strong enough with ten thousand men to encounter the one coming against him with twenty thousand?
32 "Or else, while the other is still far away, he sends a delegation and asks for terms of peace.
33 "So then, none of you can be My disciple who does not give up all his own possessions."

Luke

Luke 15

The Lost Sheep
Also in Matthew 18:12-14

This is one of the most lovely parables in the New Testament. It clearly reflects the great love that Jesus has for us. In the time of Jesus, it was an offence for the Scribes and Pharisees to associate with sinners. Jesus responded with this parable. In this parable, Jesus tells of the joy in heaven over one sinner that repents. The numbers used in this parable are staggering. The parable suggests that the shepherd leaves behind ninety-nine sheep to rescue one. The setting for this parable is also perplexing. In Palestine, sheep used to pasture in narrow and dangerous plateaux, surrounded by wild cliffs and the desert. In following the lost sheep the shepherd faced this terrible landscape and was exposed to wild animals. We can say for certain, that the Good Shepherd loves the sheep that never go stray, but that He is willing to go a great length to rescue the lost one. He will rejoice when he brings it back home.

2 Both the Pharisees and the scribes began to grumble, saying, "This man receives sinners and eats with them."
3 So He told them this parable, saying,
4 "What man among you, if he has a hundred sheep and has lost one of them, does not leave the ninety-nine in the open pasture and go after the one which is lost until he finds it?
5 "When he has found it, he lays it on his shoulders, rejoicing.
6 "And when he comes home, he calls together his friends and his neighbors, saying to them, 'Rejoice with me, for I have found my sheep which was lost!'
7 "I tell you that in the same way, there will be more joy in heaven over one sinner who repents than over ninety-nine righteous persons who need no repentance."

Luke 15

The Lost Piece of Silver

Typically, a home in Palestine has poor lighting, lit only by a mid-size circular window. The floor was beaten earth covered with dried reed and rushes. It might have been difficult to search and find a lost coin. The main focus of this parable is the joy felt by the woman when she found the lost coin. Rescuing the lost souls was a new and difficult concept to grasp by the religious institutions. Jesus settles the matter in Luke 5:32: "I have not come to call the righteous but sinners to repentance."

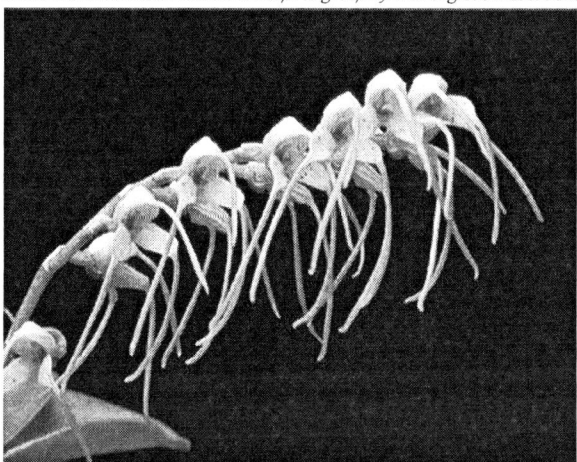

8 "Or what woman, if she has ten silver coins and loses one coin, does not light a lamp and sweep the house and search carefully until she finds it?
9 "When she has found it, she calls together her friends and neighbors, saying, 'Rejoice with me, for I have found the coin which I had lost!'
10 "In the same way, I tell you, there is joy in the

presence of the angels of God over one sinner who repents."

Luke 15

The Prodigal Son

This parable describes, in a lovely manner, the love and forgiveness that a father has for a lost son. It is clear that this parable describes the love that Our Father in heaven has for us. The parable of the Prodigal Son has three main characters. The lovely father, who gave free will to his children to shape their own destiny and unconditionally forgives when they go astray; the lost son who unwisely spends his fortune and returns home; and the second son who has served his father faithfully for many years and does not understand how his father can rejoice over the return of his sinful brother. The climax of this story is introduced by the monologue of the lost son prior to arriving home. By then, the son is ready to humble himself in front of his father. This part of the story is followed by the father welcoming him with unconditional love. In Luke 15:7, Jesus reminds us that there "will be more joy in heaven over one sinner who repents than over ninety-nine righteous persons".

11 And He said, "A man had two sons.
12 "The younger of them said to his father, 'Father, give me the share of the estate that falls to me.' So he divided his wealth between them.
13 "And not many days later, the younger son gathered everything together and went on a journey into a distant country, and there he squandered his estate with loose living.
14 "Now when he had spent everything, a severe famine occurred in that country, and he began to be impoverished.
15 "So he went and hired himself out to one of the citizens of that country, and he sent him into his fields to feed swine.
16 "And he would have gladly filled his stomach with the pods that the swine were eating, and no one was giving anything to him.
17 "But when he came to his senses, he said, 'How many of my father's hired men have more than enough bread, but I am dying here with hunger!
18 'I will get up and go to my father, and will say to him, "Father, I have sinned against heaven, and in your sight;
19 I am no longer worthy to be called your son; make me as one of your hired men."'
20 "So he got up and came to his father. But while he was still a long way off, his father saw him and felt compassion for him, and ran and embraced him and kissed him.
21 "And the son said to him, 'Father, I have sinned against heaven and in your sight; I am no longer worthy to be called your son.'
22 "But the father said to his slaves, 'Quickly bring out the best robe and put it on him, and put a ring on his hand and sandals on his feet;
23 And bring the fattened calf, kill it, and let us eat and celebrate;
24 For this son of mine was dead and has come to life again; he was lost and has been found.' And they began to celebrate.
25 "Now his older son was in the field, and when he came and approached the house, he heard music and dancing.
26 "And he summoned one of the servants and began inquiring what these things could be.
27 "And he said to him, 'Your brother has come, and your father has killed the fattened calf because he has received him back safe and sound.'
28 "But he became angry and was not willing to go in; and his father came out and began pleading with him.
29 "But he answered and said to his father, 'Look! For so many years I have been serving you and I have never neglected a command of yours; and yet you have never given me a young goat, so that I might celebrate with my friends;
30 But when this son of yours came, who has devoured your wealth with prostitutes, you killed the fattened calf for him.'
31 "And he said to him, 'Son, you have always been with me, and all that is mine is yours.
32 'But we had to celebrate and rejoice, for this brother of yours was dead and has begun to live, and was lost and has been found.'

Luke 16

The Unjust Steward

In this parable we are dealing with very imperfect characters. The manager reduced the rent of his master's debtors in order to gain their favor; the debtors agreed to steal from the master by accepting to pay a reduced rent; and the master praised the manager for acting shrewd. However, this parable has wonderful lessons. It teaches that we need to pay attention to the things of God as the unbelievers pay attention to the things of the world; it tells us that material possessions should be used for the benefit and advancement of the kingdom; it conveys that a man should be willing to undertake the smallest task for God; it asserts that God will only trust us if we make effective use of our resources; and it reveals that a man will find himself in great conflict trying to serve God and the world.

1 Now He was also saying to the disciples, "There was a rich man who had a manager, and this manager was reported to him as squandering his possessions.
2 "And he called him and said to him, 'What is this I hear about you? Give an accounting of your management, for you can no longer be manager.'
3 "The manager said to himself, 'What shall I do, since my master is taking the management away from me? I am not strong enough to dig; I am ashamed to beg.
4 'I know what I shall do, so that when I am removed from the management people will welcome me into their homes.'
5 "And he summoned each one of his master's debtors, and he began saying to the first, 'How much do you owe my master?'
6 "And he said, 'A hundred measures of oil.' And he said to him, 'Take your bill, and sit down quickly and write fifty.'
7 "Then he said to another, 'And how much do you owe?' And he said, 'A hundred measures of wheat.' He said to him, 'Take your bill, and write eighty.'
8 "And his master praised the unrighteous manager because he had acted shrewdly; for the sons of this age are more shrewd in relation to their own kind than the sons of light.
9 "And I say to you, make friends for yourselves by means of the wealth of unrighteousness, so that when it fails, they will receive you into the eternal dwellings.
10 "He who is faithful in a very little thing is faithful also in much; and he who is unrighteous in a very little thing is unrighteous also in much.
11 "Therefore if you have not been faithful in the use of unrighteous wealth, who will entrust the true riches to you?
12 "And if you have not been faithful in the use of that which is another's, who will give you that which is your own?
13 "No servant can serve two masters; for either he will hate the one and love the other, or else he will be devoted to one and despise the other. You cannot serve God and wealth."

Luke 16

The Rich Man and Lazarus

This parable juxtaposes two characters: the rich man who lived in splendor and unworried about his life after death; and Lazarus who lives in poverty and privation. This parable vividly describes the torments of those who, after death, have been separated from the kingdom and the joy of those who are part of it. One important factor in this parable, is that we alone are responsible for our life after death since God, while we are in this world, provides us with the means to learn the truth, turn to Him, and be saved for eternity. It also shows that the few years that we spend in this world are irrelevant when compared with eternity.

19 "Now there was a rich man, and he habitually dressed in purple and fine linen, joyously living in splendor every day.
20 "And a poor man named Lazarus was laid at his gate, covered with sores,
21 And longing to be fed with the crumbs which were falling from the rich man's table; besides, even the dogs were coming and licking his sores.
22 "Now the poor man died and was carried away by the angels to Abraham's bosom;

and the rich man also died and was buried.

23 "In Hades he lifted up his eyes, being in torment, and saw Abraham far away and Lazarus in his bosom.

24 "And he cried out and said, 'Father Abraham, have mercy on me, and send Lazarus so that he may dip the tip of his finger in water and cool off my tongue, for I am in agony in this flame.'

25 "But Abraham said, 'Child, remember that during your life you received your good things, and likewise Lazarus bad things; but now he is being comforted here, and you are in agony.

26 'And besides all this, between us and you there is a great chasm fixed, so that those who wish to come over from here to you will not be able, and that none may cross over from there to us.'

27 "And he said, 'Then I beg you, father, that you send him to my father's house--

28 For I have five brothers-- in order that he may warn them, so that they will not also come to this place of torment.'

29 "But Abraham said, 'They have Moses and the Prophets; let them hear them.'

30 "But he said, 'No, father Abraham, but if someone goes to them from the dead, they will repent!'

31 "But he said to him, 'If they do not listen to Moses and the Prophets, they will not be persuaded even if someone rises from the dead.'"

Luke 17

The Master and Servant

This parable tells us about the duties we have with God and that we can never put God in our debt. When we have done His work, we have only done our duty. God is our supreme Father and he owes us nothing. In the parable, the role of a servant signifies the life of the believer.

7 "Which of you, having a slave plowing or tending sheep, will say to him when he has come in from the field, 'Come immediately and sit down to eat'?

8 "But will he not say to him, 'Prepare something for me to eat, and properly clothe yourself and serve me while I eat and drink; and afterward you may eat and drink'?

9 "He does not thank the slave because he did the things which were commanded, does he?

10 "So you too, when you do all the things which are commanded you, say, 'We are unworthy slaves; we have done only that which we ought to have done.'"

Luke 18

The Unjust Judge and the Importunate Widow

This parable has two main characters: the judge and the widow. It is certain that the judge in this parable was not Jewish. In Jewish tradition, ordinary matters were taken before the elders. The widow is a symbol of poverty and helplessness. This parable contrasts God with an unjust judge. The issue is that God, differently from the judge, is willing to give to his children according to their needs. In Matthew 21:22, Jesus tells us that all things that we ask in prayer, believing, we will receive.

This parable has a similar element as the parable of "The Importunate Friend at Midnight" in Luke 11:5-8. It involves persistency. The judge finally grants the widow's petition, but not due to his desire for justice, but to avoid her persistent request. This parable closes with a puzzling question: the Lord questions how many people will remain faithful to Him by the time of His Second Coming.

1 Now He was telling them a parable to show that at all times they ought to pray and not to lose heart,
2 Saying, "In a certain city there was a judge who did not fear God and did not respect man.
3 "There was a widow in that city, and she kept coming to him, saying, 'Give me legal protection from my opponent.'
4 "For a while he was unwilling; but afterward he said to himself, 'Even though I do not fear God nor respect man,
5 Yet because this widow bothers me, I will give her legal protection, otherwise by continually coming she will wear me out.' "
6 And the Lord said, "Hear what the unrighteous judge said;
7 Now, will not God bring about justice for His elect who cry to Him day and night, and will He delay long over them?
8 "I tell you that He will bring about justice for them quickly. However, when the Son of Man comes, will He find faith on the earth?"

Luke 18

The Pharisee and the Tax Collector

In this parable, Jesus tells about the character of two men who attended the Temple for prayers. In the time of Jesus, the Pharisees were noted by their self-righteousness and their pride. In many occasions Jesus denounced them. In Matthew 3:7 they are ranked with the Sadducees as a "generation of vipers". The second character of the story is a tax collector. Tax collectors were hated by their own people. They were considered to be part of the civil service of the Roman Empire. The teaching of the parable centers on the fact that pride and self-righteousness are incompatible with prayers. No man who despises his fellowman can pray. Prayer can only reach heaven if we humble ourselves, love our fellowman, and walk in the path of God. The fundamental principle of this parable is stated in James 4:3 where James tells us that if you ask and did not receive, it is "because you ask with wrong motives".

9 And He also told this parable to some people who trusted in themselves that they were righteous, and viewed others with contempt:

10 "Two men went up into the temple to pray, one a Pharisee and the other a tax collector.

11 "The Pharisee stood and was praying this to himself: 'God, I thank You that I am not like other people: swindlers, unjust, adulterers, or even like this tax collector.

12 'I fast twice a week; I pay tithes of all that I get.'

13 "But the tax collector, standing some distance away, was even unwilling to lift up his eyes to heaven, but was beating his breast, saying, 'God, be merciful to me, the sinner!'

14 "I tell you, this man went to his house justified rather than the other; for everyone who exalts himself will be humbled, but he who humbles himself will be exalted."

Luke 19

The King's Trust in His Servants

This is a unique parable in the Bible since it is based on real facts. The narrative refers to Archelaus who inherited one fourth of the kingdom after Herod the Great died in 4 B.C. The Jews sent 50 ambassadors to Rome to persuade Augustus to allow him to enter into his inheritance. The first part of this parable refers to these historic facts. It tells us about a king who went away to receive a kingdom and whose subjects did their best to stop him. At the end, the king takes possession of his kingdom and brings justice on those who opposed him. The second part is similar to the parable of "The Talents" in Matthew 25:14-30. God gives us different gifts and we have the duty to use them according to our abilities. This second part also tells us that whatever gift we have, small or great, we must use in the service of God. It also tells us that there is no room for standing still in Christianity since Christianity implies action and labor toward honoring God.

12 So He said, "A nobleman went to a distant country to receive a kingdom for himself, and then return.

13 "And he called ten of his slaves, and gave them ten minas and said to them, 'Do business with this until I come back.'

14 "But his citizens hated him and sent a delegation after him, saying, 'We do not want this man to reign over us.'

15 "When he returned, after receiving the kingdom, he ordered that these slaves, to whom he had given the money, be called to him so that he might know what business they had done.

16 "The first appeared, saying, 'Master, your mina has made ten minas more.'

17 "And he said to him, 'Well done, good slave, because you have been faithful in a very little thing, you are to be in authority over ten cities.'

18 "The second came, saying, 'Your mina, master, has made five minas.'

19 "And he said to him also, 'And you are to be over five cities.'

20 "Another came, saying, 'Master, here is your mina, which I kept put away in a handkerchief;

21 for I was afraid of you, because you are an exacting man; you take up what you did not lay down and reap what you did not sow.'

22 "He said to him, 'By your own words I will judge you, you worthless slave. Did you know that I am an exacting man, taking up what I did not lay down and reaping what I did not sow?

23 'Then why did you not put my money in the bank, and having come, I would have collected it with interest?'

24 "Then he said to the bystanders, 'Take the mina away from him and give it to the one who has the ten minas.'

25 "And they said to him, 'Master, he has ten minas already.'

26 "I tell you that to everyone who has, more

shall be given, but from the one who does not have, even what he does have shall be taken away.
27 "But these enemies of mine, who did not want me to reign over them, bring them here and slay them in my presence."

JOHN

John 10

The Good Shepherd

Many do not consider this scripture a parable, but agree that it is one of the most lovely stories of the Bible. There is not a better picture of Jesus than the one that portrays Him as the Good Shepherd. In Palestine, it was hard to tend the sheep. The ground was rough and stony. No flock ever grazed without a shepherd, and he was never off duty. There were no dogs in Palestine and one of the means to call back a sheep was the voice of the shepherd. It is a fact that the sheep knew and understood the shepherd's voice and that they never answered to strangers. At the end of this parable, the Lord warned us about false prophets and their readiness to destroy His flock.

1 "Truly, truly, I say to you, he who does not enter by the door into the fold of the sheep, but climbs up some other way, he is a thief and a robber.
2 "But he who enters by the door is a shepherd of the sheep.
3 "To him the doorkeeper opens, and the sheep hear his voice, and he calls his own sheep by name and leads them out.
4 "When he puts forth all his own, he goes ahead of them, and the sheep follow him because they know his voice.
5 "A stranger they simply will not follow, but will flee from him, because they do not know the voice of strangers."
6 This figure of speech Jesus spoke to them, but they did not understand what those things were which He had been saying to them.
7 So Jesus said to them again, "Truly, truly, I say to you, I am the door of the sheep.
8 "All who came before Me are thieves and robbers, but the sheep did not hear them.
9 "I am the door; if anyone enters through Me, he will be saved, and will go in and out and find pasture.
10 "The thief comes only to steal and kill and destroy; I came that they may have life, and have it abundantly.
11 "I am the good shepherd; the good shepherd lays down His life for the sheep.
12 "He who is a hired hand, and not a shepherd, who is not the owner of the sheep, sees the wolf coming, and leaves the sheep and flees, and the wolf snatches them and scatters them.
13 "He flees because he is a hired hand and is not concerned about the sheep.
14 "I am the good shepherd, and I know My own and My own know Me,
15 Even as the Father knows Me and I know the Father; and I lay down My life for the sheep.
16 "I have other sheep, which are not of this fold; I must bring them also, and they will hear My voice; and they will become one flock with one shepherd."

Key for Parables

PARABLES/ LAYERS	VERSES
The House on the Rock and on the Sand	Matthew 7:24-29 Also in Luke 6:46-49
The Sower	Matthew 13:1-8 Also in Mark 4:3-20 and Luke 8:4-15
The Tares	Matthew 13:24-30
The Leaven	Matthew 13:33-35 Also in Luke 13:21
The Hidden Treasure	Matthew 13:44
The Pearl of Great Price	Matthew 13:45-46
The Drag Net	Matthew 13:47-51
The Old Gifts Used in a New Way	Matthew 13:52-53
The Unmerciful Servant	Matthew 18:23-35
The Laborers in the Vineyard	Matthew 20:1-16
The Two Sons	Matthew 21:28-31
The Vineyard	Matthew 21:33-46 Also in Mark 12:1-11 and Luke 20:9-18
Marriage of the King's Son	Matthew 22:1-14
The Ten Virgins	Matthew 25:1-13
The Talents	Matthew 25:14-30
The Sheep and Goats	Matthew 25:31-46
The Seed Growing Secretly	Mark 4:26-29
The Mustard Seed	Mark 4:30-34 Also in Matthew 13:31-32 and Luke 13:18-20
The Fig Tree	Mark 13:28-31 Also in Matthew 24:32-35 and Luke 21:29-33
Watchfulness	Mark 13:33-37
The New Cloth and an Old Garment	Luke 5:36-39 Also in Matthew 9:16 and Mark 2:21
The New Wine in Old Bottles	Also in Matthew 9:17 and Mark 2:22

Mentioned by more than one Gospel Writer

The Two Debtors	Luke 7:41-43
The Candle Under the Bushel	Luke 8:16-18 Also in Matthew 5:14-16 and Mark 4:21-23
The Good Samaritan	Luke 10:30-37
The Importunate Friend at Midnight	Luke 11:5-8
The Rich Fool	Luke 12:16-21
The Servants Watching	Luke 12:35-40
The Steward	Luke 12:42-48
The Fig Tree in the Vineyard	Luke 13:6-9
The Great Supper	Luke 14:16-24
Building a Tower and a King Going to War	Luke 14:28-33
The Lost Sheep	Luke 15:2-7 Also in Matthew 18:12-14
The Lost Piece of Silver	Luke 15:8-10

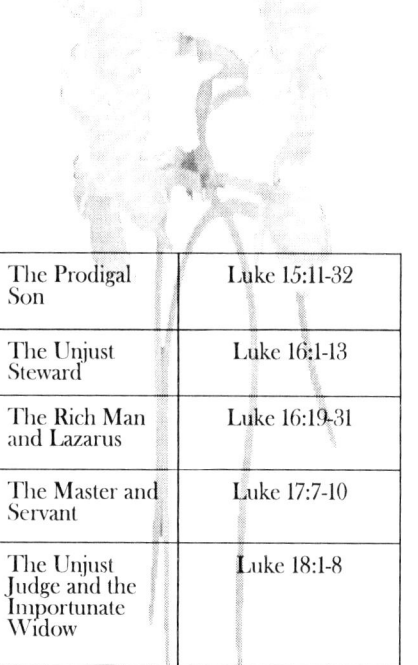

The Prodigal Son	Luke 15:11-32
The Unjust Steward	Luke 16:1-13
The Rich Man and Lazarus	Luke 16:19-31
The Master and Servant	Luke 17:7-10
The Unjust Judge and the Importunate Widow	Luke 18:1-8
The Pharisee and the Tax Collector	Luke 18:9-14
The King's Trust in His Servants	Luke 19:12-27
The Good Shepherd	John 10:1-16

Mentioned by more than one Gospel Writer

APPENDIX 1

Rare words and ancient places from the Bible found in this book

ABBA

This Syriac or Chaldee word is found three times in the New Testament and in each case is followed by its Greek equivalent, which is translated "father." It is a term expressing warm affection and filial confidence. It has no perfect equivalent in our language. It has passed into European languages as an ecclesiastical term, "abbot."

ABADDON

Destruction, the Hebrew name of "the angel of the bottomless pit". This word may be regarded as a personification of the idea of destruction, or as sheol, the realm of the dead.

ARARAT

Sacred land or high land, the name of a country on one of the mountains of which the ark rested after the Flood subsided. The "mountains" mentioned were probably the Kurdish range of South Armenia. At the close of the seventh century B.C. the kingdom of Ararat came to an end, and the country was occupied by a people who are ancestors of the Armenians of the present day.

BABYLON

An ancient city which stood on the Euphrates, about 200 miles above its junction with the Tigris, which flowed through its midst and divided it into almost two equal parts. Under Nebuchadnezzar it became one of the most splendid cities of the ancient world. After passing through various vicissitudes the city was occupied by Cyrus, king of Elam, 538 B.C., who issued a decree permitting the Jews to return to their own land. It then ceased to be the capital of an empire. It was again and again visited by hostile armies, till its inhabitants were all driven from their homes, and the city became a complete desolation, its very site being forgotten among men. Babylon is mentioned in the Bible as a support of tyranny and idolatry. In modern times the word Babylon is associated with a city devoted to materialism and sensual pleasure.

BASHAN

An ancient country. At the time of Israel's entrance into the Promised Land, Og (the king of Bashan, who was defeated by Moses) came out against them, but was defeated. This country extended from Gilead in the south to Hermon in the north, and from the Jordan on the west to Salecah on the east. Golan, one of its cities, became a city of refuge. Argob, in Bashan, was one of Solomon's commissariat districts. The cities of Bashan were taken by Hazael, but were soon after reconquered by Jehoash, who overcame the Syrians in three battles. From this time Bashan almost disappears from history, although we read of the wild cattle of its rich pastures, the oaks of its forests, and the beauty of its extensive plains. Soon after the conquest, the name "Gilead" was given to the whole country beyond Jordan.

EDOM

An ancient country which extended from the head of the Gulf of Akabah, the Elanitic Gulf, to the foot of the Dead Sea, and contained, among other cities, the rock-hewn Sela, generally known by the Greek name Petra. It is a wild and rugged region, traversed by fruitful valleys. Its old capital was Bozrah. The early inhabitants of the land were Horites. They were destroyed by the Edomites, between whom and the kings of Israel and Judah there was frequent war. At the time of the Exodus they refused permission to the Israelites to pass through their land, and ever afterwards maintained an attitude of hostility toward them. They were conquered by David and afterwards by Amaziah. But they regained their independence, and in later years, during the decline of the Jewish kingdom, made war against Israel. They took part with the Chaldeans when Nebuchadnezzar captured Jerusalem, and afterwards they invaded and held possession of the south of Palestine as far as Hebron. At length, however, Edom fell under the growing Chaldean power (the inhabitants of the country of which Babylon was the capital). There are many prophecies concerning Edom, which have been remarkably fulfilled. The present desolate condition of that land is a standing testimony to the inspiration of these prophecies. After an existence as a people for seventeen hundred years, they have utterly disappeared, and their language is forgotten for ever.

EPHESUS

The capital of proconsular Asia, which was the western part of Asia Minor. It was colonized principally from Athens. Many Jews took up their residence in this city. At the end of his second and during his third missionary journey, Paul spent time in Ephesus. John also spent many years in Ephesus, where he died and was buried.

GATH

One of the five royal cities of the Philistines on which the ark brought calamity. It was famous as being the birthplace or residence of Goliath. David fled from Saul to Achish, king of Gath, and his connection with it accounts for the words in 2 Samuel 1:20. It was afterwards conquered by David. It occupied a strong position on the borders of Judah and Philistia. Its site has been identified with the hill called Tell esSafieh, the Alba Specula of the Middle Ages, which rises 695 feet above the plain on its east edge.

GAZA

A city on the Mediterranean shore, remarkable for its early importance as the chief centre of a great commercial traffic with Egypt. It is one of the oldest cities of the world. Its earliest inhabitants were the Avims, who were conquered and displaced by the Caphtorim, a Philistine tribe. In the division of the land it fell to Judah. It was the southernmost of the five great Philistine cities which gave each a golden tumor as a trespass-offering unto the Lord. Its gates were carried away by Samson. Here he was afterwards a prisoner, pulled down the temple of Dagon, and slew the lords of the Philistines, also perishing in the ruin.

GIBEON

A hill city and one of the royal cities in ancient times. Its inhabitants were Hivites. Here the tabernacle was set up after the destruction of Nob, and here it remained until the temple was built by Solomon. It is represented by the modern el-Jib, to the south-west of Ai, and about 5 1/2 miles north-north-west of Jerusalem. This city was connected with the victory Joshua gained over the kings of Palestine and as the scene of a battle between the army of Ish-bosheth under Abner and that of David led by Joab. After Solomon became king, he paid a visit to Gibeon to offer sacrifices. On this occasion the Lord appeared to him in a dream, recorded in 1 Kings 3:5-15; 2 Chr. 1:7-12. When the temple was built the men of Israel assembled themselves to king Solomon, and brought up from Gibeon the tabernacle and the holy vessels that were in the tabernacle to Jerusalem, where they remained until they were carried away by Nebuchadnezzar.

HERMON

An eastern prolongation of the Anti-Lebanon range, reaching to a height of 9,200 feet above the Mediterranean. It marks the north boundary of Palestine and is seen from a great distance. It is about 40 miles north of the Sea of Galilee. Its modern name is Jebel-esh-Sheikh, "the chief mountain." It is one of the most conspicuous mountains in Palestine or

Syria. In whatever part of Palestine the Israelite turned his eye northward, Hermon was there, terminating the view. Our Lord Jesus and his disciples climbed this high mountain and remained on its summit all night. During the night he was transfigured before them.

IO

Related to Canaanite mythology.

JERICHO

Place of fragrance, a fenced city in the midst of a vast grove of palm trees, in the plain of Jordan, where that river was crossed by the Israelites. Its site was near the 'Ain es-Sultan, Elisha's Fountain, about 5 miles west of Jordan. It was the most important city in the Jordan valley, and the strongest fortress in all the land of Canaan. It was the key to Western Palestine.

JERUBBESHETH

Contender with the shame; i.e., idol, a surname also of Gideon.

KADESH

A sacred desert of wandering, a place on the south-eastern border of Palestine, about 165 miles from Horeb. From this place, Moses sent forth twelve spies to spy the land. After examining it in all its districts, the spies brought back a discouraging report. Disappointed by this report, the people abandoned all hope of entering into the Promised Land. They remained a considerable time at Kadesh. Because of their disbelief, they were condemned by God to wander for thirty-eight years in the wilderness. They took their journey from Kadesh into the deserts of Paran, "by way of the Red Sea". However, some believe that during these thirty-eight years they remained in and about Kadesh.

KING

When used with capital letters the word is a title applied to God. In the New Testament it also refers to Our Lord Jesus.

LEVIATHAN

A transliterated Hebrew word, meaning "twisted," "coiled." This word is used figuratively for a cruel enemy and it may refer to the Assyrian and the Babylonian empires.

MAMRE

The name of the place in the neighborhood of Hebron where Abraham dwelt. The site of Mamre has been identified with Ballatet Selta, i.e., "the oak of rest", where there is a tree called "Abraham's oak, about a mile and a half west of Hebron. Others identify it with er-Rameh, 2 miles north of Hebron.

MASKIL

Maskil is a favorite wisdom word. It means instructing. The word Maskil occurs in the title of thirteen Psalms. It denotes a song enforcing some lesson of wisdom or piety, a didactic song.

MEDES

In Genesis 10:2 the Hebrew word occurs in the list of the sons of Japheth. But probably this is an ethnic and not a personal name, and denotes simply the Medes as descended from Japheth.

MIKHTAM

A poem or song found in the titles of Psalms 16:56-60. Some translate the word "golden", i.e., precious. The root of the word means to stamp or grave, and it is regarded as denoting a composition so precious as to be worthy to be engraven on a durable tablet for preservation; or, as others render, "a psalm precious as stamped gold."

MORIAH

Probably, one of the hills of Jerusalem where Solomon's temple was built. It is usually included in Zion, to the north-east of which it lays. This was the land of Moriah to which Abraham went to offer up his son Isaac. It was probably the highest point of the temple. Here also, one thousand years after Abraham, David built an altar and offered sacrifices to God.

MOUNT SINAI

The mountain where the Law was given to Moses; thought to be in the Gebel Musa on Sinai Peninsula.

Nephilim

This word means giants. A Hebrew word left untranslated in Genesis 6:4. One of the Canaanitish tribes.

Nineveh

This ancient great city lay on the eastern or left bank of the river Tigris, along which it stretched for some 30 miles, having an average breadth of 10 miles or more from the river back toward the eastern hills. This whole extensive space is now one immense area of ruins. Occupying a central position on the great highway between the Mediterranean and the Indian Ocean, thus uniting the East and the West, wealth flowed into it from many sources, so that it became the greatest of all ancient cities.

Patmos

A small rocky and barren island, one of the group called the "Sporades," in the Aegean Sea. It is mentioned in Scripture only in Rev. 1:9.

Pi-Hahiroth, in front of Baal-Zephon

Place where the reeds grow. The name of a place in Egypt where the children of Israel encamped. Some have identified it with Ajrud, a fortress between Etham and Suez. The condition of the Isthmus of Suez at the time of the Exodus is not exactly known. The isthmus has been formed by the Nile deposits. In the maps of Ptolemy (of the second and third centuries A.D.) the mouths of the Nile are forty miles further south than at present.

Pit

In the psalms the word is used as a grave and as a figure for mischief. It is a hole, shaft, or cavity in the ground. In the Bible it also refers to the unseen place of woe.

Philistines

The Philistines were sea people who came from the Aegean and settled along the southern coast of Canaan in the twelfth century B.C. They posed a serious threat to Israel during the time of the judges (before King David).

Rabbath

Rabbath was the city of the Ammonites (this tribe hired Balaam to curse Israel). It was located among the eastern hills, some 20 miles east of the Jordan. After David had subdued all their allies in a great war, he sent Joab with a strong force to take their city. For two years it held out against its assailants. It was while his army was engaged in this protracted siege that David was guilty of that deed of shame which left a blot on his character and cast a gloom over the rest of his life. David directed the final assault of the city. The city was given up to plunder, and the people were ruthlessly put to death. The conquest and destruction of Rabbath was the last of David's battles.

SELAH

A word frequently found in the Book of Psalms. Its meaning is doubtful. Some interpret it as meaning "silence" or "pause;" others, "end," "a louder strain."

SHEOL

The invisible world of departed souls. Sheol is a grave, a place of murky silence and of no return, with little or no contact with God. In the psalms, there is the notion of God's presence with the dead in Sheol.

SOREK

The name of a valley which drains the western Judean hills, and flowing by Makkedah and Jabneel, falls into the sea some eight miles south of Joppa. This was the home of Delilah, whom Samson loved.

TABOR

A cone-like prominent mountain, 11 miles west of the Sea of Galilee. The view from the summit of it is said to be singularly extensive and grand. There is an old tradition, which, however, is unfounded, that it was the scene of the transfiguration of our Lord. The prominence and isolation of Tabor, standing, as it does, on the border-land between the northern and southern tribes, between the mountains and the central plain, made it a place of note in all ages, and evidently led the psalmist to associate it with Hermon, the one emblematic of the south, the other of the north.

TARSHISH

The name of a place which first comes into notice in the days of Solomon. Some think there was a Tarshish in the East, on the Indian coast. There can be little doubt, however, that this is the name of a Phoenician port in Spain, between the two mouths of the Guadalquivir. It was founded by a Carthaginian colony, and was the farthest western harbour of Tyrian sailors. It was to this port Jonah's ship was about to sail from Joppa.

THEVEZ

A place some 11 miles north-east of Shechem, on the road to Scythopolis, the modern Tabas. Abimelech led his army against this place, because of its participation in the conspiracy of the men of Shechem; but as he drew near to the strong tower to which its inhabitants had fled for safety, and was about to set fire to it, a woman cast a fragment of millstone at him to brake his skull. His armor bearer thereupon thrust him through, and he died.

ZION

One of the eminences on which Jerusalem was built (the city was built on two mountains Zion and Moriah). It was surrounded on all sides, except the north, by deep valleys, that of the Tyropoeon separating it from Moriah, which it surpasses in height. It was the south-eastern hill of Jerusalem. When David took it from the Jebusites he built on it a citadel and a palace, and it became "the city of David." In the later books of the Old Testament this name was sometimes used to denote Jerusalem in general, and sometimes God's chosen Israel. The name Zion (or Sion) appears to have been, like Ariel ("the hearth of God"), a poetical term for Jerusalem.

ZOAR

A town on the south-east of the Dead Sea, to which Lot and his daughters fled from Sodom. It was originally called Bela. It is referred to by the prophets Isaiah and Jeremiah. Its ruins are still seen at the opening of the ravine of Kerak, the Kir-Moab referred to in 2 Kings 3, the modern Tell esh-Shaghur.

APPENDIX 2

Brief biographies of the main characters in the Old Testament found in this Book

AARON

The eldest son of Amram and Jochebed, a daughter of Levi. He was born in Egypt three years before his brother Moses, and a number of years after his sister Miriam. He married Elisheba, the daughter of Amminadab of the house of Judah, by whom he had four sons, Nadab and Abihu, Eleazar and Ithamar. When the time for the deliverance of Israel out of Egypt drew close, he was sent by God to meet his long-absent brother, that he might cooperate with him in all that they were required to do in bringing about the Exodus. He was to be the "mouth" or "prophet" of Moses because he was a man of a ready utterance. He was faithful to his trust, and stood by Moses in all his interviews with Pharaoh.

ABRAHAM (ABRAM) AND SARAH (SARAI)

Father of a multitude, son of Terah, named before his older brothers Nahor and Haran, because he was the heir of the promises. Till the age of seventy, Abram lived among his kindred in his native country of Chaldea. He then, with his father and his family and household, left the city of Ur where he lived fifteen years. The cause of his migration was a call from God. There is no mention of this first call in the Old Testament; it is implied, however, in Genesis 12. At this point, Abram received a second and more definite call, accompanied by a promise from God; whereupon he took his departure, taking his nephew Lot with him. He was unsure where to go but trusted God's calling. Abram entered on a migratory life, and dwelt in tents. Passing along the valley of the Jabbok, in the land of Canaan, he formed his first encampment at Sichem, in the vale or oak-grove of Moreh, between Ebal on the north and Gerizim on the south. Here he received the great promise, "And I will bless you, And make your name great; And so you shall be a blessing." (Genesis 12:2) He was the chosen ancestor of the great Deliverer whose coming had been long ago predicted. He married his half-sister Sarai who became the mother of his son Isaac. They settled in Mamre, where, the promises already made to him by God were repeated and enlarged. "The word of the Lord" (an expression occurring here for the first time) "came to him." (Gen. 15:1) He now understood better the future that lay before the nation that was to spring from him. Sarai, now seventy-five years old, in her impatience, persuaded Abram to take Hagar, her Egyptian maid, as a concubine, intending that whatever child might be born should be reckoned as her own. Ishmael was accordingly thus brought up, and was regarded as the heir of these promises. When Ishmael was thirteen years old, God again revealed yet more explicitly. In token of the sure fulfillment of that purpose the patriarch's name was now changed from Abram to Abraham, and the rite of circumcision was instituted as a sign of the covenant. It was then announced that the heir to these covenant promises would be the son of Sarai, though she was now ninety years old; and it was directed that his name should be Isaac. At the same time, in commemoration of the promises, Sarai's name was changed to Sarah. On that memorable day of God's thus revealing his design, Abraham and his son Ishmael and all the males of his house were circumcised. Three months after this, as Abraham sat in his tent door, he saw three men approaching. They accepted his proffered hospitality, and, seated under an oak-tree, partook of the fare which Abraham and Sarah provided. One of the three visitants was none other than the Lord, and the other two were angels in the guise of men. The Lord renewed on this occasion his promise of a son by Sarah, who was rebuked for her unbelief. Abraham accompanied the three as they proceeded on their journey. The two angels went on toward Sodom; while the Lord tarried behind and talked with Abraham, making known to him the destruction that was about to fall on that guilty city. The patriarch interceded earnestly in behalf of the doomed city. But as not even ten righteous persons were found in it, for whose sake the city would have been spared, the threatened destruction fell upon it; and early the next morning Abraham saw the smoke of the fire that consumed it. After fifteen years' residence at Mamre, Abraham moved southward, and pitched his tent among the Philistines, near Gerar. From Gerar, the patriarch moved down to Beer-sheba. It was probably here that Isaac was born, Abraham being now an hundred years old. A feeling of jealousy now arose between Sarah and Hagar, whose son, Ishmael, was no longer to be regarded as Abraham's heir. Sarah insisted that both Hagar and her son should be sent away. This was done, although it was a hard trial for Abraham. At this point there is a blank in the patriarch's history of perhaps twenty-five years. These years of peace and happiness were spent at Beer-sheba. The next time we see him his faith is put to a severe test by the command that suddenly came to him to go and offer up Isaac, the heir of all the promises, as a sacrifice on one of the mountains of Moriah. His faith stood the test. He proceeded in a spirit of unhesitating obedience to carry out the command; and when about to slay his son, whom he had laid on the altar, his uplifted hand was arrested by the angel of Jehovah, and a ram, which was entangled in a thicket near at hand, was seized and offered in his stead. From this circumstance that place was called Jehovah-jireh, i.e., "The Lord will provide." The promises made to Abraham were again confirmed (and this was the last recorded word of God to the patriarch); and he descended the mount with his son, and returned to his home at Beer-sheba, where he resided for some years, and then moved northward to Hebron. Some years after this Sarah died at Hebron, being 127 years old. Abraham acquired now the needful possession of a burying-place, the cave of Machpelah, by purchase from the owner of it, Ephron the Hittite; and there he buried Sarah. His next care was to provide a wife for Isaac, and for this purpose he sent his steward, Eliezer, to Haran, where his brother Nahor and his family resided. The result was that Rebekah, the daughter of Nahor's son Bethuel, became the wife of Isaac. Abraham then himself took to wife Keturah, who became the mother of six sons, whose descendants were afterwards known as the "children of the east", and later as "Saracens." At length all his wanderings came to an end. At the age of 175 years, 100 years after he had first entered the land of Canaan, he died, and was buried in the old family burying-place at Machpelah.

ABSALOM

Son of David, he was noted for his personal beauty and for the extra-ordinary profusion of the hair of his head. The first public act of his life was the blood-revenge he executed against Amnon, David's eldest son, who had basely wronged Absalom's sister Tamar. David's other sons fled from the place in horror, and brought the tidings of the death of Amnon to Jerusalem. Alarmed for the consequences of the act, Absalom fled to his grandfather at Geshur for three years. David mourned his absent son, now branded with the guilt of fratricide. After a while, David invited Absalom to return to Jerusalem. He returned accordingly, but two years elapsed before his father admitted him into his presence. Absalom was now probably the oldest surviving son of David, and as he was of royal descent by his mother as well as by his father, he began to aspire to the throne. His pretensions were favoured by the people. He gained their affection; and after his return from Geshur he went up to Hebron, the old capital of Judah, along with a great body of the people, and there proclaimed himself king. The revolt was so successful that David found it necessary to quit Jerusalem and flee to Mahanaim, beyond Jordan; where upon Absalom returned to Jerusalem and took possession of the throne without opposition. Absalom marched out against his father, whose army, under the command of Joab, he encountered on the borders of the forest of Ephraim. Twenty thousand of Absalom's army were slain and the rest fled. Absalom fled on a swift mule; but his long flowing hair, or more probably his head, was caught in the bough of an oak, and there he was left suspended till Joab came up and pierced him through with three darts. His body was then taken down and cast into a pit dug in the forest, and a heap of stones was raised over his grave. When the tidings of the result of that battle were brought to David, he gave way to the bitter lamentation: "O my son Absalom, my son, my son Absalom! Would I had died instead of you, O Absalom, my son, my son!" (2 Samuel 18:33) " Absalom's three sons had all died before him, so that he left only a daughter, Tamar.

ADAM

Adam was the first man whom God created. He was formed out of the dust of the earth (and hence his name), and God breathed into his nostrils the breath of life, and gave him dominion over all the lower creatures. He was placed after his creation in the Garden of Eden. Being induced by the tempter in the form of a serpent to eat a forbidden fruit, Eve, his helper and wife, persuaded Adam to also eat from the fruit. Thus man fell, and brought upon himself and his posterity all the sad consequences of his transgression.

ABEL

The second son of Adam and Eve. He was put to death by his brother Cain. Guided by the instruction of their father, the two brothers were trained in the duty of worshipping God. Each of them offered up to God of the first fruits of his labours. Cain, as a husbandman, offered the fruits of the field; Abel, as a shepherd, of his flock. The Lord was pleased with Abel's offering but not with Cain's. Cain was angry with his brother and put him to death. Abel was the first martyr, as he was the first man to die.

AMNON

The eldest son of David, by Ahinoam of Jezreel. Absalom caused him to be put to death for his great crime in the matter of Tamar, a daughter of David, whom Amnon shamefully outraged and afterwards "hated exceedingly." One of the sons of Shammai, of the children of Ezra.

BATHSHEBA

She was the daughter of Eliam Ammiel and wife of Uriah the Hittite. David committed adultery with her. The child born in adultery died. After her husband was slain she was married to David, and became the mother of Solomon. She took a prominent part in securing the succession of Solomon to the throne.

CAIN

The first son of Adam and Eve. Guided by the instruction of their father, Cain and his brother Abel were trained in the duty of worshipping God. Each of them offered up to God of the first fruits of his labours. Cain, as a husbandman, offered the fruits of the field; Abel, as a shepherd, of his flock. The Lord was pleased with Abel's offering but not with Cain's. This caused in Cain feelings of murderous hatred against his brother who he eventually put to death. This was the first time that human blood soiled the ground. For this crime he was expelled from Eden, and led the life of an exile, bearing upon him some mark which God had set upon him in answer to his own cry for mercy, so that thereby he might be protected from the wrath of his fellow-men. Doomed to be a wanderer and a fugitive in the earth, he went forth into the "land of Nod", i.e., the land of "exile", which is said to have been in the "east of Eden," and there he built a city, the first we read of, and called it after his son's name, Enoch. His descendants are enumerated to the sixth generation.

DARIUS

Darius the Mede, the son of Ahasuerus, of the seed of the Medes. On the death of Belshazzar the Chaldean he "received the kingdom" of Babylon as viceroy from Cyrus.

During his brief reign, Darius was promoted to the highest dignity and the story of "Daniel in the Lions' Den" unfolded. On the account of the malice of his enemies Daniel was cast into the den of lions. After his miraculous escape, a decree was issued by Darius enjoining reverence to Daniel's God. Some are of the opinion that the name "Darius" is simply a name of office, equivalent to "governor."

DAVID

David was the eighth and youngest son of Jesse, a citizen of Bethlehem. His early occupation was that of tending his father's sheep on the uplands of Judah. While David was a young man, Samuel paid an unexpected visit to Bethlehem. There he offered up sacrifice, and called the elders of Israel and Jesse's family to the sacrificial meal. Among all who appeared before him he failed to discover the one he sought. David was sent for, and the prophet immediately recognized him as the chosen of God— chosen to succeed Saul, who was now departing from the ways of God, on the throne of the kingdom. David went back again to his shepherd life, but "the Spirit of the LORD came mightily upon David from that day forward," (1 Samuel 16:13) and "the Spirit of the LORD departed from Saul." (1 Samuel 16:14) Not long after this, David was sent to soothe with his harp the troubled spirit of Saul, who suffered from a strange melancholy dejection. He played before the king so skillfully that Saul was greatly cheered, and began to entertain great affection for the young shepherd. After this, he went home to Bethlehem. However, he soon again came into prominence. The armies of the Philistines and of Israel were in battle in the valley of Elah. David was sent by his father with provisions for his three brothers, who were then fighting on the side of the king. On his arrival in the camp of Israel, David (now about twenty years of age) was made aware of the state of matters when the champion of the Philistines, Goliath of Gath, came forth to defy Israel. David took his sling, and with a well-trained aim threw a stone "out of the brook," which struck the giant's forehead, so that he fell senseless to the ground. David then ran and slew him, and cut off his head with his own sword. The result was a great victory to the Israelites. David's popularity turned Saul against him. Saul tried to kill him and David fled, and for years was a fugitive in the mountains. Saul was finally killed by the Amalekites and David became the king of Judah under divine direction. Later, he was anointed king over all Israel, and sought out a new seat of government, more suitable than Hebron, as the capital of his empire. At this time there was a Jebusite fortress on the hill of Zion, called also Jebus. David took it from the Jebusites, made it Israel's capital, established his residence, and afterwards built for himself a palace. While king of Israel, David entered on a series of conquests, which greatly extended and strengthened his kingdom. He ruled over a vast empire, and his capital was enriched with the spoils of many lands. However, in the midst of all this success, he fell, and his character became stained with the sin of adultery. He became guilty of murder. Uriah, whom he had wronged, an officer of the Gibborim, the corps of heroes, was, by his order, sent in the front of the hottest battle at the siege of Rabbath, in order that he might be put to death. Bathsheba became his wife after Uriah's death. The result of these sinful actions were devastating: his first child with Bathsheba died; the people's respect for David was lowered; he entered in battles with neighboring countries; he was not allowed to build the Temple; and his beloved son Absalom revolted against him. After the death of his first son, Bathsheba gave birth to a second son, whom David called Solomon, and who ultimately succeeded him on the throne. After the successful termination of all his wars, David formed the idea of building a temple for the ark of God. He was not permitted to carry it into execution, because he had been a man of war. God, however, sent Nathan to him with a gracious message. On receiving it, he went into the sanctuary, the tent where the ark was, sat before the Lord, and poured out his heart in words of devout thanksgiving. The building of the temple was reserved for his son Solomon, who would be a man of peace. After his son Absalom revolted and was killed --which caused great grief to the heart of David-- he enjoyed ten years of peace. During those years he was mainly engaged in accumulating treasures of every kind for the great temple at Jerusalem, which it was reserved to his successor to build, a house which was to be "exceeding magnifical, of fame and of glory throughout all countries". After a reign of forty years and at the age of seventy, David became an enfeebled man, prematurely old. David died in 1015 B.C. and his tomb is still pointed out on Mount Zion. The book of Psalms commonly bears the title of the "Psalms of David," from the circumstance that he was the largest contributor (about eighty psalms) to the collection.

Daniel

One of the four great prophets, although he is not once spoken of in the Old Testament as a prophet. His life and prophecies are recorded in the Book of Daniel. He was descended from one of the noble families of Judah, and was probably born in Jerusalem about 623 B.C., during the reign of Josiah. Cyrus, who was now master of all Asia from India to the Dardanelles, placed Darius, a Median prince, on the throne, during the two years of whose reign Daniel held the office of first of the "three presidents" of the empire, and was thus practically at the head of affairs, interesting himself in the prospects of the captive Jews, whom he had at last the happiness of seeing restored to their own land, although he did not return with them. His fidelity to God exposed him to persecution, and he was cast into a den of lions, but was miraculously delivered; after which Darius issued a decree enjoining reverence for the God of Daniel. He prospered in the reign of Darius, and in the reign of Cyrus the Persian, whom he probably greatly influenced in the matter of the decree which put an end to the Captivity (536 B.C.).

Delilah

A Philistine woman who dwelt in the valley of Sorek. She was bribed by the "lords of the Philistines" to obtain from Samson the secret of his strength and the means of overcoming it. She tried on three occasions to obtain from him this secret in vain. On the fourth occasion she received it from him. She made him sleep upon her knees, and then called the man who was waiting to help her; who shaved off "seven locks of his hair," and so his "strength left him." (Judges 16:19)

EVE

The name given by Adam to his wife. The account of her creation is given in Genesis 2:21, 22. The Creator declared that it was not good for man to be alone and created him a companion. The Lord caused a deep sleep to fall upon Adam, and while in an unconscious state took one of his ribs, and closed up his flesh again; and of this rib he made a woman, whom he presented to him when he awoke. Adam received her as his wife, and said, "This is now bone of my bones, And flesh of my flesh; She shall be called Woman, Because she was taken out of Man." (Genesis 2:23) He called her Eve, because she was the mother of all living. Through the subtle temptation of the serpent she violated the commandment of God by taking of the forbidden fruit, which she also gave to her husband. Thus man fell, and brought upon himself and his posterity all the sad consequences of his transgression. They were expelled from Eden, and at the east of the garden God placed a flame, which turned every way, to prevent access to the tree of life. Shortly after their expulsion Eve brought forth her first-born, and called him Cain. Although we have the names of only three of Adam's sons, Cain, Abel, and Seth, it is obvious that he had several sons and daughters.

EZRA

The scribe who led the second body of exiles that returned from Babylon to Jerusalem 459 B.C. In the second year after the return, he erected an altar and laid the foundation of the temple on the ruins of that which had been destroyed by Nebuchadnezzar. Tradition connects his name with the collecting and editing of the Old Testament canon. The final completion of the canon may have been the work of a later generation; but Ezra seems to have put much into the shape in which it is still found in the Hebrew Bible. After the ruined wall of the city had been built by Nehemiah, there was a great gathering of the people at Jerusalem preparatory to the dedication of the wall. On the appointed day the whole population assembled, and the law was read aloud to them by Ezra and his assistants. There was a great religious awakening. For successive days they held solemn assemblies, confessing their sins and offering up solemn sacrifices. They kept the feast of Tabernacles with great solemnity and joyous enthusiasm, and renewed their national covenant with the Lord. Abuses were rectified, and arrangements for the temple service completed, allowing for the dedication of the walls of the city.

GOLIATH

A famous giant of Gath, who for forty days openly defied the armies of Israel, but was slain by David with a stone from a sling. He was probably descended from the Rephaim who found refuge among the Philistines after they were dispersed by the Ammonites. His height was six cubits and a span, which, taking the cubit at 21 inches, is equal to 10 1/2 feet. David cut off his head and brought it to Jerusalem, while he hung the armor which he took from him in his tent. His sword was preserved at Nobas as a religious trophy. David's victory over Goliath was the turning point in his life. He came into public notice now as the deliverer of Israel.

ISAAC

The only son of Abraham by Sarah. He was the longest lived of the three patriarchs. The most memorable event in his life is connected with the command of God given to Abraham to offer him up as a sacrifice on a mountain in the land of Moriah. When he was forty years of age Rebekah was chosen for his wife. After the death and burial of his father he took up his residence at Beer-lahai-roi, where his two sons, Esau and Jacob were born.

JOAB

One of the three sons of Zeruiah, David's sister, and "captain of the host" during of the whole of David's reign. His character is stained by the part he willingly took in the murder of Uriah. He also put Absalom to death, apparently acting from a sense of duty. David was unmindful of the many services Joab had rendered to him, and afterwards gave the command of the army to Amasa, Joab's cousin. When David was dying Joab espoused the cause of Adonijah in preference to that of Solomon. He was afterwards slain by Benaiah, by the command of Solomon, in accordance with his father's injunction, at the altar to which he had fled for refuge. He was buried in his own property in the wilderness, probably in the north-east of Jerusalem.

JONAH

He was a prophet of Israel, and predicted the restoration of the ancient boundaries of the kingdom. He exercised his ministry very early in the reign of Jeroboam II. His personal history is mainly to be gathered from the book which bears his name. This book professes to give an account of what actually took place in the experience of the prophet. The book gives an account of: a) Jonah's divine commission to go to Nineveh, his disobedience, and the punishment (the Lord appointed a great fish to swallow Jonah, a fact that finally brought him into obedience); b) his prayer and miraculous deliverance (Jonah was in the stomach of the fish and prayed three days and three nights); and c) the second commission given to him (he arouse and went to Nineveh to proclaim the message of the Lord).

JOSHUA

Moses' minister or servant who accompanied him part of the way when he ascended Mount Sinai to receive the two tablets. Under the direction of God, Moses, before his death, invested Joshua in a public and solemn manner with authority over the people as his successor. Joshua carried out many battles in the early stages of Israel. Six nations and thirty-one kings were conquered by him. He died, at the age of one hundred and ten years, twenty-five years after having crossed the Jordan. He was buried in his own city of Timnathserah.

LEVI

The third son of Jacob by Leah. The origin of the name is found in Leah's words, "Now this time my husband will become attached to me, because I have borne him three sons." Therefore he was named "Levi." (Genesis 29:34) He is mentioned as taking a prominent part in avenging his sister Dinah He and his three sons went down with Jacob into Egypt, where he died at the age of one hundred and thirty-seven years .

LOT

The son of Haran, and nephew of Abraham. On the death of his father, he was left in charge of his grandfather Terah, after whose death he accompanied his uncle Abraham into Canaan, into Egypt, and back again to Canaan. After this he separated from him and settled in Sodom. At length, when the judgment of God descended on the guilty cities of the plain, Lot was miraculously delivered. When fleeing from the doomed city his wife "looked back from behind him, and became a pillar of salt." There is to this day a peculiar crag at the south end of the Dead Sea, near Kumran, which the Arabs call Bint Sheik Lot, i.e., Lot's wife. It is "a tall, isolated needle of rock, which really does bear a curious resemblance to an Arab woman with a child upon her shoulder."

MOSES

Moses was a great spiritual leader of the Israelites who received the Law from God that has guided Judeo-Christian traditions throughout centuries. He was born to a Levite named Amran and his wife Jochebed. While captive in Egypt, the Israelites began to exceedingly multiply. The Pharaoh conceived a plan to destroy all the Hebrew male children to be born. Moses' mother was able to conceal him in the house for three months. However, when the task of hiding the child became impossible, Jochebed allowed her child to be noticed by the daughter of the Pharaoh. She constructed an ark of bulrushes, which she laid among the bushes, which grew on the edge of the river at the spot where the princess came down and bathed. Her plan was successful. Pharaoh's daughter saw the child crying, had pity on him, took the child, and brought him up as her adopted son. When Moses became a man, he learned of the fate of the Israelites in Egypt. They were made to serve in hard bondage. Moses was a shy and humble man who did not seek notoriety. One day the angel of the Lord appeared to him in the burning bush, and told him to go down to Egypt and bring forth the children of Israel out of bondage, he was at first unwilling to go. He expressed to God that he lacked the require eloquence, being slow of speech and of tongue. The Lord agreed to allow Aaron --Moses' elder brother-- to act as his spokesman. Moses was obedient and he and Aaron were faced with the hard task commanded by the Lord. Moses confronted the Pharaoh and pleaded with him to let his people free to go and worship God. At each petition from Moses, the Pharaoh refused. At each refusal, God, as an act of judgment, sent plagues: all water in Egypt turned into blood; frogs; insects, Egyptian cattle died; boils; hail; locusts; and darkness over the land. (Exodus: 7-11.) After all these hardships, the heart of Pharaoh still remained unchanged and he refused to let the Israelites leave Egypt. At last, God brought the last plague: the first born of all humans and animals were to die. The Hebrews were instructed to save their children and flocks by sacrificing an unblemished young lamb and daubing its blood on the two doorposts and the lintel at the front of each house. At midnight God struck dead all of Egypt's' firstborn, including Pharaoh's child. After this last plague and after 430 years in captivity, the Israelites were allowed to leave Egypt. However, Pharaoh had a change of heart and decided to send his army after the Israelites and force them to return to Egypt. Moses and his people became trapped between Pharaoh's army and the Red Sea. God intervened and protected the Israelites in a pillar of cloud, thus hiding the Israelites from their persecutors. Moses followed a divine command and raised his shepherd's rod over the sea. Miraculously, the Israelites escaped as the Red Sea was divided at Moses' command. They were able to walk through the open path while the pursuing army became trapped in the returning waters of the sea. After their escape from Egypt, Moses and the Israelites entered on a long journey through the Sinai Peninsula, a largely barren and sparsely occupied land. Moses received the tablets of the Ten Commandments from God at the same time that he had to struggle with the Israelite's faith in God. When he returned from Mount Sinai carrying the tablets, he found his people adoring a Golden Calf. Moses becomes furious and "shattered" the tablets which, later, were reengraved by God. As a result of this incident 3,000 people were killed, at Moses' command. Throughout the journey in the wilderness, as they marched toward Mount Sinai, at Kadesh, the people were frightened and refused to invade Canaan. This brought condemnation on part of the Lord. For 38 years they wandered in the wilderness. Most of that long part of the journey was spent in the region around Kadesh and in the area north of Ezion-Geber. The final months of Israel's journey were filled with conflict, as the Israelites swept up the eastern side of the Dead Sea and conquered the territory north of Moab. Finally, the long journey ended, as the tribes reached the Jordan and prepared to enter the Promised Land. However, Moses never entered into the land of promise as this was denied by God. After blessing the tribes, he ascended to the mountain of Nebo, to the top of Pisgah. Deuteronomy 34:1-4 tells us: "And the Lord showed him all the land, Gilead as far as Dan, and all Naphtali and the land of Ephraim and Manasseh, and all the land of Judah as far as the western sea, and the Negev and the plain in the valley of Jericho, the city of palm trees, as far as Zoar." Then the Lord said to him, "This is the land which I swore to Abraham, Isaac, and Jacob, saying, 'I will give it to your descendants'; I have let you see it with your eyes, but you shall not go over there." After that, Moses died. Deuteronomy 34:5-8 tells us the following in regard to the death of Moses: "So Moses the servant of the Lord died there in the land of Moab, according to the word of the Lord. And He buried him in the valley in the land of Moab, opposite Beth-peor; but no man knows his burial place to this day. Although Moses was one hundred and twenty years old when he died, his eye was not dim, nor his vigor abated. So the sons of Israel wept for Moses in the plains of Moab thirty days; then the days of weeping and mourning for Moses came to an end." The life and spiritual leadership of Moses is recorded in the Pentateuch.

NATHAN

A prophet in the reigns of David and Solomon. He is first spoken of in connection with the arrangements David made for the building of the temple, and next appears as the reprover of David on account of his sin with Bathsheba. He was charged with the education of Solomon, at whose inauguration to the throne he took a prominent part. His two sons, Zabad and Azariah, occupied places of honour at the king's court. He last appears in assisting David in reorganizing the public worship.

NOAH

The grandson of Methuselah, who was for two hundred and fifty years contemporary with Adam, and the son of Lamech, who was about fifty years old at the time of Adam's death. This patriarch is rightly regarded as the connecting link between the old and the new world. He is the second great progenitor of the human family. He lived five hundred years, and then there were born unto him three sons, Shem, Ham, and Japheth. He was a "righteous man, blameless in his time." (Genesis 6:9) However, in the time of Noah, the descendants of Cain and of Seth began to intermarry, and then there sprang up a race distinguished for their ungodliness. Men became more and more corrupt, and God determined to sweep the earth of its wicked population by sending rain for forty days and forty nights. The Lord instructed Noah to build an ark for the saving of himself and his house. An interval of one hundred and twenty years elapsed while the ark was being built, during which Noah bore constant testimony against the unbelief and wickedness of that generation. When the ark of "gopher-wood" (Genesis 6:14) was at length completed according to the command of the Lord, the living creatures that were to be preserved entered into it; and then Noah and his wife and sons and daughters-in-law entered it, and "the Lord closed it behind him". (Genesis 7:16) When Noah entered the ark, the judgment of the Lord began. The ark floated on the waters for one hundred and fifty days, and then rested on the mountains of Ararat; but not for a considerable time after this was divine permission given him to leave the ark, so that he and his family were a whole year shut up within it. On leaving the ark Noah's first act was to erect an altar. He made offers and sacrifices to the Lord who promised Noah to "never again destroyed every living thing, as I have done."

SAMSON

The first recorded event of his life was his marriage with a Philistine woman of Timnath. Such a marriage was not forbidden by the law of Moses, as the Philistines did not form one of the seven doomed Canaanite nations. It was, however, an ill-assorted and unblessed marriage. His wife was soon taken from him and given "to his companion". (Judges 14:20) For this Samson took revenge by burning the corn of the Philistines, who, in their turn, in revenge burnt her and her father with fire. Her death he terribly avenged. During the twenty years following this he judged Israel; but we have no record of this period. Probably these twenty years may have been simultaneous with the last twenty years of Eli's life. Along the way, he becomes infatuated with Delilah. Delilah was bribed by the "lords of the Philistines" to obtain from Samson the secret of his strength and the means of overcoming it. She tried on three occasions to obtain from him this secret in vain. On the fourth occasion she received it from him. She made him sleep upon her knees, and then called the man who was waiting to help her; who shaved off "seven locks of his hair," and so his "strength left him". (Judges 16:19) He perished in the last terrible destruction he brought upon his enemies. "So the dead whom he killed at his death were more than those whom he killed in his life." (Judges 16:30)

SARAH

(See Abraham and Sarah)

SAUL

The son of Kish, of the tribe of Benjamin, the first king of the Jewish nation. The singular providential circumstances connected with his election as king are recorded in 1 Sam. 8-10. His father's asses had strayed, and Saul was sent with a servant to seek for them. During this trip he consulted the "seer". Saul visited Samuel who had been divinely prepared for his coming. When Saul arrived, Samuel anointed Saul as king over Israel, giving him three signs in confirmation of his call to be king. When Saul reached his home in Gibeah the last of these signs was fulfilled, and the Spirit of God came upon him, and "he was turned into another man." At length, Saul is anointed as the king, first in secret and later on in front of the nation. Saul's reign was constantly confronted and attacked by enemies. The war against the Amalekites is the only one which is recorded at length. These oldest and hereditary enemies of Israel occupied the territory to the south and south-west of Palestine. Samuel summoned Saul to execute the "ban" (In Joshua 7:11 the Lord expressed that "Israel has sinned, and they have also transgressed My covenant which I commanded them. And they have even taken some of the things under the ban and have both stolen and deceived.") Saul proceeded to execute the divine command; and gathering the people together, marched from Telaim against the Amalekites, whom he smote from Havilah until Shur, utterly destroying all the people with the edge of the sword. He was, however, guilty of rebellion and disobedience in sparing Agag their king, and in conniving at his soldiers' sparing the best of the sheep and cattle; and Samuel, following Saul to Gilgal, in the Jordan valley, said unto him, "Because you have rejected the word of the Lord, He has also rejected you from being king." At this point, the Spirit of the Lord departed from Saul. The kingdom was taken from Saul and was given to David. Before Saul and David became enemies, Saul had great affection for David. David was now sent for as a player on an harp to play before Saul when the evil spirit troubled him, and thus was introduced to the court of Saul. He became a great favorite with the king. When David defeated Goliath, Saul now took David permanently into his service. Not long after that, David's popularity turned Saul against him. Saul tried to kill him and David fled, and for years was a fugitive in the mountains. Saul was finally killed by the Amalekites. Saul died when he took a sword and fell upon it. After Saul's death, David became the king of Israel.

SOLOMON

David's second son by Bathsheba, the first after their legal marriage. He succeeded his father on the throne in early manhood, probably about sixteen or eighteen years of age. Nathan, to whom his education was entrusted, called him Jedidiah, i.e., "beloved of the Lord." His father chose him as his successor, passing over the claims of his elder sons: "Assuredly Solomon my son shall reign after me." His history is recorded in 1 Kings 1—11 and 2 Chr. 1—9. His elevation to the throne took place before his father's death, and was hastened on mainly by Nathan and Bathsheba. During his long reign of forty years the Hebrew monarchy gained its highest splendor. Solomon's reign was a period of great material prosperity and equally remarkable for its intellectual activity. However, that golden age of Jewish history passed away. The bright day of Solomon's glory ended in clouds and darkness. His decline and fall from his high estate is a sad record. Chief among the causes of his decline were his polygamy and his great wealth. As he grew older, he lived among 1,000 idle women. He did not, indeed, cease to believe in the God of Israel with all his heart and mind. He did not cease to offer the usual sacrifices in the temple at the great feasts. But his heart was not right with God; his worship became merely formal; his soul, left empty by the dying out of true religious fervor, sought to be filled with any religious excitement which offered itself. This brought upon him the divine displeasure. His enemies prevailed against him and one judgment after another fell upon the land. And now the end of all came, and he died, after a reign of forty years, and was buried in the City of David and with him died the short-lived glory and unity of Israel. One of the major accomplishments of Solomon was the building of the Temple of God. For some years before his death, David was engaged in the active work of collecting materials for building a temple in Jerusalem as a permanent abode for the Ark of the Covenant. He was not permitted to build the house of God; that honor was reserved to his son Solomon. After the completion of the temple, Solomon engaged in the erection of many other buildings of importance in Jerusalem and in other parts of his kingdom. He was well known for his thirst and search for wisdom.

Uriah

Uriah the Hittite was one of the band of David's mighty men. He was the husband of Bathsheba, whom David first seduced, and then after Uriah's death married. Uriah was an officer of the Gibborim, the corps of heroes. He was, by David's order, sent to the front of the hottest battle at the siege of Rabbath, in order that he might be put to death. The thirty-second and fifty-first Psalms reveal the deep struggles of David's soul due to his crime.

APPENDIX 3

Brief biography of Jude, James Matthew, Mark, Luke, John, Paul, and Peter

JUDE (JUDAS)

A brother of Jesus. His name appears in the Gospels of Matthew and Mark on the occasion of Jesus coming to Nazareth. Many believe that Jude was Joseph's son from a previous marriage. Jude is known as the author of the epistle of Jude. The name Judas also refers to Judas Iscariot who betrayed Jesus and turned Him over to those who considered him dangerous and wanted his death.

JAMES

The Lord's brother and one of the twelve apostles. He was one of the three pillars of the Church. Many believe that James was the eldest brother of the Lord but his importance in the Christ seems to have derived from his closeness to Jesus.

MATTHEW

Very little is known about Matthew other than he was a tax gatherer and that he must therefore have been a bitterly hated man, for the Jews hated the members of their own race who had entered the civil service of their conquerors. Matthew would be regarded as nothing better than a quisling. But there was one gift which Matthew possessed. Most of the disciples were fishermen. The disciples would have little skill and little practice in putting words together on paper; but Matthew would be an expert in that. When Jesus called Matthew, as he sat at the receipt of custom, Matthew rose up and followed him and left everything behind him except one thing—his pen. Matthew used his literary skill to become the first man ever to compile an account of the teaching of Jesus. Matthew is the gospel which was written for the Jews. Matthew was responsible for the first collection and the first handbook of the teaching of Jesus. It is to him that we owe the Sermon on the Mount and nearly all we know about the teaching of Jesus. Matthew does everything possible to arrange the teaching of Jesus in such a way that people will be able to assimilate and remember it.

MARK

Mark is considered by many, the most important of the all the gospels. It is the earliest of all the gospels; if it was written just shortly after Peter died about A.D. 65. It embodies the record of what Peter preached and taught about Jesus. Mark is the nearest approach we will ever possess to an eyewitness account of the life of Jesus. Mark was the son of a prosperous woman whose name was Mary, and whose house was a meeting place of the early church. Mark stood close to Peter, and so near to his heart, that Peter could call him " Mark, my son." (1 Peter 5:13) Like no other gospel Mark tells us about the divine side of Jesus and his emotions. He begins his gospel with the declaration of faith, "The beginning of the gospel of Jesus Christ, the Son of God." He leaves us in no doubt what he believed Jesus to be. The sheer humanity of Jesus in Mark's picture brings him very near to us. Over and over Mark's gospel inserts vivid details into the narrative which is the trademark of an eyewitness.

LUKE

The gospel according to Luke has been called the loveliest book in the world. Luke was a Gentile; and he was the only New Testament writer who was not a Jew. Luke's gospel is an exceedingly careful bit of work. He was a trusted companion of Paul so it is believed that he must have known all the great figures of the church and heard from them the stories about Jesus. For two years, Luke was Paul's companion in imprisonment in Caesarea. In those long days he had every opportunity for study and research. Luke wrote mainly for Gentiles and his gospel centers around prayer. At all the great moments of his life, Luke shows us Jesus at prayer. Through his gospel, Luke shows us the role of women during the life of Jesus. It is Luke that tells the birth narrative from Mary's point of view; it is in Luke that we read of Elizabeth, of Anna, of the widow at Nain, of the woman who anointed Jesus' feet in the house of Simon the Pharisee; and it is Luke who makes vivid the pictures of Martha and Mary and of Mary Magdalene.

JOHN

For many Christian people the Gospel according to John is the most precious book in the New Testament. It is the book of love and the most penetrating search into the mysteries of eternal truths and the mind of God. Reading John, one is able to take a quick glimpse into the minds of God and our Lord Jesus Christ. John's gospel is quite different from the other three. In the other gospels Jesus speaks either in these wonderful stories or in short, epigrammatic, vivid sentences. But in the Fourth Gospel the speeches of Jesus are often a whole chapter long; and are often involved, argumentative pronouncements quite unlike the pithy, sayings of the other three. The Fourth Gospel was written in Ephesus about the year A.D. 100. John was the younger son of Zebedee, who possessed a fishing boat on the Sea of Galilee and was well off to be able to employ hired servants to help him with his work. His mother was Salome, and it seems likely that she was the sister of Mary, the mother of Jesus. With his brother James he obeyed the call of Jesus. It would seem that James and John were in partnership with Peter in the fishing trade. He was one of the inner circle of the disciples, for the lists of the disciples always begin with the names of Peter, James and John, and there were certain great occasions when Jesus took these three with him. Tradition identifies John as the beloved disciple of Jesus, the one that Jesus loved most. John was well known to be a man of a clearly turbulent and ambitious character. How can a man like that write so much about love and be loved in such a way by Jesus? This clearly shows that the Lord uses common people and sinners to carry his message.

Paul

The letters of Paul constitute the most important parts of the New Testaments. In these letters, Paul establishes the framework for the Christian Church. His letters usually contain prayers, thanksgivings, special contents (the body of the letters), special salutations, and personal greetings. Paul wrote his letters, not as an academic exercise, but as documents written to friends. Paul was born about the same time as our Lord. His name was Saul and was a native of Tarsus, a Roman province in the southeast of Asia Minor. Though a Jew, his father was a Roman citizen. When Paul was a young man, Christianity was quietly spreading its influence in Jerusalem. Persecution arose against Christians in which Paul took a prominent part. Paul was converted as a Christian on his way to Damascus where Christian fugitives had taken refuge. He had reached the last stage of his journey, and was within sight of Damascus. The Bible tells us that suddenly, at mid-day, a brilliant light shone round Paul and his companion. Paul was laid prostrate in terror on the ground while a voice sounding in his ears said, "Saul, Saul, why persecutes thou me?" This is the only recorded appearance of the Lord Jesus Christ after his ascension to the Father. The risen Savior was there, clothed in the vesture of his glorified humanity. "Who art thou, Lord?" he said, "I am Jesus whom thou persecutes." (Acts 9:5; 22:8; 26:15) This was the moment of his conversion. Blinded by the dazzling light, his companions led him into the city, where Ananias, a disciple living in Damascus, was informed by a vision of the change that had happened to Saul, and was sent to him to open his eyes and admit him by baptism into the Christian church. The whole life of Paul was permanently changed becoming the living force of the emerging Church. After Paul has been a Christian for more than 12 years and had become a leader of the Antioch Church, Paul initiated his missionary journeys. Paul had three major missionary trips during which he founded many churches and preached the gospel extensively. While at Jerusalem, at the feast of Pentecost, he was almost murdered by a Jewish mob in the temple. Rescued from their violence by the Roman commandant, he was conveyed as a prisoner to Caesarea, where he was a prisoner for two years. Paul was finally acquitted. He set out on his missionary labors, visiting western and Eastern Europe and Asia Minor. The year of his release was signalized by the burning of Rome, which Nero saw fit to attribute to the Christians. A fierce persecution now broke out against the Christians. Paul was seized, and once more conveyed to Rome as a prisoner. Though a prisoner, he was allowed to live in is own hired house with his guard, freedom to receive visitors, and to teach Christianity. These two years were very fruitful. While there he wrote the Epistles to the Ephesians, Philippians, Colossians, Philemon, and possibly Hebrew. It is generally accepted that Paul was acquitted about A.D. 63 or 64. Whether he went on to Spain, as had planned (Romans 15:28), is not known. However, if he did, he did not remain long. It seems certain that he was back in Greece and Asia Minor about A.D. 65 to 67 in which period he wrote the Epistles to Timothy and Titus. Then rearrested, he was taken back to Rome and beheaded about A.D. 67. His ministry lasted about 35 years during which he won vast multitudes to Christ; and to this day, still does.

Peter (Simon)

He was the son of Jona and originally was called Simon. He had a younger brother called Andrew, who first brought him to Jesus. His native town was Bethsaida, on the western coast of the Sea of Galilee. He was trained in occupation of a fisherman. His father had probably died while he was still young, and he and his brother were brought up under the care of Zebedee and his wife Salome. There the four youths, Simon, Andrew, James, and John, spent their boyhood and early manhood in constant fellowship. It would seem that Simon was married before he became an apostle. He was living in Capernaum at the time Christ entered His public ministry. The Lord recognized Peter as the "living rock of the church." In Matthew 16:15-18, Jesus asked His disciples, "But who do you say that I am?" Peter answered, "You are the Christ, the Son of the living God." Jesus responded: "Blessed are you, Simon Barjona, because flesh and blood did not reveal this to you, but My Father who is in heaven. I also say to you that you are Peter, and upon this rock I will build my church; and the gates of Hades will not overpower it." The name Simon does not occur again, but the name Peter gradually displaces the old name Simon, though our Lord himself always uses the name Simon when addressing him. Peter was known for his independence, energy and bluntness of speech. He was the dominant personality among the disciples and regularly acted as their spokesman. He was part of the inner circle of the Lord. He accompanied Jesus and was a witness of the transfiguration. Peter was the first of the apostles whom Jesus chose to appear after Mary Magdalene announced Jesus' resurrection. Peter was present in several resurrection appearances and during the ascension. When Christ was arrested, some bystanders asked Peter if he was a follower of Jesus and Peter denied the Lord three times. Matthew 26:75 tells us that after this happened he "wept bitterly." However, after Christ death, Peter's ministry helped to form the early church and he actively pursued the inclusion of the Gentiles. He was in prison several times for voicing his Christian views. On one occasion he was cast into prison by Herod Agrippa but that night, an angel of the Lord opened the prison gates, and he went forth and found refuge in the house of Mary. Important events in his ministry can be found in the book of Acts. There is no certainty how and when Peter went to Rome. Peter is said to have died in Rome during the persecution under Nero around A.D. 64. Tradition tells that in Rome he was arrested and crucified and that he asked to be placed head downward to show his subordination to the Lord.

Bibliography

Barclay, William, *The Daily Study Bible Series*, the Westminister Press, Philadelphia, Pennsylvania, 1975

Gardner Associates, *Who's Who in the Bible*, Reader's Disgest Assocation, Pleasantville, New York, 1994

Halley, Henry H., *Halley's Bible Handbook*, Regency Reference Library, Zondervan Publishing House, 1965

Mays, James L., *The Harper's Bible Commentary,* Harper & Row, Publishers, San Francisco, 1988

The New American Standard Bible (updated edition), The Lockman Foundation, Foundation Press Publications, La Habra, California, 1995

Softwares:
    Bible Link at www.biblelink.us, *The New American Standard Bible 1995*

    Quick Verse Essentials, Parsons, Nebraska

Website/Photos:
    Greg Allikas at www.orchidworks.com

BVG